Claudia Mesch is Associate Professor at the School of Art, Arizona State University. Her publications include *Joseph Beuys: The Reader* (edited with Viola Michely, I.B.Tauris and MIT Press, 2007); and *Modern Art at the Berlin Wall: Demarcating Culture in the Cold War Germanys* (I.B.Tauris, 2008). She is founding editor of the e-journal *Journal of Surrealism and the Americas* (jsa.asu.edu).

ART AND POLITICS

A SMALL HISTORY OF ART FOR SOCIAL CHANGE SINCE 1945

CLAUDIA MESCH

BLOOMSBURY VISUAL ARTS
LONDON · NEW YORK · OXFORD · NEW DELHI · SYDNEY

BLOOMSBURY VISUAL ARTS
Bloomsbury Publishing Plc
50 Bedford Square, London, WC1B 3DP, UK
1385 Broadway, New York, NY 10018, USA
29 Earlsfort Terrace, Dublin 2, Ireland

BLOOMSBURY, BLOOMSBURY VISUAL ARTS and the Diana
logo are trademarks of Bloomsbury Publishing Plc

First published in Great Britain by I.B. Tauris 2103
Reprinted 2014, 2016, 2017
This edition published by Bloomsbury Visual Arts 2020
Reprinted 2021

Bloomsbury Publishing Plc does not have any control over, or responsibility for,
any third-party websites referred to or in this book. All internet addresses given
in this book were correct at the time of going to press. The author and publisher
regret any inconvenience caused if addresses have changed or sites have
ceased to exist, but can accept no responsibility for any such changes.

A catalogue record for this book is available from the British Library.

A catalog record for this book is available from the Library of Congress.

ISBN: HB: 978-1-8488-5109-2
PB: 978-1-3501-8129-8
ePDF: 978-0-7556-0621-4
eBook: 978-0-8577-3410-5

Typeset by Scala & Scala Sans by Tetragon, London

To find out more about our authors and books visit
www.bloomsbury.com and sign up for our newsletters.

contents

list of illustrations

Every effort has been made to secure copyright on illustrations that are included in this book. In cases where information might be incomplete, the author requests that such instances be communicated so that they might be remedied.

acknowledgments

I wish to thank my editors at I.B.Tauris, Susan Lawson, who encouraged me to develop and pursue this book, and Liza Thompson, for her understanding and good advice while I carried through with it. I have benefited from the careful editing of this text by Alex Middleton and the assistance of Alex Billington. I am grateful for the considerable support extended to me by my institution, the School of Art at Arizona State University, which made the book in its current form possible. I am especially indebted to the following scholars and artists whose work has proven most important to me in my quest to navigate the highly complex and nuanced connection between contemporary art, culture, and politics: Albert Boime, Loren Kruger, Stuart Hall, Francis Frascina, Trinh T. Minh-ha, Griselda Pollock, Yolanda López, Jack Burnham, Terry Smith, Masumi Hayashi, Okwui Enwezor, and David Craven.

introduction

This book considers how artists visually or otherwise have engaged with political and grassroots movements in the era after 1945. In the wake of the major world events that marked the beginning of the post-colonial era, politically engaged, activist, or guerrilla art has increasingly come to characterize a key new direction in art production. This book will examine postwar modern and contemporary art, mostly from the US and Europe, but also as it is practiced and exhibited in the West by African and Middle Eastern artists. This art is explicit in its combative stance, or in its tone of political dissent, and does not shrink from making direct reference to the social problems and issues that are unique to the postwar era. At times this engaged art took on the advanced forms, techniques, and mediums of the art world, such as photomontage or the strategies of conceptual art, but it frequently also turned to traditional modes of figuration to communicate the artist's, or a public's, point of view regarding social and political issues of common interest.

After 1960 politics began to have less to do with nationalist narratives or class-based collectives—though certainly the latter still played a considerable role in the unrest of 1968. Rather, a "grassroots" politics anchored in still-forming notions of protest (against war, imperialism, or corporate crime), and in the ethnic, gender, and sexual identifications of the "personal," began to define multiple public discourses or discussions that gave voice to difference and heterogeneity within the collective. This book argues that certain artists and the works they created intentionally contributed to the construction of new political or social consciousness, and that artists continue to believe, to the present day, that their art can be and is political in nature.

The book uses the language of art history and political theory to examine the long history of postwar art's commitment to politics. In this introduction I map a number of categories of modern and contemporary political art that remain operative but that require attention to their distinctive and often historically determined notions of the "political." It is also useful to consider how modern art historians have recently charted the interrelation of modernism and politics, and to deliberate modes of political visual modernism that still have not been addressed. High-modernist critics often overlooked the role of dissent in both art-making and art criticism. However, the position of dissent, and the reconsidering of the boundaries of human social relationships established by modernism, continued to be important to visual art during the Cold War, the historical period that encompasses much of the art that is discussed in this book. As should also be clear from its subtitle, borrowed from the pen of the philosopher Walter Benjamin, this book reconsiders or retrieves what has been devalued and marginalized—in this case, political art after 1945—as a major component within a larger, and shifting, cultural/historical constellation since the late twentieth century.

Political art is certainly not unique to the moderns; it can also be found among the ancients. One needs only to see a single triumphal arch to be reminded of the power relations of ancient politics. But it can be argued that the political content of visual art becomes increasingly specific in modernity and that it has become more pervasive in art during the era of globalization. Politics, in the way I will use the term in this book, has to do with the activity of collective or group decision-making that also affects other groups within that social body. These decisions have to do with pressing, current problems confronting a particular group.

The philosopher Michel Foucault suggested that decisions made on the part of a given social group not only deal with particular concerns and problems, but also form discourses that regulate the flow or circulation of power in a society or social collective at any given time.[1]

After the French Revolution the dominant shape taken by social collectives in the West was that of "nation," an entity constructed by the State; the defining of the contours of national identity or collectivity became a major cultural activity.[2] Of course, visual art played a central role in these constructions. In France, for example, Jacques-Louis David and Jean Auguste Dominique Ingres among others literally envisioned the founding myths of modern France. In this early modern period politics and political art were subsumed within nation-building. This casting of politics and of the collective as nation is an aspect of modernism that continued into the twentieth century and still animates culture today. Early on the State's construction of nation was contested in multiple ways, but most importantly by the rise of socialism and the many schools associated with it, beginning with Claude Henri de Rouvroy, Comte de Saint-Simon, known as Saint-Simon, and his early followers or adherents, like Auguste Comte or the German poet in exile Heinrich Heine.[3] Saint-Simon advocated a rethinking of the collective toward a new and utopian social order in which the situation of the poor would be redressed and the ranking of social classes (of the propertied and the working classes) would lead to class-based conflict. Within this rethinking, Saint-Simon, or possibly a disciple, Olinde Rodrigues, suggested that, along with scientists and industrialists, *artists* would become the "avant-garde" or elite that would enable such social transformation.[4]

In the nineteenth century numerous artists across Europe and beyond answered the call for an engaged or political art practice that touched upon these socialist ideas, including Heine, Eugène Delacroix, Gustave Courbet, and Édouard Manet. Other artists later became associated with related schools of thought: Marxism and, finally, communism and Leninism. Of course, after World War I the last of these, Leninism, was successfully put into practice in gaining control over the Czarist State in Russia, with innovative and sometimes abstract artists like the constructivists, the productivists, the Dadaists, the surrealists, Pablo Picasso, and Mexican muralists like Diego Rivera using their art to embody and advocate the realizing of State socialism. At times the Soviet State directly solicited these artists' support. Dada and surrealism would contribute to the rise of Western Marxism, an intellectual, cultural, and political development. These intellectual circles, particularly surrealism and the Western Marxists, would also take up a serious critique of colonialism—a foundation of national expansion or imperialism in the nineteenth and twentieth centuries—as another means of dissenting from the goals and actions of the nation state. The artistic advocacy of State socialism within political modern art was not without ambivalence, particularly after 1949, when Joseph Stalin's genocidal abuses of power became known. For these reasons among others, the art historian T.J. Clark has convincingly argued that modern art has had a dialectical relation to socialism.[5]

Clark believes that the era of modern (political) art and of socialist dissent with the politics of nationalism ended with the beginning of the Cold War. It is indeed the case that after 1949 the "superpowers" of the US and the USSR and their satellite countries such as West Germany and Poland began to position and deploy modern art politically. During the Cold War both the US and the Soviet States used modern art as a means of persuading a world public of their new global identification with one or the other side of the conflict, either US-style democracy or Soviet-style State socialism. This politicizing of modern art—and it has been argued that even the most abstract modern art became an advertisement for Cold War affiliations with either the US or the USSR—was realized in the US in the 1950s, and most prevalently in the defeated countries of Western and Central Europe after World War II, such as West Germany or the former Yugoslavia. However, at least for a time the Soviet Bloc promoted the work of certain Western modern artists, most visibly Picasso.[6] At the same time, critics like Clement Greenberg in the US pronounced that modern art was completely autonomous or independent of society and of politics more generally. This position might be understood as modernist criticism's denial of the State's ongoing (re)politicizing of modern art; the critic Moira Roth noted the "indifference" that Greenberg's position generated in American contemporary art of the time.[7] Thus it appeared that the State had severed modern art's association with the position of (socialist) dissent toward the vested interests of the nation state, a legacy well established by World War II.

During the Cold War the US successfully deployed and (re)politicized the forms of dissenting modern art in order to promote its own goals within global, Cold War alliances. As Chapter 1 discusses, the cultural events of this period make clear that formally advanced or completely abstract art proved to be quite available for appropriation, since the State, particularly in the US, could fill this art, apparently without subject matter, with *any* subject matter it found most persuasive of its own goals. In short, even the most abstract modernist artworks were politicized in the twentieth century, as many art historians have argued, for example, about US abstract expressionist painting in the late 1940s and 1950s.

On the other side of the Iron Curtain, most pervasively in the Soviet Union and the Soviet Bloc, visual culture was not just appropriated but dictated by Stalin's cultural ministry. Andrei Zhdanov's crude decrees and censorship of artists extended into all of the Soviet spheres of influence, including its distant interests in the Soviet Republics and Angola. For Zhdanov, visual and indeed all art, including music, was limited to one purpose: to represent to the public the inherent goodness of socialism under Stalin. This goodness had to be rendered as legible as possible; therefore visual art could use only naturalistic or figurative visual forms. The style of socialist realism has recently been ironically described as a "dream factory" akin to escapist Hollywood musicals of the 1930s, since its methods of persuasion actually mirrored those of consumerist and profit-driven capitalist culture, something that was otherwise anathema to the communist State.[8] Socialist realism's repertoire of subject matter—strapping young workers and their beaming children, often grouped around Joseph Stalin—is well known. The first chapter discusses how socialist realism was also practiced by Western European communist artists such as André

Fougeron and Renato Guttuso, and by artists in Angola and other African countries. This official style of State socialism became intriguing to the West German painters Eugen Schönebeck and Jörg Immendorff, and the Icelandic artist Erró. These Western artists appeared to be attracted to this mode either because post-Stalinist (or Maoist) notions of State socialism refused Western politics, or simply because socialist realism was deemed to be taboo or the ultimate kitsch within the Western art world and market. To take up the style of socialist realism in the West became an avant-garde gesture. Artists also realized that new forms and mediums for political art could deliver dissent or critique more effectively in that they would be less inclined to be appropriated by the State—which possibly might not recognize these forms and objects as art to begin with. Artists who sought to voice dissent, or to protest against the positions and politics of the Cold War nation, began to devise new techniques and even mediums to do so. In the USSR and beyond, samizdat art gained currency as a rejection of official dictates, and socialist realism was openly dismantled in the works of Soviet artists such as Erik Bulatov.

In the period after 1960, newly established countries declared their independence. India (1947), Ghana (1957), and Algeria (1962) repudiated colonialism as it had been practiced by major Western nations, and thereby realized post-colonial states. Nevertheless, many post-colonial African nations still played assigned roles within global Cold War conflict and were at least in part still controlled by the superpowers and their satellites, despite their independence. Cultural and other forms of racism were similarly rejected. Chapter 2 examines the widespread artistic manifestations of post-colonialism in the work of African and African-diaspora artists Ernest Mancoba, Tshibumba Kanda Matulu, Gavin Jantjes, Betye Saar, David Hammons, Yinka Shonibare, and Georges Adéagbo, among others. In the US, anti-colonialism manifested itself in the form of the civil-rights movement. Although primarily committed to the advancement of equal rights for African Americans, many in this camp shared the concerns of the anti-war lobby. Both US protest movements disapproved of mounting Western aggression toward Vietnam, a former French colony whose struggle for independence soon devolved into an extended Cold War conflict. Because of this wide rejection of colonialism in the 1960s, the notion of collectivity based on nationhood shifted into a more fragmented and individualized landscape in which identity was based less on social and economic class than on personal traits. Race or ethnicity became central to the way individuals thought about their identity. Of course, ethnic identity was frequently tied to modern-era migrations, or to the diasporas generated by colonialism, the largest of which was the forced migration of millions of Africans to the New World and North America as part of the slave trade. The ethnic consciousness encouraged by the civil-rights movement, along with the practice of segregation—or of concentrating and limiting certain ethnic populations to specific areas and neighborhoods of urban centers—heightened the African American population's understanding of one's place within a new shared-ethnicity collective. Building on this newly formed core of identity based on ethnicity, liberation movements that emerged from the foundational civil-rights movement similarly began to define identity around other characteristics: gender, generational affiliation (such as the youth-based student movement), or sexual orientation.

It is often said that a new form of political engagement based on personal identity grew from the atmosphere of post-colonialism and protest. An entire range of postwar protest movements—the civil-rights movement, anti-war sentiment, feminism, and gay rights—sought to persuade individuals to become participants. This call for engagement was also an appeal for solidarity that could be established by means of shared aspects of personal identity. For the first time, political engagement came to be understood differently, giving rise to the famous phrase "the personal is political." As a newly individuated notion of protest, grassroots activism differed from earlier notions of collectivity. The term "community" became a common designation, a notion that understands solidarity as the proximity of other individuals—either in sharing a particular (personal) identity, or in terms of co-existing in actual physical spaces or neighborhoods in urban centers. "Community-building" became an activist goal that sought to channel personal identifications and/or neighborhoods into participation in an agenda for social change, because of common interest shared by a community on specific social issues. The sit-in or street protest increased in popularity, events based on actual physical participation at a particular place and the performance of those attending there. Participants or activist community members also included advocates, those individuals who by reason of their deep sense of identification or sympathy align themselves with a given social group, but perhaps do not physically share the identity of the group in question.

Community-building of the 1960s and 1970s, then, was no longer based on an idea of collectivity as a fantasy or abstraction of belonging, but often involved embodied participation and alliances with actual individuals who sought change and justice for a social group. It has been argued that the very idea of collectivity—of a nation, of a class, or of a "collectivism after modernism"—is in truth a fantasy projection, or a kind of utopia.[9] This notion suggests that artists who contributed to the widening of communities through their allegiance to given dissident or protesting communities were not so much sharing a social bond as taking part in an unrealizable "dream of redemption" that characterizes social change. This idea of social change as an unrealizable fantasy is drawn from key tenets of orthodox post-modernism, which has rejected as totalizing or quasi-dictatorial any "master narrative" that privileges or "honors" a specific subject of history as an engine for old-fashioned modernist revolutionary change, of the kind that Marx constructed around his subject of history, the "proletariat."

Yet long after the waves of grassroots activism and protest that characterized the 1960s and 1970s, social, political, and economic inequality continues to galvanize direct cultural and artistic participation that recognizes the *current* concerns of certain social groups. Artists still use their work to convince a larger public of injustice that necessitates a social change that would lead to the improved lives of these individuals, families, and nations, and even to the amelioration of global relations. Terry Smith has argued that our current vantage point is in many ways beyond orthodox post-modernism; certainly the global crisis precipitated by the terrorist attacks of September 11, 2001 has distanced us in many ways from that earlier cultural moment.[10] Furthermore, many artists recognize current injustice and social problems experienced by specific groups in order to realize a condition of living in the present or, as Smith says, of "being up-to-date" as an *artist*. Artists may also critique the structures that enable globalization per se, or the cultural homogenization that globalization spreads by means of Western consumerism, mass culture, and digital networks.

In order to render politics visible, or the relations and concerns of social groups at a particular moment, many artists make use of the quick legibility of illusionism or the traditional text-and-image combinations used in propaganda. But this is not always the case; by the 1960s artists had already begun to expand the entire field of mediums beyond those of painting and sculpture—in performance, the ready-made, installation, site-based artworks and film, conceptual art—at times to counter the State's Cold War manipulation of traditional forms of visual art. In 1968 the critic Jack Burnham perceptively argued that, due to the new scientific and mathematical developments of systems theory, cybernetics, and computer science, a sea change had occurred in social and cultural notions of the object. Burnham stated that objects could no longer be thought of as completely independent and autonomous entities, which had earlier been the central tenet of high-modernist art according to formalist critics like Clement Greenberg and his disciples. He claimed, "We are now in transition from an *object-oriented* to a *systems-oriented* culture. Here change emanates, not from *things*, but from the *way things are done*." The new needs or concerns that animate art after cybernetics have to do with "the creation of stable, ongoing relationships between organic and non-organic systems, be these neighborhoods, industrial complexes, farms, transportation systems, information centers, recreation centers, or any of the other matrices of human activity."[11] The new "artist of significance" began to think about the proximity of what she does to the "productive means of society." As Burnham himself noted, the shift into postformalism in art had also been taken up by other critics, most notably Donald Judd. But Burnham recognized that artists' new concern with deploying art as a kind of "psychic preparedness" connected to the stability of organic and inorganic systems also signaled the rise of a political element within art production.

Since Burnham's time, critics have argued that new grassroots or community-based activist art is positioned or staged in public spaces and not the gallery or museum, thereby emphasizing the process of art instead of an object.[12] These artists furthermore make temporary or ephemeral works, and use collaboration or collectives of various kinds to produce or execute the artwork itself. Finally they also appropriate the devices and techniques of mass media for art. All of these were new strategies artists devised in part to facilitate community solidarity, and to make art relevant to community goals of social change. Yet within this group some advanced artists pursued a kind of high-modernist art production that focused on the autonomy of the art process, the art object, and the art medium, as a realm very distinct and independent of any other aspect of everyday life. This book does not discuss the work of artists who work exclusively in this tradition of high modernism.

The remaining chapters of the book, along with the Epilogue, examine specific case studies of artists' allegiances, on an international scale, to specific social communities or subpopulations since 1960. Art that participated in anti-war protest concerning the US war in Vietnam, and since that time has targeted other conflicts, is the subject of Chapter 3, which includes the work of Nancy Spero, Ed Kienholz, Leon Golub, Dinh Q. Lê, Martha Rosler, Joana Hadjithomas and Khalil Joreige, Walid Ra'ad, and Harun Farocki. The impact of new forms and techniques, particularly in terms of performance-based or embodied art, is apparent in the artworks that evidence artists' commitment to the feminist goal of the equality of women in various societies around the world. Feminist artists whose work was innovative in this formalist sense include Miriam Schapiro and Judy Chicago, Carolee Schneemann, Yolanda López, Hannah Wilke, Joan Jonas, Barbara Kruger, Cindy Sherman, Trinh T. Minh-ha, and Le Groupe Amos. Works by these artists are discussed in Chapter 4.

Chapter 5 details how artists contributed to a general cultural shift away from repressed homophile notions of homosexuality, or what the theorist Eve Kosofsky Sedgwick has termed the "relations of the gay closet." One component of the sexual revolution that marked the 1960s was the fading of the ideology of heterosexuality as the only recognized or permissible aspect of human sexuality in Western societies. This rejection also took place within the realm of art; artists more openly articulated their own homosexuality within their production, or acknowledged their partners within artworks. This is the case in key artworks by Jasper Johns, Andy Warhol, Rainer Fetting, Salomé, and Catherine Opie, and by the filmmaker Rainer Werner Fassbinder, that are presented in this chapter. The chapter also includes David Wojnarowicz and the collective AIDS Coalition to Unleash Power (ACT UP), artists who aligned themselves with the gay-rights movement's increasing focus, during the 1980s, on AIDS activism and, in a further echo of the AIDS crisis, on the themes of mortality, loss, and death.

Community ecological and environmental awareness, and community engagement with the environmental movement, gained currency after the colossal environmental disasters of the late 1980s: the catastrophic nuclear-power-plant disaster in Chernobyl, Ukraine, in 1986, and the 1989 Exxon Valdez oil spill off the Alaska coast. Environmental art and its contribution to the environmental movement is the subject of Chapter 6, which focuses on key works and/or actions by Joseph Beuys, Helen Mayer Harrison and Newton Harrison, Mel Chin, Ines Doujak, Sokari Douglas Camp, and Beatriz da Costa, among others.

During the 1990s, however, many of these activist and artistic strategies seemed compromised by the economic and technological developments of globalization. Newly empowered Euro-American and Japanese transnational corporations snaked out over national borders to cultivate "emerging markets" in under-developed countries and elsewhere. Global corporations such as Exxon/Mobil, Monsanto, or Philip Morris advertised their interest in the "community" and touted their "community investment"; in other words, corporate entities have taken on the mantle of community-building that was once the preserve of grassroots activism. Often this is done by public-relations executives and serves to mask the environmental and fiscal disasters that many of these same corporations have unleashed in specific communities. Chapter 7 discusses artists who have countered this corporate appropriation of community-building. It focuses on the intersection of art with two distinct protest movements that foreground the consequences of globalization: the migrants' rights/anti-poverty movements, and anti- or alter-globalization. The chapter begins with the works of the early alter-globalization artists Thomas Hirschhorn, Alfredo Jaar, and Alighiero Boetti. Other artists and collectives reference the increasing burden on the lower-income worker that resulted from globalization, especially on migrant workers, and the persistence of poverty in the globalizing economy. Therefore the chapter also includes art by Mierle Laderman Ukeles, Chantal Akerman, Santiago Sierra, and the collective the Border Film Project.

The internet is the great enabler of the new market-driven neocolonialism of globalization; worldwide networks quasi-instantaneously facilitate huge economic transactions across the globe. Artists allied with alter-globalization participate in informatics resistance, in occupying or interrupting digital functions where possible, by deploying other means of dissent toward the technology of the World Wide Web, or in other mass media like television and film. Chapter 7 concludes by discussing related media-based and "culture jamming" artworks by Mel Chin, the Yes Men, Radical Software Group, and Raqs Media Collective. Artists who oppose corporate control of the digital mass media are also active in the now-global Occupy Wall Street protest movement by means of innovative digital "augmented reality" artworks that are disseminated via smartphones; these works are discussed in the Epilogue.

In its broadest sense political art seeks two things: to comment on, and also to elicit a reaction to, an issue or development that is of current concern to a social group in the decision-making process that is politics. As the reader will discover, both realms—politics and art—have changed considerably since the beginnings of modernity. High-modernist art criticism after 1945 often trivialized the intersection of social concerns and political goals with "advanced" visual art. Yet it is the case that the continued engagement of visual artists with dissent, protest, resistance, and community-building after 1945 points to the dynamic interrelation between visual culture and the history of social and political change. By emphasizing the political component of modern art, the art profiled in this volume serves as a unique introduction to twentieth- and twenty-first-century art history, in that it points to the fact that "difficult" or seemingly inaccessible art is very often relevant to the struggles of daily life in the present.

state-sponsored art during the cold war

The expanding cultural dimension of the Cold War brought about a major revival of political art. This chapter will focus on the politicization of figurative and abstract art that was carried out by each of the "superpowers" as part of the culture war of the period. It will address the institutional involvement of governmental agencies with artworks produced at the time, and also consider how certain artists and their individual artworks responded to State intervention or pursued an explicitly politicized message within the context of Cold War conflict. This chapter, then, does not offer a comprehensive survey of all State-sponsored art during the Cold War, but concentrates on case studies that are particularly striking or significant. I believe the general conclusions that I draw from the case studies presented in this chapter might also apply to other instances of art supported by the State during the period.

Socialist Realisms

During the Cold War art was rendered political mostly through its manipulation by the two opposing poles of this post-World War Two conflict, the US and the USSR. Generally it has been assumed in the West that only the art of the USSR and the Soviet Bloc states was explicitly politicized by the State, in taking up the forms and stylistic conventions of socialist realism. Soviet bureaucrat Andrei Zhdanov had established this genre in the late 1930s, and he revised it as a Cold War directive in 1947. In that year Zhdanov reaffirmed that socialist realism had as a goal the depiction of the revolutionary advancement and victory of the industrial and rural working class over those of other established interests. According to Zhdanov it is the duty of art to reveal, through an easily understandable depiction of everyday reality, evidence of the steady progress of the working class to a position of social and economic power.[1] Therefore postwar socialist realism in its Soviet formulation meant to represent a traditionally Marxist notion of class-based struggle, as well as the inevitable victory of the working class in that conflict.

Zhdanov's pronouncement concerning visual art's relation to the good life promised by Soviet State socialism was already operative in the USSR at the start of the Cold War, as well as in its expanding roster of satellites, occupied countries in Eastern Europe, and the Soviet republics. The Soviet artist Alexander Deineka, among others, produced paintings that exemplified Soviet artists' interpretation of Zhdanov's directive. Deineka had already established a considerable reputation in 1928 with his painting *The Defense of Petrograd*; he was furthermore a member of the "October" group. While he studied at Vkhutemas in Moscow with leading practitioners of constructivism, he did not take up the constructivist style, as is already evident in his 1928 history painting. In the new postwar USSR, Deineka's paintings returned to the subject matter that had concerned him during the 1920s and 1930s.[2] This is true of his paintings *The Relay Baton round the Ring B* and *Donbas*, both from 1947. In *The Relay Baton* (**Figure 1.1**) Deineka presents a sporting event, a relay or team-based foot race that features both male and female competitors on a clear, sunny afternoon, with flags waving crisply in the wind overhead. The painting's subject does not so much underscore the athletic talent of the individual as the teamwork that makes victory possible, a theme that surely pleased party functionaries who pressed for greater collective productivity of worker brigades. In certain areas of this composition Deineka points to his own handling of paint, as some brushstrokes are prominent, particularly in his depiction

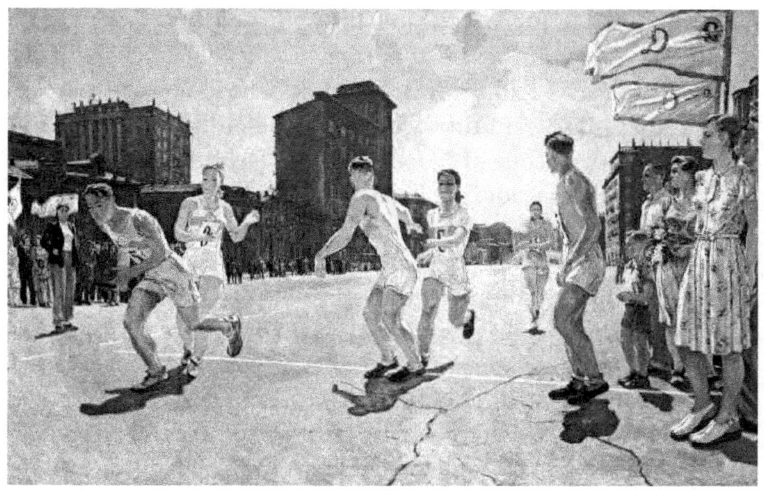

1.1   Alexander Deineka, *The Relay Baton round the Ring B* (1947)

of the slightly clouded sky. He also focuses the painting on the spectators of this event, whom he depicts in considerable detail in the right foreground. The athletes at the center of the painting are shown more schematically. This is a clever device on Deineka's part to reference the visual effect of a moving body, or the speed of a track athlete. Other Deineka paintings of the immediate postwar years reveal the burden of Soviet reality, one that did not conform to Zhdanov's new declarations of the continuous goodness of life that art was to deliver. Deineka's *Donbas* depicts laborers working at a coal-processing plant in the famed region of Ukraine (Donbas or the Donets Basin is a major coal-producing area of that country). Again the bright and sunny day Deineka depicts sets an upbeat atmosphere, along with the efficient locomotive that waits to be loaded with coal behind two female workers. The task that Deineka represents these Ukrainian workers performing in their brightly colored, neatly clean dresses belies the soot and hard physical labor this largely female working brigade was asked to perform in transporting mountains of coal; other women workers can be seen in the background, where they struggle to push cartloads of coal to other transport points on a bridge. At the same time Deineka indicates the spoils of their labor in the curling, diagonal plumes of steam and smoke that belch from the locomotive and a factory chimney stack behind it. For Deineka, this exhaust is as beautiful in form as the clouds in the sky. It is certainly a sunny scene of "goodness," but Deineka also points to the cracks in this façade: the hard labor Ukrainian women faced, and the loss of male workers that was surely widespread in the immediate postwar years due to the millions of war casualties suffered by the Soviet Union. Nevertheless, Deineka's paintings were considered prime examples of successful socialist realism; his art was reproduced in publications of Soviet Bloc states such as the German Democratic Republic (GDR), and was emulated by other artists. He was awarded the Lenin Prize in 1964 for his mosaics, as well as the Order of Lenin. He furthermore served in various positions at the Decorative Arts Department of the Arts Academy of the USSR before his death in 1969. His complex paintings can therefore be considered as exemplary of Soviet notions of socialist realism during the Cold War period.

Zhdanov's rather old-fashioned Marxist message of 1946 meant to unify and buttress the intense efforts underway in Europe to rebuild old socialist, or Western communist, parties in the wake of the destruction of the war, and after their considerable persecution during the years of conflict by German and Italian fascists. This policy may have struck some European leftists as antiquated, particularly those who were no longer affiliated with various national communist parties. Also known as the "independent Left," these groups had rejected the strictures of (Stalinist) Soviet Communist ideology after 1945. Communist parties in France (the PCF) and Italy (the PCI), as well as in North American countries such as the US (the CPUSA) and Mexico (the PCM), struggled to re-establish themselves during these years. As will be clear in this chapter, the complex restructuring of socialist ideas into organized communist parties (the "old Left") on the one hand, and into an independent Left on the other, varied greatly from country to country after 1945. Another challenge to the re-establishment of communist parties in Western Europe was US pressure to purge communist-party members from national governments there in exchange for

Marshall Plan funds; this diplomatic action on the part of the US was certainly successful in France, where the government of the Fourth Republic expelled all communist-party members in order to receive US reconstruction aid. It is generally accepted that the independent Left's recalibration of socialist ideas involved an intellectual shift away from militaristic notions of Marxist class-based conflict toward one of socialist or leftist opposition that was largely played out within the realm of culture.[3]

The recasting of socialist ideas became important for leftist intellectuals, artists, and critics in Western Europe, some of whom repositioned themselves within the new political, intellectual, and cultural landscape of the late 1940s. This intellectual realignment greatly influenced the course of visual art during the Cold War. The "official" Soviet style of socialist realism was refined in a multitude of different ways, by theorists such as Georg Lukács and Ernst Fischer, and softened by sympathetic leftist European painters. After their initial enthusiasm for it, critics in the US and Mexico (such as Clement Greenberg), as well as a number of surrealist artist-exiles, re-evaluated Leon Trotsky's position on visual art—this was mostly carried out in the journal *Partisan Review*, and in the pages of Wolfgang Paalen's *Dyn*. In France, Albert Camus and Jean-Paul Sartre continued to adhere to socialist notions in their development of existentialist thought, but both made an official break with the PCF. Sartre chose to promote the art of a painter devoted to complete abstraction, Wols (Alfred Otto Wolfgang Schulze), and the former surrealist Alberto Giacometti. Art historian Serge Guilbaut has argued that independent-leftist painters working in Paris, such as Pierre Soulages and Jean Dubuffet, similarly used the formalist innovations of their "humble" paintings to advocate for the working class, as much as official PCF artists did. These painters rejected Soviet standards for politically oriented painting.[4]

There were French artists who continued their loyalty to the old Left. The PCF promoted artists it found most useful to Stalinist-Zhdanovian goals, often lifting its prescriptions for visual art directly from the pages of *Pravda*. A Stalinist mouthpiece, this publication remained rigidly dismissive of even slightly abstract painting, those that still made some reference to recognizable forms (as Picasso's art continued to do). For example, in 1947 it published an article that condemned the modernists Matisse and Picasso as decadent; soon afterward the article appeared in translation in *Les Lettres françaises,* the party newspaper in France. This occurred despite the fact that world-class artists such as Picasso and Fernand Léger had joined the PCF in 1944 and 1945, respectively.[5] Instead the *art de parti* was to be found in the work of a naïve worker-artist and former member of the Resistance, André Fougeron. On the basis of one of his least interesting paintings, Fougeron became the artist whom the PCF valued most within class struggle. When Fougeron exhibited his painting *Parisian Women at the Market* (1947–8, **Figure 1.2**) at the 1948 Salon d'Automne in Paris, it was panned by much of the Parisian press as insignificant or worse. Fougeron's painting depicts stern women, one of whom looks aggressively toward the viewer, evaluating the meager offerings of a Parisian fish market. Fougeron implies that the paltry selection of food is overpriced; as though completing a measurement of

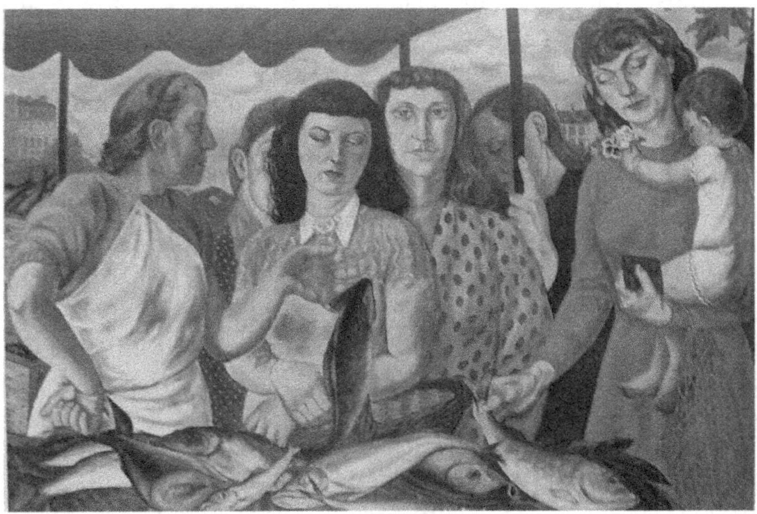

1.2   André Fougeron, *Parisian Women at the Market (Les Parisiennes au marché,* 1947–8)

some kind, the figure on the right attempts to balance the needs of her child against her ability to pay (she also holds her wallet in the same hand). She is then forced to consider whether or not to buy food. Fougeron critiques the hardship that market shortages and high prices inflicted on the average working-class French family. It has also been suggested that his painting points to the declining quality of everyday life of the French under increasing American control. Fougeron's other paintings, like his dramatic tribute to a PCF martyr, *Homage to André Houllier* (1950), are more successful compositions.[6] Also active for the PCF were painters like Édouard Pignon, who proved to be, like Picasso, more difficult for the party to deal with, because of his concern with modernist distortion and technique; and the Holocaust survivor and party member Boris Taslitzky. But it was the *Parisian Women* painting that made Fougeron the primary proponent of French, and arguably also of Western European, socialist realism.

For the 1953 Salon d'Automne—a crucial year because of Stalin's death—Fougeron submitted *Atlantic Civilization*, a far more explicit condemnation of American and French militarism, and the American or capitalist way of life. In this painting Fougeron takes up techniques of the classical avant-garde, such as collage; yet even within this format he remained a strictly figurative painter. Nevertheless, this modernist turn away from perspectival space and a simple realist style cost him the support of his champion, the critic Louis Aragon. Cartoon-like figures punctuate the composition, which is centered around a hulking American car that a GI pokes out of as he aims his rifle at an unseen target. The car is pulled up before an electric chair, raised on a pedestal as though it were art; the execution of Julius and Ethel Rosenberg had perhaps just taken place. In his depiction Fougeron foregrounds the ugly American way of life, but also presents its visual implications in France, in the unhealthy results of thoughtless reindustrialization, and in the cost of French military actions in Vietnam (referenced in the coffins being lowered into the ground on the painting's right). This content must have pleased the party, as well as intellectuals like Aragon and Sartre, who both continued to voice sharp criticism about a perceived Americanization of France. However, Aragon dismissed the painting as caricature, and said a simple sign that said "go home" would be more effective.[7] Aragon's about-face may have had more to do with political uncertainty within the PCF as it restructured in this year after Stalin's death. Perhaps Aragon thought that it was not the best time for him to take chances on art that might not please Moscow.

By the late 1950s and early 1960s, other Western and Eastern European artists, including Willi Sitte in the GDR and the Italian painters associated with the PCI, Renato Guttuso and Gabriele Mucchi, adopted socialist realism as a style and incorporated modernist elements and techniques into it, such as the look of collage, or the refusal of linear perspective. Guttuso, a Sicilian, joined the PCI during the late 1930s when the party operated underground, and later joined the Resistance. In a conscious rejection of Zhdanovian directives, Guttuso founded the Fronte Nuovo delle Arti (New Arts Front) in 1946 with Emilio Vedova and several other Italian artists, whose purpose was to pursue socialist goals in a new political painting that used modern form and a "post-cubist," if not expressionist, style.[8] In works such as *Massacre* (1943), in his series depicting workers at leisure at the seashore beginning in 1955, and also in his innovative *The Discussion* (1959–60, **Figure 1.3**), Guttuso continued to take an anti-fascist and anti-war position. The last of these works makes use of collage elements (an explicit *papier collé*, in homage to his friend Picasso), and became very influential in the GDR. The discussion, a depiction of citizens and party members debating the challenges faced by State socialism, became an official painting genre in the GDR. Guttuso became a corresponding member of the Akademie der Künste in Berlin in 1955. Though he remained in Italy, he exhibited his art in East Germany. Gabriele Mucchi, another painter affiliated with the PCI, would teach at the Kunsthochschule in Weissensee, East Berlin.

Guttuso's widening influence there arguably contributed to the East German turn against orthodox Zhdanovism. Several German monographs were published on his art in the GDR, including John Berger's book (1957), translated by Wolfgang Martini, and another in 1975 by the Leipzig critic Lothar Lang. Guttuso received

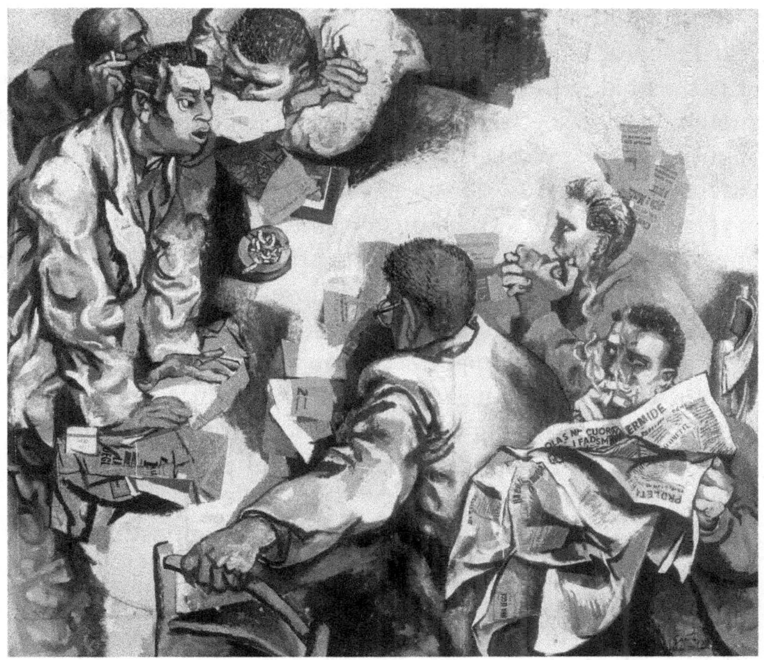

1.3   Renato Guttuso, *The Discussion* (*La discussione*, 1959–60)

retrospectives in New York as well as at the Pushkin Museum and the Hermitage; it is said that his art "straddled" the Iron Curtain. His friend the novelist Alberto Moravia said of his paintings:

> the attitudes of the people in Guttuso's pictures are not those of men and women who want to move and know why they're moving of their own free will, but of people who are pushed and forced to move by some eternal agent against their own free will. [...] Hence Guttuso's crowds are like objects thrown in confusion and borne away by a hurricane, or hurled in all directions by an explosion. In this sense Guttuso is a real Marxist. He firmly believes that the representation of reality is not enough; he has to introduce movement and dialectical impulse into reality.[9]

Guttuso first met Picasso on a trip to Paris in 1946, the same year he became involved with the Fronte Nuovo, and the two artists visited each other frequently over the years. Guttuso is another of Picasso's friends (like the poet Paul Éluard) who was aligned with the old Left's party structure in Western Europe. Famously, Picasso is said to have joined the PCF in the last days of World War Two because of these friends. Picasso was one of the most renowned modern artists in the West of this era—another was Diego Rivera—whose art had already been associated with anti-fascism or the old Left. Both continued to use their painting to support leftist oppositional politics, and to counter US Cold War policy in Korea and Latin America. Both used figurative painting to refer to and even to comment in a positive way on the aesthetic and political positions of Soviet communism after 1945.

Picasso proved to be a bigger problem for almost the entire political spectrum, for the West as well as for the USSR. Like Guttuso, he bridged the cultural Cold War divide. He was a new PCF member in the 1940s. He produced the iconic image for the new Soviet-backed "peace movement" of 1949. The "national congresses" for this movement took place exclusively in major cities in Western Europe; it was the USSR's anti-militarist response to the formation of NATO that same year. Picasso's peace dove became ubiquitous throughout Eastern Europe, and he reinterpreted it in prints well into the 1960s. He made activist appearances for Stalinist causes during the 1950s; he showed his work at the Pushkin Museum in Moscow in 1956.[10] Of course, there was no shortage of retrospective exhibitions devoted to Picasso in either the West or the East, even during the 1960s, the most repressive period in the Soviet Bloc states.

During the Cold War Picasso became a contested icon of the modern artist per se. In the increasingly harsh climate of anti-communism in the US in the 1950s, it became deeply troubling to many Americans that he had unequivocally aligned himself with communism. After his first retrospective at the Museum of Modern Art (MoMA) in New York in 1939, two exhibitions devoted to the artist at the same institution followed, in 1946 and 1957.

Picasso's most overtly anti-fascist and political commentaries on wartime Spain, his painting *Guernica* and the etching series *The Dream and Lie of Franco* (1937), had already been included in the 1939 MoMA exhibition. To mark his joining of the PCF, Picasso published a short statement titled "Why I became a communist" in the US in 1944 (in both the *New Masses* and the *Art Digest*). The statement apparently did not attract much consternation or even interest in the art world at the time; MoMA curator Alfred Barr mentioned Picasso's new political affiliation in a museum publication of 1945.[11]

Soon there were challenges mounted to the validity of modern art from both the American Right and the Left. Picasso became an icon for the Right's suspicions about the connection of modern art to Soviet-style State socialism, argued most viciously by State representative George A. Dondero of Michigan beginning in 1948. In a speech to the US House of Representatives in 1949, Dondero notoriously pegged Picasso as the "hero of all the crackpots in so-called modern art"; Picasso came under investigation by the US Federal Bureau of Investigation.[12]

The American old Left also attacked Picasso; echoes of the "decadence" charge leveled against modern art by Soviet critics can be found in American discourse of this period. CPUSA member Rockwell Kent condemned Picasso as an elitist whose art was not accessible and therefore not suited to the populism of communism.[13] Some American exhibitions were canceled, and certain public collections were purged of Picasso's works. Curator Alfred Barr came under increasing pressure by Kent, Dondero and others. Because MoMA itself was coming under attack, Barr began to tell his museum colleagues that Picasso's art did not conform to the kind of art promoted by the Soviet State. This became obvious when Americans learned of the fallout generated in France and in the USSR by Picasso's infamous Stalin portrait, a memorial drawing Picasso completed in 1953. The portrait was published on the front page of *Les Lettres françaises* (Picasso had also drawn a festive greeting to Stalin on the latter's 70th birthday in 1949). Picasso faced reprimands from the PCF and Soviet officials because of it. Barr and US journalists such as Joseph A. Barry began to portray

Picasso the man—as distinct from the artist—as a gullible, passive follower of communist politics.[14]

In addition to his misunderstood but admiring tributes to Stalin, Picasso produced other works highly critical of US actions after 1946. For example, his *Rape of Europa* of that year has been read as Picasso's critique of the expanding US presence in France, exemplified by the opening of French markets to American products and the subsequent forgiveness of the French war debt under the Blum-Byrnes agreement of 1946. Best known is the *Massacre in Korea* (**Figure 1.4**), shown at the Salon de Mai in Paris in 1951. The painting has been discussed as Picasso's reaction to either an American-led ambush in the Korean War during which Korean civilians, women, and children were killed, or the PCF's consistent preference for Fougeron and his attempt to appease it. The painting has been described as "a new *Guernica*" in which America had replaced Germany, or as a condemnation of an atrocity and State-supported violence.[15] The painting apparently bewildered the New York art world, where Picasso the communist blithely continued to sell his work at the Samuel Kootz Gallery. A clumsy composition, Picasso nevertheless makes multiple art-historical references in *Massacre in Korea* to Goya and Manet, and to his own *Guernica*, and attempts to integrate cubistic or geometric

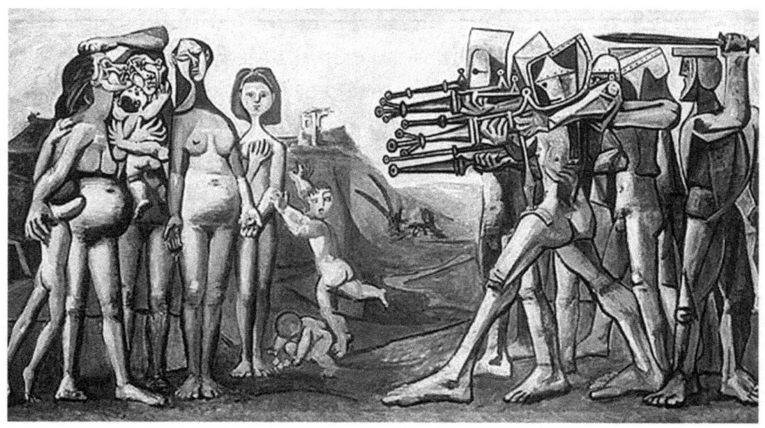

1.4   Pablo Picasso, *Massacre in Korea* (*Massacre en Corée*, 1951)

forms with the figure. The American troops on the right are improbably clad in armor and are shown wielding swords against the defenseless pregnant women and infants to the left. Picasso was certainly aware of the technological superiority of the US armed forces by the 1950s. It is not too difficult to speculate that in using these archaic forms of war and violence, Picasso meant to portray with a "broad brush" the US military apparatus as uncivilized, barbaric, and cruel in its stance toward "hot" Cold War conflicts like the Korean War. Despite its critical content, the painting was also controversial in the Soviet Bloc because of its modernist forms. For example, an extended exchange of opinion on the painting took place in the East German art journal *Bildende Kunst* in 1955–6; several authors presented spirited defenses of Picasso's work, which they understood as a "new realism" that refused Stalinist proscription against modernist form. The Italian painter Gabriele Mucchi, a colleague of Guttuso's, later stated that Picasso's art must not be as inaccessible as many had claimed, since Italian authorities removed the *Massacre in Korea* from a Rome exhibition in 1953 with the statement that a State ally might be offended by it.[16]

Not letting up on his criticism of the US, Picasso, like Fougeron, portrayed and memorialized the Rosenbergs in 1953. Picasso's political and highly critical artworks of these years would make it easier for the New York art world to reject him as obsolete and simply old in terms of biological age, though the discourse stated that this negative pronouncement was based not on the political content but rather on the formalist "failings" of his late work. In the end one might speculate as to which aspect of Picasso proved the most troubling and led to a final and negative evaluation of his late art. The most influential American art critic of the period, Clement Greenberg, would comment frequently on Picasso's late art over the next 20 years (his last essay on Picasso is dated 1980). In his writing Greenberg constructs Picasso as the primary link between American art and European modernism, but also as the figure who precipitates American art's turn away from European precedents. In his *Arts Magazine* review of MoMA's 1957 Picasso retrospective Greenberg foregrounds the artist's advanced age as an index of the breadth of his artistic production but also as an indicator of his decline. Greenberg sees this palpably demonstrated in the exhibition's (flawed) focus on Picasso's art after *Guernica*.[17] The Picasso who could be accepted by New York art institutions was therefore the young, pre-PCF Picasso, and not the political Picasso of *Guernica* and after. This was all the more awkward given the imposing physical presence of that painting in New York—Picasso had arranged for MoMA to keep *Guernica* beginning in 1939, and it was not returned to Spain until 1981 (it is now at the Museo Reina Sofía in Madrid). First established by Greenberg, it became a wider practice among New York art circles not to discuss Picasso's picture as a representation of atrocity and trauma. Instead critics' statements focused on the painting's formalist elements. But most often they preferred to take up other paintings, preferably Picasso's early canvases, which could be found in other galleries at MoMA.

Like Picasso, the modern-art celebrity and leftist Diego Rivera produced a major painting critical of the US military even as the Korean War was just beginning. Rivera completed the mural-sized and transportable *Nightmare of War and the Dream of Peace* (1951) for the Instituto Nacional de Bellas Artes (INBA) in Mexico City, with the understanding that it would be shipped abroad as part of an exhibition of Mexican art in Paris and other cities. It never got there, since the INBA decided not to include it in the Paris exhibition and instead returned it to Rivera, most likely because of its highly sympathetic depictions of Mao and Stalin and harsher treatment of icons of France, Britain, and the US.[18] (The location of this painting has recently again come into question; it was rumored to have been destroyed by Mao in China during the Cultural Revolution, or to be in the collections of the Pushkin Museum in Moscow, which the latter has denied.[19]) Along with Rivera's other Cold War painting *Glorious Victory* (1954)—which is a protest against the CIA-backed military coup in Guatemala of the same year, one that removed the elected president Jacobo Árbenz Guzmán—*Nightmare of War* is so explicit as to be crass in its condemnation of American foreign policy. In *Glorious Victory*, for example, Rivera depicts John Foster Dulles, the US Secretary of

State, grasping a bomb emblazoned with a likeness of Eisenhower, and surrounded by corpses of Guatemalan children. Far more so than Picasso's *Massacre*, these Rivera paintings function like political or satirical cartoons in that they ridicule both the workings of US foreign policy and the profiteering of the US United Fruit Company (thereby implying that the two are closely related). Furthermore, they do not have the positive view of "dialectical" reality that was demanded by socialist realism. They also lack the intricate fusing of Mesoamerican motifs with modernist forms and structures that made Rivera's equally political Radio Corporation of America (RCA)/Rockefeller Center mural so notable as modern art; the latter was of course painted over (and therefore destroyed) by RCA in New York in 1934.

Since his earliest appearance on the national stage in Mexico, when secretary of public education José Vasconcelos granted him his first public commissions of the 1920s, Rivera had a tortuous relation with the PCM, the Mexican Communist Party. The fact that no post-revolutionary government in Mexico has ever been tied to the USSR and its party structure, even during the Cold War, points to Mexico's sustained neutrality toward Stalin. This unaligned Mexican Left is probably a legacy of Lázaro Cárdenas, president from 1934 to 1940, who granted exile to Leon Trotsky, perhaps as a means to distance himself from Stalin on the world stage. Rivera had allied himself with and befriended Trotsky in Mexico, but the two fell out, perhaps due to political disagreements, before the latter's assassination there by the KGB in 1940 (which was allegedly assisted by the painter and Stalin sympathizer David Siqueiros; if this were true, it would prove that Stalinists were quite active in Mexico). After these traumatic events and the increasing involvement of the CIA in Latin America during the 1950s, Rivera concluded, in the works *Glorious Victory* and *Nightmare of War and the Dream of Peace*, that Latin America itself was under siege. In his commentary on the then recent US intervention in Guatemala in *Glorious Victory*, Rivera is most interested in constructing, from his position in Mexico, a sense of pan-American solidarity with that nation. Rivera depicts the visual alliance with Stalin and Mao as an anti-colonial statement, understanding both figures as bridges toward Latin American solidarity. While these works may be crassly literal, in them Rivera formulates an emerging notion of an independent Latin America, one that has in some ways outlived the Cold War conflict and the artist himself.

The Cold War culture war also made its way into Africa, where the USSR was active in cultivating Soviet-style State socialism in many countries, even during the momentous events that marked the independence of different African nations and the beginning of the post-colonial era (see also Chapter 2). This campaign for influence was most successful in Angola, Congo, Mozambique, and Ethiopia, but State socialism had support in almost every country in the continent. For example, the post-revolutionary Cuban government famously sent Ernesto "Che" Guevara to Congo to help support socialism during their period of political crisis in 1965. The history of modernism in Africa is an important and highly complex topic that was examined in the epic 2001 exhibition *The Short Century: Independence and Liberation Movements in Africa 1945–1994* by curator Okwui Enwezor.[20] In a parallel to the marginalization that socialist realism has received in art histories of the West, this exhibition largely avoided the subject of State-sponsored African art during this period. However, as an example of the spread of Cold War conflict in visual culture there, one is able to trace most clearly the general promotion of socialist-realist motifs and subject matter in visual art in the countries of Congo and Angola.

Some of the most interesting art of Cold War Africa is that produced in Congo referencing the rise and presumed assassination of elected prime minister Patrice Lumumba, the leader of the Mouvement National Congolais (MNC) and the first African leader of the country after its independence from Belgium in 1960. Lumumba was executed in January 1961 along with two other members of his government, Maurice Mpolo and Joseph Okito. His death was covered up for weeks, and it is alleged that US and Belgian interests played a role in it. Lumumba is memorialized in the painting series *History of Zaire* (1973–4) by Congolese artist Tshibumba Kanda Matulu, in the works *The Deaths of Lumumba,*

Mpolo, and Okito (On January 17, Bob Denard killed Lumumba, Mpolo, and Okito), and *Lumumba Indépendance* (**Figure 1.5**). The latter has as its subject Lumumba's legendary speech on Congo delivered on June 30, 1960 after he had been left off of the official program for the independence-day celebration; the crowd that day included the king of Belgium. Tshibumba clearly presents Lumumba as a martyr; the Christian iconography of these paintings also points to the Christlike elements he ascribes to the former leader. Also of interest are later paintings devoted to Lumumba, by, for example, the Belgian painter Luc Tuymans, who painted him from a photograph in 2000, at a time when public debate in Belgium had only just begun concerning the details of Lumumba's death several decades before. Lumumba then becomes a potent and tragic symbol of post-colonial Cold War Africa *in toto*. Tuymans' and Tshibumba's paintings serve as a bitter reminder of the continuing injustice and victimization faced by Africans after independence from colonial control.

In countries with socialist governments like Mozambique and Angola, public, monumental socialist-realist art was created during the Cold War to celebrate political leadership and the events around national-independence movements. Perhaps best known in Angola is the dramatic monument in Independence Square, Luanda (2002), to Agostinho Neto, the first Angolan president (1975–9) and leader of the socialist Popular Movement for the Liberation of Angola (MPLA) party. This monument also reveals, in its orthodox socialist-realist and militaristic motifs, Neto's ties and alliances with the USSR (he died in Moscow in 1979). It features a sculptural depiction of Neto, fist raised, crowning a tall pedestal. Large-scale mosaic murals decorate the rounded base (**Figure 1.6**). As is visible on recent photographs of the monument, parts of these mosaics are accented or outlined with a string of lights to make them more visible in darkness. Three separate mosaics depict a troop of fatigues-clad African soldiers and independence fighters waving automatic weapons and leading a charge into the foreground; a smiling woman with her child gestures toward the figure of Neto. Behind her a crowd waves placards and Angolan flags, and to her left is a large depiction of a 1950s-era Picasso peace dove. Most dramatically,

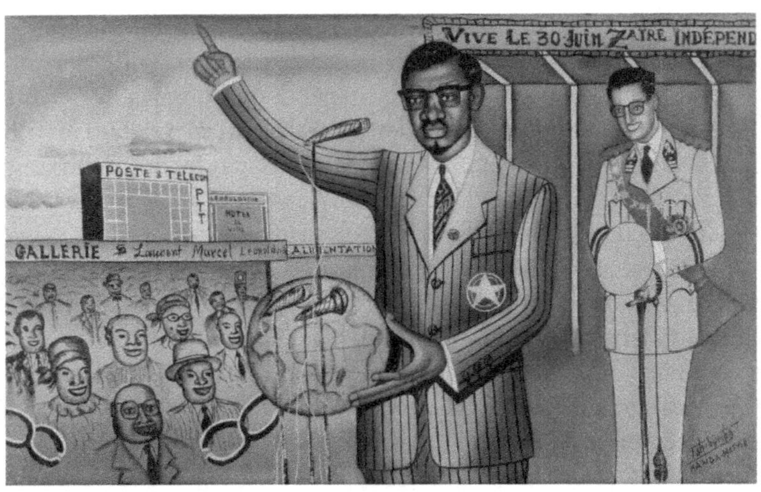

1.5   Tshibumba Kanda Matulu, *Lumumba Independance* (*Lumumba Indépendance*, from the series *History of Zaire*, 1973–4)

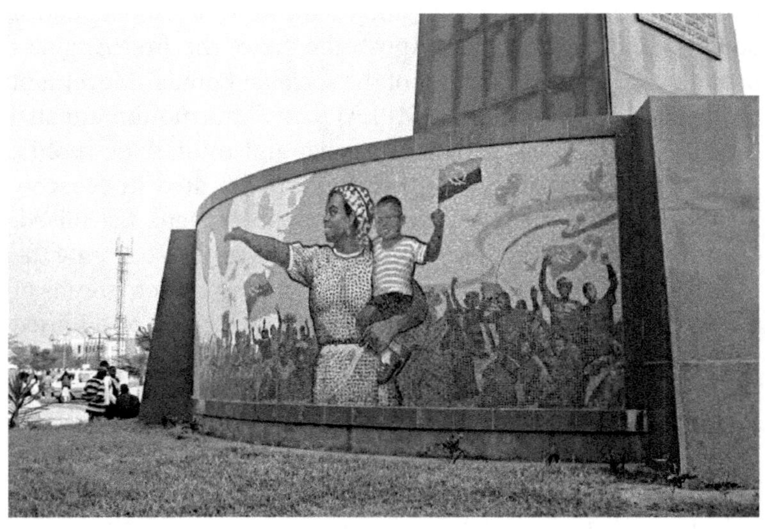

1.6   Independence Square monument mosaics (2002), Luanda, Angola

the final mosaic depicts a scene of enslaved Africans, some toiling, others shackled and being led on a march to a slave ship that can be seen in the distance. Over these figures a large-scale, bare-chested man breaks the chains on his hands and looks upward, presumably also at the figure of Neto. Therefore, in this monument Neto is positioned as the culmination of the colonial history of the region, and also as the deliverer of freedom to Angolans. Delinda Collier discusses other monuments and murals dedicated to Neto in Angola and elsewhere in Africa. As she has noted, these official monuments are usually not attributed to individuals, as many artists who worked on them now decline to recognize these projects as their own work or otherwise disown their Cold War commissions. This hesitation on the part of artists may have to do with larger debates on African art, and with changing notions of what proper Angolan, and also African, art should foreground.[21]

American Art and the Cold War

In the early Cold War, the situation of art and politics in the US was highly complex and has been vigorously debated by art historians. In the 1970s American critics and art historians argued that a politicization of art had also occurred in the US, centered on the government's use of large-scale American abstract painting of the 1940s and 1950s—that is, the movement known as abstract expressionism. Before this wave of 1970s revisionist scholarship, US art historians seem to have assumed that US abstraction as it was practiced after 1950 retained a status of autonomy and a measure of distance from crude references to explicit political goals that figurative and/or realist art could not. In his 1976 history of abstract expressionism, Irving Sandler described US abstraction as nothing less than a "triumph."[22] Nancy Jachec has argued that as the US took up an extreme domestic anti-communism, and modern art became a political target of extremist anti-communists in the US Congress like Joseph McCarthy and Dondero, US art critics, curators, and art institutions defensively recast Marxist or Trotskyite notions of political radicalism that had earlier been associated with avant-garde or abstract painting in New York. Instead, abstract painting was related to a generalized notion of existentialist cultural dissent, or what Jachec calls "new radicalism." For a time, the US government found the "third way" leftism or socialism newly associated with abstract expressionism useful in galvanizing US support among the growing, unaligned leftist intelligentsia in Western Europe (mostly in Italy and France), and possibly also in the USSR.[23]

The United States Information Agency (USIA) was founded in 1953 as the Marshall Plan began to wind down. It in part intended to counter the anti-American claims of the Soviet-backed peace movement; its promotion of aspects of American culture in Europe was meant to refute these claims and, it has been argued, to garner sympathy for the US, particularly among leftists critical of Stalin. The International Council (IC) of MoMA, established in the same year as a private initiative on the urging of Nelson Rockefeller, was to replace the former "International Program." At one key point in that decade, 1958, the USIA coordinated with the IC in exhibiting and promoting abstract expressionist painting in Europe; the International Program's earlier exhibitions had otherwise been more diverse in the kind of American high art it toured abroad, as in the 1953 *Twelve Modern American Painters and Sculptors* exhibition, which included early American figurative painters.[24] The launch of major traveling exhibitions on abstract expressionism and Jackson Pollock also came shortly after Pollock's death in an automobile accident in August 1956. US media focus on his death—which has been described as an "existentialist suicide"— made Pollock the most famous "Ab Ex" painter, and cemented the MoMA curators' decision to foreground him as a sophisticated and European-influenced contemporary painter abroad.

In the late 1950s the IC exported exhibitions of American abstract expressionist painting to numerous venues. For example, the 1956 Tate Gallery *Modern Art in the US* exhibition, organized in London and featuring work drawn from MoMA collections, traveled to 12 additional European cities including Vienna and Belgrade. In 1958–9 MoMA's twin exhibitions *The New American*

Painting and *Jackson Pollock 1912–1956* went to eight European cities, including Madrid, Amsterdam, and Berlin. The Pollock exhibition and catalog presented him as an existentialist or Europeanized painter; *The New American Painting* took the additional step of associating Pollock's style, along with that of the other abstract expressionist painters, with democracy. In West Germany, Werner Haftmann, the curator of the new international exhibition Documenta in Kassel, also made gestural abstraction and especially American abstract expressionist painting the centerpiece of his 1959 show. Haftmann established special galleries in this exhibition to highlight paintings by Pollock (16 altogether), the German artist Willi Baumeister, and French painters Nicolas de Staël and Wols, and to create an association between them. Haftmann's 1959 Documenta included additional paintings by the Americans Helen Frankenthaler, Robert Motherwell, Mark Rothko, Clyfford Still, Willem de Kooning, and Philip Guston. A British critic called the new American painting "inspiring," but he simultaneously characterized its broad exposure in Europe as an "invasion."[25] In regard to this charge it is interesting to note, for example, that Porter A. McCray, the director of MoMA in New York, had been called in to coordinate all of the American works for this West German exhibition.[26] It did then appear that by 1959 the US—that is to say New York's MoMA, in conjunction with the federal USIA—had in some ways "stolen the idea of modern art" from Europe, or had at least established itself for the first time as the major center of a progressive modernism in the West.[27] This latter category had also been redefined as consisting exclusively of the kind of gestural abstract painting that had become very successful on the international art market. Nevertheless, as it was presented to the European Left, this cultural victory on the part of the US was related to recent European philosophy and to existentialism's individualized and anti-collective—that is, an independent-leftist—notion of political dissent.[28]

Some art historians have related the shift to an independent Left in the late 1940s and 1950s to a new and dominant "liberal ideology" of the Cold War US, or have claimed that in the immediate postwar years, liberalism monolithically appropriated and neutralized any dissent from the US Left and leftist artists. However, the art historian Nancy Jachec has argued for the cultural significance of the exile to the US in these years of the sociologists of the Frankfurt School, Leo Lowenthal, Herbert Marcuse, Erich Fromm, and Theodor Adorno—who, along with Hannah Arendt, had a close familiarity with the work of their deceased friend Walter Benjamin. These intellectuals brought to their US university appointments new ideas of Western Marxism (often termed "post-Marxism"), based in cultural expression and in the modernist forms of literature, music, and visual art. They furthermore contributed to the American understanding of both the phenomenon of fascism and the related dimensions of the Holocaust during World War Two in Europe.[29] This growing awareness led some to realize, like the painter Barnett Newman, that the modes and goals of engaged art or dissent pursued by the surrealists, for example, had resolutely failed during fascism's rise to power. Artists like Newman had already begun to explore alternative modes within visual art, like complete abstraction, as a means toward an individualized notion of political change outside the strictures of the old Left. Newman and others continued to view engagement as a key aspect of modern art. This intellectual and artistic redefinition of engaged modern art within the US would become quite useful for a time in the US Cold War culture war in Europe and even as far as the USSR, where the USIA again displayed American abstract expressionist painting, at the National Exhibition in Moscow in 1959. But by 1961, another traveling exhibition, *American Vanguard Painting*, flatly stated that this style of art had nothing to do with dissent, but rather with experiments in form.[30] By 1964 this characterization of the "best" contemporary American painting took on the weight of a prescription for American art. It is another cultural legacy that has outlived the Cold War.

Political Cold War Painting in the West

It is certainly the case that many artists refused to conform to the strict Cold War split in the ideology of painting: figurative "socialist realism" in the State-socialist East and the USSR, and a formalist or stylistic "abstraction" in the capitalist West, which satellite states were to import from their corresponding superpower. Some Western painters criticized the notion that abstraction must function as a kind of idealized period style of the Cold War West: West German artists Jörg Immendorff and Sigmar Polke, for example, used painting to question such polarizing declarations for abstraction, in works such as Polke's *The Higher Powers Command: Paint the Upper Right Corner Black!* (1969, **Figure 1.7**). In an extended painting series combining image and text of 1973, Immendorff chastised a number of fellow West German artists—Wolf Vostell, Joseph Beuys, Klaus Staeck, and Blinky Palermo—for using their art to be "enablers for capitalism," when they should have been "presenting real life" in the struggle against "imperialism" instead.

In addition to artists in the Soviet Bloc, dissident artists in the West including Immendorff and Eugen Schönebeck, but also the Icelander Erró, radically stretched the genre of socialist realism in using iconography that directly referenced tenets of socialism or communism that were otherwise shunned. Schönebeck, who defected from the GDR to West Germany, created a series featuring icons of Comintern socialism and socialist culture culled from photographs. In 1965–6 Schönebeck painted, in his familiar block-like forms, *Mayakovsky, Mao Tse-tung* (**Figure 1.8**), the anonymous *The Red Army Soldier*, and *Siqueiros*; one of his drawings features Ho Chi Minh. More so than an expression of celebration, these paintings underscore the West's aversion to the socialist icon. They thereby reveal the ideological bent of Western media culture more generally.[31] The Icelandic artist Erró worked extensively from collage in order to unify forcefully, onto one painted surface, the opposing mass-culture sign systems propagated in the Cold War. He did not make use of pasted-paper collage, but instead painted the assembled collages into seamless compositions on canvas.

Some of these images, like those by the French painter Bernard Rancillac, make explicit anti-war statements that connect with the Vietnam War. His painting series *American Interior* of 1968 inserts Chinese war propaganda imagery into sterile American domestic interiors as they are presented in advertisements. In a

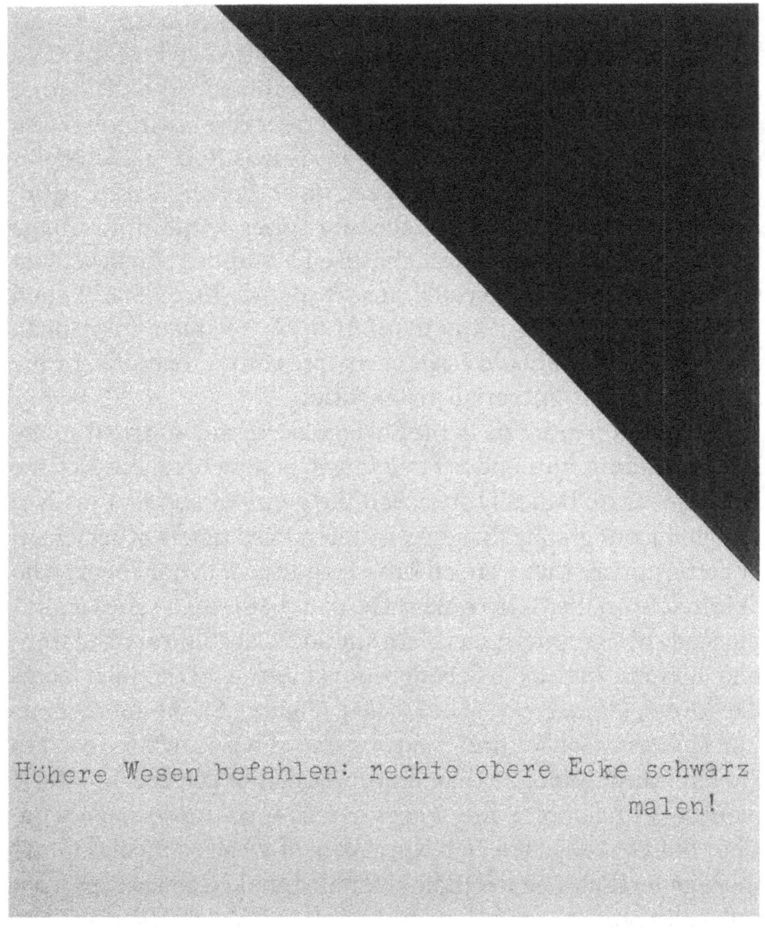

1.7   Sigmar Polke, *The Higher Powers Command: Paint the Upper Right Corner Black!* (*Höhere Wesen befahlen: rechte obere Ecke schwarz malen!*, 1969)

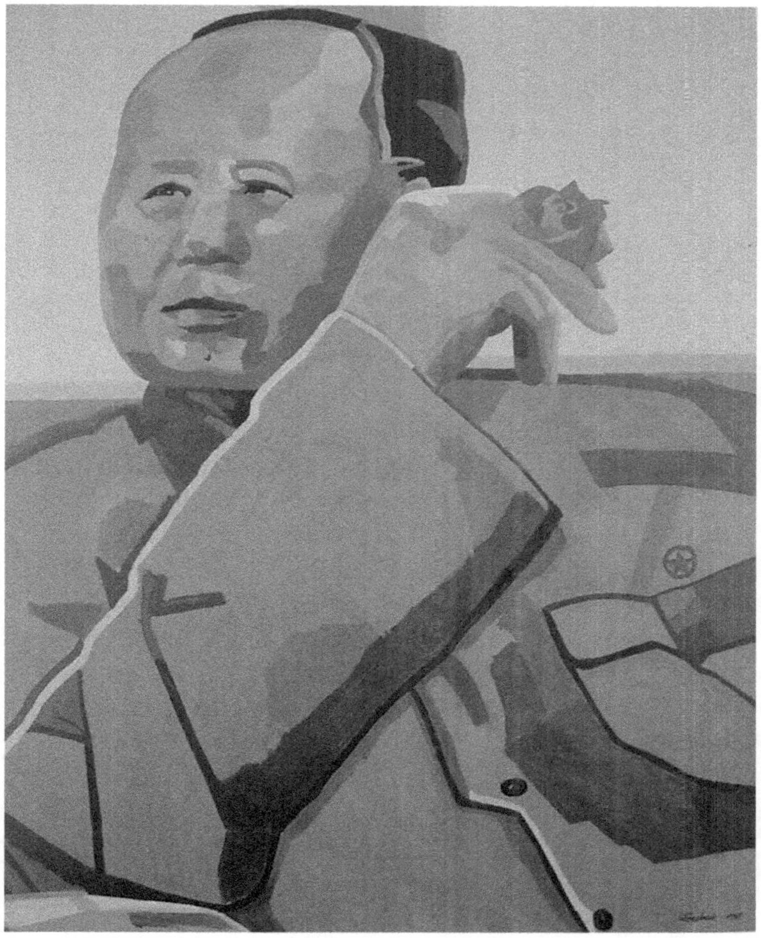

1.8   Eugen Schönebeck, *Mao Tse-tung* (1965)

visually violent refusal of Cold War borders, his later work *New Jersey* (1979–80), an extension of his series *Chinese Paintings* of 1974–9, likewise integrates recognizable views or mass-media representations of American cities and skylines with Maoist propaganda (**Figure 1.9**). In a later appropriation of Erró's technique, the Chinese-Canadian photographer Tseng Kwong Chi creates a persona in his series of photographic self-portraits. In them he

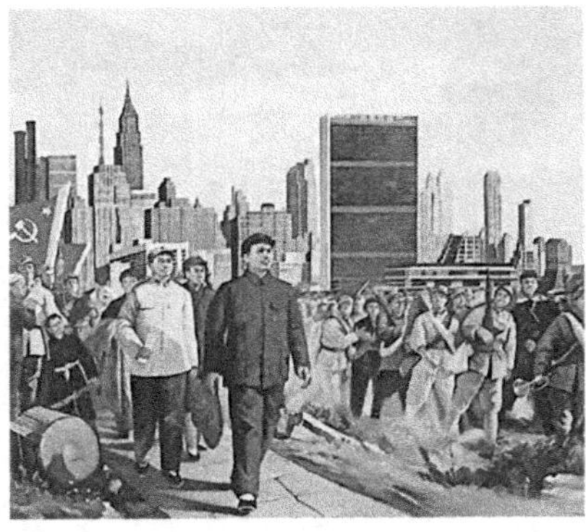

1.9 Erró (Guðmundur Guðmundsson), *New Jersey* (1974)

appears in a traditional and over-starched Mao suit, frequently grasping a cable release, or a remote shutter, and posed in front of an array of tourist destinations around the world, including Paris, New York (**Figure 1.10**), and Mount Rushmore. Tseng presents a persona that is a banal icon or even a surrogate of "Red" China, since it uses the familiar iconography of tourist photography but is at the same time exotic, as it appears as a (fictional) political representative of the Chinese nation. Tseng's images present Cold War stereotypes of the Chinese as the (racial, political) Other while they suggest that the West (Europe, the US) might itself become an exotic or fetishized Other for the Chinese. Tseng's images, then, compellingly reverse a power relation central to Cold War culture.

Sots Art

Socialist realism was furthermore critiqued in the USSR by artists such as Erik Bulatov and the collaborators Vitaly Komar and Alexander Melamid, by means of what this team termed "Socialist Pop Art" or "Sots Art," also called "Russian post-utopianism" by the critic and art historian Boris Groys.[32] Some of these paintings seem ambivalent enough to suggest to the viewer that in fact they may celebrate or continue socialist realism—Komar and Melamid are said to have declared the latter. This direction of a critical

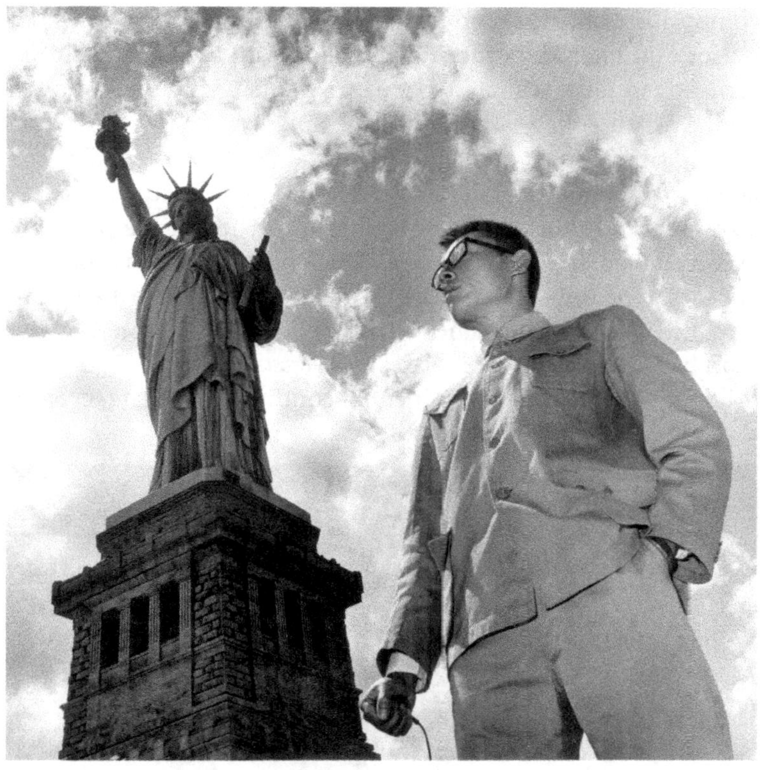

1.10   Tseng Kwong Chi, *New York, NY (Statue of Liberty)* (1979) (frcm
Expeditionary Self-Portrait Series, 1979–89)

Russian socialist realism in some ways parallels what has been
called "*Ostalgie*," or nostalgia for the everyday life of communist
East Germany. At least one feature film, *79 qm DDR*, released
with the English title *Good Bye Lenin!* (Wolfgang Becker, 2003),
has also been devoted to this genre. However, unlike the film's
cheery and humorous depiction of life in East Germany, the nostalgia that lurks in these Sots paintings, particularly Bulatov's, is
far more ambivalent. Bulatov positions his paintings to examine
the legacies of Soviet constructivism; he mingles constructivist
iconography and forms, as in his combining of dynamic geometric

compositions and the merging of text and image (as was practiced by, for example, Alexander Rodchenko), with the later, idealized forms of socialist realism. Like Erró's maneuvering between the mediums of collage and painting, Bulatov also synthesizes a painted surface from photographic images, texts, or the hackneyed landscapes of Sunday painters. In *Beware* (1973) he superimposes a severely foreshortened, doubled text, the title of the painting, over a clichéd, bucolic landscape. The effect is such that Bulatov appears to be unveiling for the viewer, like René Magritte before him, the ideological treachery that can be unleashed on even the most banal painted surface. *Revolution-Perestroika* (1988, **Figure 1.11**) brilliantly visualizes the engine that continued to create, even as

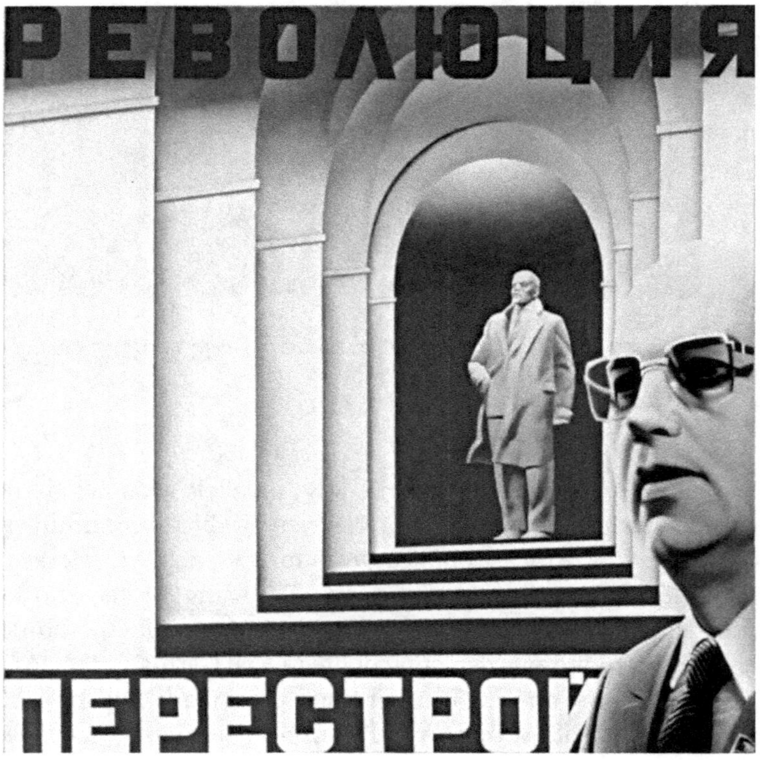

1.11   Erik Bulatov, *Revolution-Perestroika* (1988).

late as 1988, the ideal and fiction that was the USSR. The composition presents the parallel alpha and omega of that construct: the figure of Lenin in red-toned grisaille, next to that of Mikhail Gorbachev; and the words "revolution" and "perestroika" framing them. Bulatov presents two additional visual components essential to the construction of Soviet identity: constructivist forms, which he integrates in strong geometric shapes and in the Cyrillic text, and the icon of the party leader in the figurative style. In that it is copied from a photographic source, his depiction of Gorbachev both introduces and foregrounds a photorealist element, and it interrupts the otherwise monochrome—of course it must be red—composition. The painting recasts the entire notion of revolution, the foundational concept of the USSR and Marxism-Leninism, as now having to do with the "restructuring" action that was the agenda of perestroika, a series of reforms tied to another party leader. The painting seems to shift its focus from the comfortable, even museological visual clichés of the Soviet nation to the less certain present. Bulatov could not have known that the USSR was entering its final years. But in suggesting that revolution of the sort that established it had become an historical concept, he visually points to the possibility of a monumental change.

post-colonial identity and the civil-rights movement

While India's independence from British control in 1947 preceded it, the decolonization of African countries in the years following the 1945 Pan-African Congress in Manchester marked the ideological rejection of modern imperialist colonialism, and the beginning of what has been called the post-colonial era of the later twentieth century. Enormous cultural change also contributed to independence movements in Ghana, Algeria, Nigeria, Kenya, and Zaire (now Congo), among other countries. As Chika Okeke has stated, the story of the emergence of the multiple modernisms of the African continent hinges upon the fact that "modern artistic subjectivity is limited to political independence."[1] Art by modern artists in each of these countries, both before and since independence, certainly has a complex relation to African social and political developments, but the agency that is necessary for African artists to take up and rework Western notions of modernism was only achieved with the rejection of the ideology of colonialism. This made it possible for African artists to construct an autonomous notion of African identity. I will, then, argue that African modern art must generally be understood as engaging with politics.

As this chapter lays out, modern art pursued by African artists in Nigeria, Ethiopia, Ivory Coast, South Africa, and Benin collectively rejected Western, colonialist notions of "primitivism." Even in its beginnings in the notion of "Negritude" (discussed later in this chapter), modern African art sought to "mak[e] Africanness (whatever that may entail) part of the repertory of modern art."[2] It must, however, be noted that the very idea of "Africanness" is a problem, since it is a highly complex notion that has to do with the diverse cultures that make up the African continent— the Maghreb, West Africa, Northern Africa, sub-Saharan Africa. Perhaps the single unifying characteristic of African modern art is its anti-colonialism, and its resulting quest to rethink the African subject. One indication and example of this cultural diversity is the fact that South Africa alone has 11 official languages. The African diaspora, another dimension of post-colonial African culture and identity and a very concrete result of the development of the slave trade by colonialist nation states, further contributes to the staggering diversity of culture and identity that can be understood as "African." Colonialism not only enslaved Africans but set into motion the enormous displacement, or a diaspora, of Africans to the "new world," which included the Caribbean, the US, and elsewhere. This chapter also examines significant art that emerged around the US civil-rights movement in the 1960s and since, and that had as its subject both an emphatic rejection of institutionalized racism and a reformulation of African American identity. I recognize, however, that the African diaspora and its cultures must be traced in the art history of many nations. The chapter concludes with a consideration of several important African and pro-civil-rights artists working within the contemporary art world.

Decolonization in Africa; Independence; Resistance Art under Apartheid

African visual art foreshadowed the new ideology of post-colonialism: the work of several artists from the continent anticipated the cultural and political changes of the African era of independence. Ernest Mancoba (born 1904) and Gerard Sekoto (born 1913), two important pre-independence South African painters, both began to merge visual modernism with forms unique to

African culture, either in painted scenes from everyday life in the black townships of South Africa (Sekoto) or, in Mancoba's case, in referencing the rich traditions of African textiles in abstract compositions. Like Sekoto, Mancoba was largely self-taught while he still lived in his native South Africa, where he finished a degree at the Catholic teacher's college in Pietersburg (now Polokwane). In order to obtain proper artistic training in a period before the founding of modern African art schools that were open to black Africans, Mancoba received a grant or award to attend the École Nationale Supérieure des Arts Décoratifs in Paris. This is despite the fact that Mancoba was fairly successful with commissions for his sculptural work by the 1930s. Sekoto chose to go into exile in France. Therefore both of these painters had to be exiled from Africa in order to be trained as modern artists. Significantly, both artists died in France: Sekoto in 1993, and Mancoba in 2002.

During his years in Paris in the 1940s, Mancoba came to know several other painters who like him worked in an expressionistic, gestural, and highly colorful style. With them he founded, in 1948, the artists' group CoBrA, an acronym that was famously derived from only the European members' home cities—Copenhagen, Brussels, and Amsterdam—since Mancoba's home town of Boksburg outside Johannesburg seems to be missing from it, as was that of another group member, Jean-Michel Atlan, an Algerian artist. It is perhaps the case that CoBrA's interest in Mancoba's paintings had to do with their general enthusiasm for outsider art as their preferred route to authenticity in postwar art. Mancoba's *Composition* (1940, **Figure 2.1**) pursues a kind of decorative abstraction that does not adhere to the strict geometric forms of De Stijl, for example, and possibly refers to the bright patterning of African textiles.

In participating in CoBrA exhibitions Mancoba shared, at least for a time, the group's insistence that art of the postwar period continue its connection to revolutionary socialist goals, including the enlightenment of the population. Surely Mancoba also hoped for such radical social change in South Africa. As he continued to work in France, finally also as a French citizen, his engagement with decolonization in South Africa was at best indirect. However,

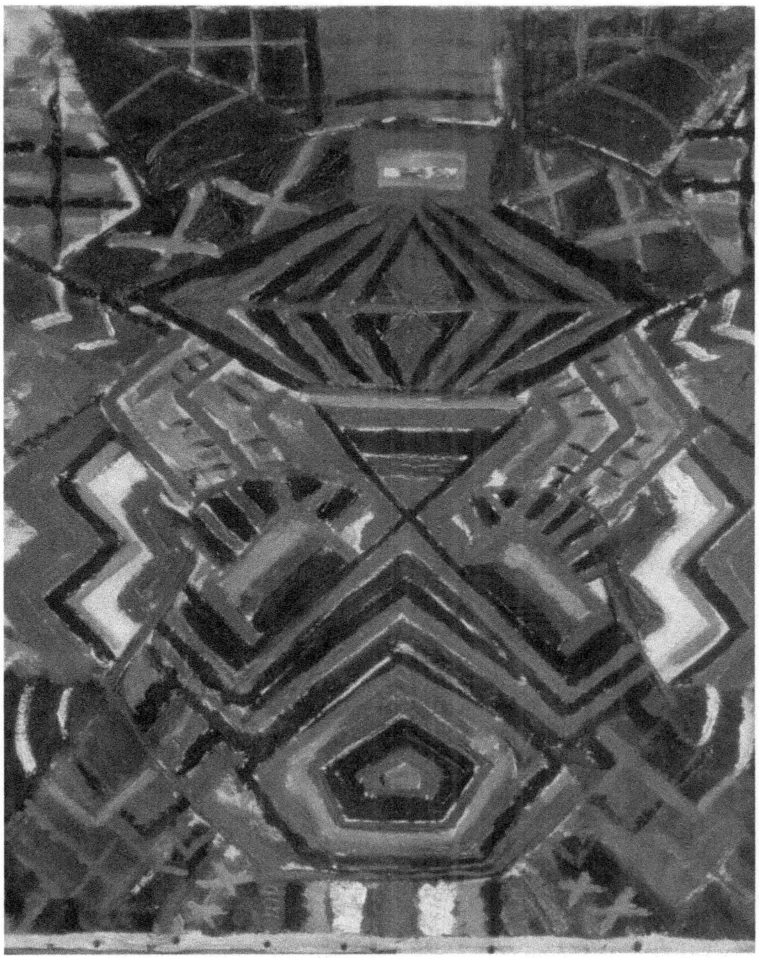

2.1   Ernest Mancoba, *Composition* (1940), oil on canvas, 59 x 50 cm

his work has yet to be fully understood in its rejection of European postwar painters' notions about the "primitivism" of African art, and in establishing an African modern and abstract painting in Europe.[3] Mancoba's art, then, initiated what Okwui Enwezor has called the "African systemization, deployment, and usage of modern forms, values, and structures."[4]

During Mancoba and Sekoto's exile the pursuit of independence gained momentum as a result of other intellectual developments relating to black African identity beyond colonialist strictures and specifically, from the developing philosophy of Negritude, an African humanism that rejected European philosophical and cultural models of the universality of the European subject, and of subjectivity itself. Negritude was theorized in Paris by the exiled Caribbean writers Aimé Césaire and Léon Damas and the Senegalese poet and statesman Léopold Sédar Senghor beginning in 1934, all of whom shared African ethnicity; Césaire is credited with first using the term, in his poem "Cahier d'un retour au pays natal" (1938).[5] In part, Negritude had to do with the construction and celebration of an African subject who rejected colonialism and assimilation to white culture, and who looked to African culture for new notions of black or Negro identity. Arguably Negritude, which was theorized in French, also took up Alain Locke's ideas about African culture and consciousness as they were presented in his writings on the Harlem Renaissance writers and artists of the 1920s in his book *The New Negro* (1925). The emergence of the independence leaders in Africa of the 1950s and 1960s was one outcome of this new philosophical construction of an African subject. Nnamdi Azikiwe of Nigeria, Kwame Nkrumah of Ghana, Jomo Kenyatta of Kenya, and, perhaps most famously, Patrice Lumumba of Zaire, were elected national presidents in the wake of independence from European control. As I discussed in Chapter 1, Lumumba was imprisoned and executed shortly after he took office. He became the primary and tragic icon of the first wave of African independence through Tshibumba Kanda Matulu's 1973–4 painting series *History of Zaire* (**Figure 1.5**) and more recently, a painting completed in 2000 by the Belgian Luc Tuymans (Zaire was a Belgian colony). Sadly, Tshibumba himself went missing sometime after leaving Lubumbashi in the early 1980s.

Looking beyond the icon of the fallen independence leader, some African artists took up the ideas of Negritude in reconfiguring visual modernism to deal with their own local, indigenous cultures. With the slow establishment of African art schools that were open to black African students in Ghana, Sudan, Uganda, and Nigeria,

African artists no longer had to be exiled to Europe in order to study modern art. Another system of art education, the workshop, was established by European expatriates like Ulli and Georgina Beier in Nigeria, but workshops were founded in other countries as well, including Mozambique, Zimbabwe, and Namibia. Prince Taiwo Olaniyi Wyewale-Toyeje Oyekale Osuntoki, who took the pseudonym Twins Seven Seven, trained in the Beier workshop in Osogbo, Nigeria in the early 1960s. Seven Seven's art focuses on the sacred figures and iconography of Yoruba culture, and possibly his own personal mythology, presented in compositionally dense drawings, paintings, and batiks. His pseudonym points to a general Nigerian interest in numerology. It is a reference both to the fact that he was said to be the only surviving child of his parents' seven sets of twins, and to the number two, which also has significance within Yoruba belief.[6] His drawing *The Goddess of Eternity* (1984) is characteristic of his compositions in its web of ornament and figure that fills the entire picture plane. The nine heads of the figure possibly reference the Yoruba goddess Oya, who is known as the "Queen of the Nine," after the nine tributaries of the Niger River. Seven Seven furthermore surrounds her in a swirl of fish and sea life; she grasps some of these animals in her hands. It seems certain that Seven Seven worked in a rich environment of artistic discovery in Osogbo with expatriate artists like Beier and Susanne Wenger, who likewise were drawn to the sacred aspects of Yoruba culture and were likely influenced by Seven Seven's art.

The noted Ethiopian artist Alexander "Skunder" Boghossian trained in London and Paris in the late 1950s before he returned briefly to Addis Ababa to teach. In 1969 he took a position at Howard University in Washington DC, where he taught until his death in 2003. He was first recognized as an artist of note in 1954 when he won a prize for his work during the jubilee celebrations for the Emperor Haile Selassie. In an interview Boghossian noted that during his time in Europe he was impressed by paintings by Paul Klee, Wifredo Lam, and particularly Roberto Matta. This statement, along with what can be argued to be the dream-image iconography in some of his paintings, has led commentators to conclude that Boghossian was something of a surrealist, while others strongly deny any connection to that movement. An early painting with collage, *Night Flight of Dread and Delight* (1964, **Figure 2.2**), suggests that Boghossian had multiple sources for his forms and techniques of painting. The bird and owl forms that he positions before a star-filled sky in this work recall the animal and plant forms in Lam's paintings, or Max Ernst's presentations of his bird-man alter ego Loplop. Boghossian's use of collage might also reference the medium used by the surrealist painter. At the same time Boghossian evokes the tight texture and subtle palette of Coptic mosaics of north-east Africa and of the neighboring Middle East, as some have claimed for his painting more generally.[7] It is thought that other Boghossian paintings, particularly *The End of the Beginning* (1972–3), make reference to

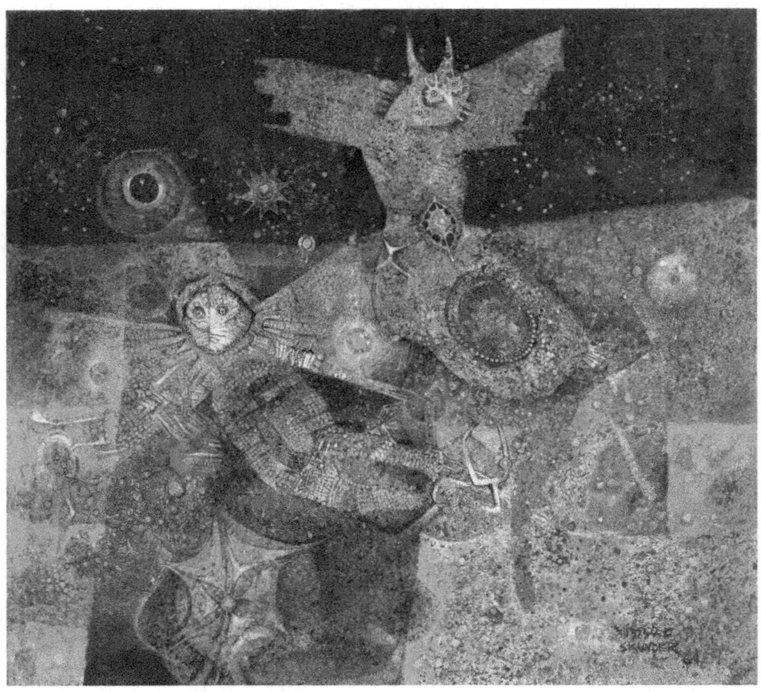

2.2   Alexander "Skunder" Boghossian, *Night Flight of Dread and Delight* (1964)

a specifically Ethiopian landscape and cityscape in flux that also touched upon the political changes and instability of the country around 1974 and the Ethiopian Revolution. It must be noted that surrealism had, by the 1940s, established a network of world artists stretching well beyond Western Europe, and involved figures of the African diaspora such as Lam, and Egyptian modernists such as the anti-fascist group Art and Freedom, organized in 1939 by Georges Henein, which held exhibitions in Cairo beginning that same year.[8] There was, then, a legacy of African artists who in advocating independence from occupying and colonizing powers had also discovered the forms of surrealism. This movement, an avant-garde that engaged with ideas of social change, was relevant to their own artistic work and, more generally, to the cultural and political struggle against the inequities of colonialism. Within his hybrid compositions that drew from both African and surrealist traditions, Boghossian was clearly also aware of these interconnecting legacies.

South African modern art similarly addressed the localized system of apartheid—an Afrikaans word for segregation—in place there from 1948 to 1994, which assured that a white minority would remain in control of the State and its institutions. South African artists, black and white, mounted resistance to this system and ideology, as did cultural institutions: the Amadlozi Group, for instance, founded by Cecil Skotnes, Sydney Kumalo, and the gallerist Egon Guenther, had as a major goal the exploration of African identity by both white and black artists through the forms of modern art. Amadlozi came out of a community art center or workshop, the Polly Street Art Centre in Johannesburg, of the type that remained the only option for black South Africans to receive art training in the 1940s and 1950s.[9]

Gavin Jantjes attended art school in his native Cape Town. He has worked across many different mediums but is perhaps best known for his print portfolios. His series *A South African Colouring Book* of 1974–5 (**Figure 2.3**) consists of collages of text and image that directly address the results and ideology of apartheid. A conceptual artist, Jantjes appropriates documentary photographs as a foundation for his work in this series, turning them into a moral

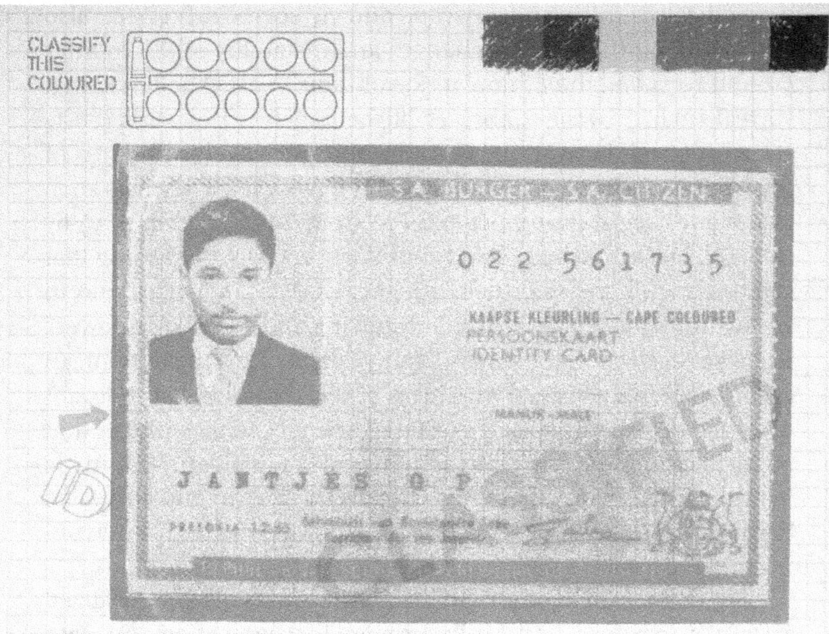

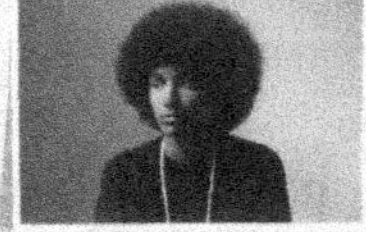

2.3 Gavin Jantjes, *Classify this Coloured* (from the series *A South African Colouring Book*, 1974–5)

statement against the injustice of institutionalized racism. In several prints Jantjes presents journalistic photographs of the 1960 Sharpeville township massacre, in which 69 unarmed apartheid protesters were killed by police and a further 185 were injured; in one print Jantjes uses text and diagrams to point to black policemen who participated in this brutal repression. Other prints in the series play on the word "colour," with the phrases "the true colour of the state"; "colour these people dead"; and "colour these blacks white." The last phrase, already intimated in one of Jantjes' other Sharpeville prints, is juxtaposed with photographic-negative images of activities of daily life, a wedding and a beauty pageant, and a quote from Frantz Fanon, the first psychoanalyst to access the self-loathing of the colonized subject:

> Having judged, condemned, abandoned his cultural forms, his language, his food habits, his sexual behaviour, his way of sitting down, of resting, of laughing, of enjoying himself, the oppressed flings himself upon the imposed culture with the desperation of a drowning man.

Jantjes then points to how the colonized black African has internalized the racist value systems of colonialism, and has come to reject black culture in favor of that of the colonizer. By means of the multicolored bars he includes in the corner of each print in the series, Jantjes also points to apartheid as a racial, or color-coding, system, whereby some lives are categorized as more valuable than others. One print features Jantjes' own identity card, stamped with the word "classified" with a text below it regarding the 1960 Population Registration Act's requirement that South Africans be categorized as either "colored," "native," or "white." As Jantjes' inserted autobiographical text in the print points out, the language of these identification cards gives rise to the same lack of self-esteem in the colonized that Fanon had described a decade earlier. The print remains one of the most powerful self-portraits of an African artist subjected to the oppression of apartheid.

Art of the Civil-Rights Movement and its Legacies

The African diaspora, a product of the slave trade and a central consequence of colonialist expansion during the early modern period, can especially be tracked across the countries of the so-called "new world" of the Americas and the Caribbean. The visual art and philosophy that grew around the US civil-rights movement arguably also connected with the main ideology behind independence in Africa, namely pan-Africanism and the notion of Negritude. The latter, as I have already stated, had its roots in the art and literature of the Harlem Renaissance of the 1920s, as it was articulated by Alain Locke's notion of the "new Negro." It appears that early steps toward desegregation in public education as well as in public transport in the US—the 1954 court decision of Brown vs. the Board of Education, Topeka, Kansas, and the Montgomery bus boycott of 1955–6—led to an at times violent backlash by parts of the white population, particularly in the south of the US where most of the early protests against segregation were staged. African American protesters generally followed the Gandhian strategy of protest through non-violence and civil disobedience to the State, a view shared by the Rev. Martin Luther King, Jr., the most important leader of the US civil-rights movement.

Mary Schmidt Campbell has tracked the early interaction between visual artists and civil-rights protest in the Spiral group, and particularly in the work of its most famous member, Romare Bearden. Formed in 1963 by the African American painters Bearden, Norman Lewis, and Hale Woodruff in New York, Spiral would ultimately have 14 members. Two of these, Bearden and Lewis, were known for their large-scale abstract works. The group began to read and discuss Senghor on Negritude as a philosophical position, surely a response to events of that year, such as King's historic "I have a dream" speech, delivered in Washington DC on August 28, 1963. Campbell recounts that the three artists thought one strategy of solidarity with the growing civil-rights movement would be to create collective works, with Bearden suggesting that they might work collaboratively with the additive process of collage.[10] He was apparently the only member who carried through with this idea, which transformed the rest of his oeuvre. Bearden turned to photomontage in his 1964 work *Conjur Woman* (**Figure 2.4**), part of his *Projections* series, a title that points to his

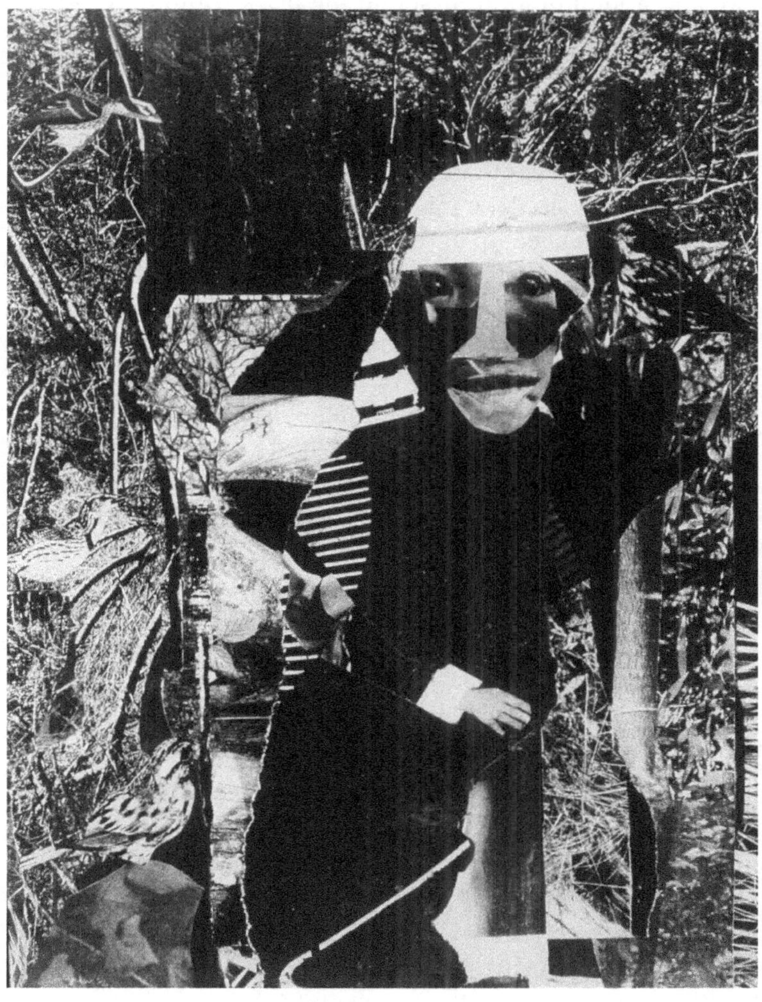

2.4   Romare Bearden, *Conjur Woman* (1964)

artistic process, since the artist had his original small-sale collage photographically enlarged and mounted for exhibition. As he completed more photomontages the series was shown in 1964 under the subtitle *The Prevalence of Ritual.* In this and other works Bearden took up the theme of his own childhood in the south (North Carolina) that he evokes through the figure of the "conjur woman," a kind of local mystic in the black community whom Bearden shows surrounded by flora and fauna, beckoning to the viewer. In manipulating the photographic fragment in his projections, Bearden also exploited the mnemonic associations of the photographic image. As a medium it could bring together his own personal memories with those of an entire generation of African Americans who similarly migrated north, and whose past in the south could be called up or "conjured" as a collective or cultural memory. Bearden then strives to represent the shared nature of African American experience as one united in a common spirituality and with a strong sense of community. In Bearden's projections this representation of black community and spirituality takes on further power and significance through the medium of painting.

The artist Charles Wilbert White, best known for his skill as a draftsman and his work in graphic art, used his artwork to celebrate positive images of prominent African Americans throughout American history, such as Frederick Douglass, Sojourner Truth, Harriet Tubman, and Paul Robeson. White also mounted a critique of slavery in the US and some of its legacies, including the widespread practice of lynching that had continued into the twentieth century. White was an activist for socialism, a connection other black American intellectuals such as the novelist Richard Wright had also made. White appears to have discovered the links between socialism and the struggle against racism around 1947, during the years that he studied at the Taller de Gráfica Popular in Mexico, where he came into contact with engaged socialist Mexican artists such as Diego Rivera and supporters such as Elizabeth Catlett. (White was married at one time to Catlett, who became a Mexican citizen and remained in Mexico throughout her life.) White trained at the Art Institute of Chicago and became active in projects by the Works Progress Administration (WPA), the US government agency set up as part of the New Deal that was dedicated to public-works projects, and the public murals it commissioned. This surely heightened his attraction to Mexican modernism and its tradition of public-mural painting. Another indicator of White's ties to socialism, and also his involvement and exploitation in the Cold War culture war, is the monograph and autobiography *Charles White, Ein Künstler Amerikas* (Charles White: An American Artist) published by the East German publisher VEB Verlag der Kunst in Dresden in 1955. White received accolades from the Akademie der Künste in East Berlin where he lectured, as well as from other Soviet Bloc countries. It has been noted that in addition to the racism White struggled against, he was also subjected to the blacklisting and other repression exerted on the US Left by McCarthyism.[11]

White returned to the US, where he lived and taught in both New York City and Los Angeles during the 1950s. In California he was able to show his work at Benjamin Horowitz's Heritage Gallery, one that promoted and exhibited both white and black artists. Throughout his career White took on the most difficult subjects for work that consistently sought to revise and clarify American history. This is most evident in artworks such as his 1947 drawing *Freeport*, which addressed the horrendous practice of the lynching of African Americans, sometimes veterans, by white mobs and the Ku Klux Klan. Like Bearden, White sought to underscore the historical references and mnemonic functions of his art. He did so by often using sepia-toned charcoals in his drawings and prints. This formalist invocation of memory is especially pronounced in White's *Wanted Poster* series of 1970 (**Figure 2.5**). On one level White uses these prints in order to point to the very medium itself as having played an historical role in perpetuating the injustice of slavery. In these prints White references the history of other prints or posters used before the civil war to announce slave auctions or to give notice of missing or runaway slaves, for example. One print features carefully rendered likenesses of two young people, one male and one female, framed by the dates "1619" and "19??." These sensitive portraits point not only to the continuity of prejudice and racism, but also

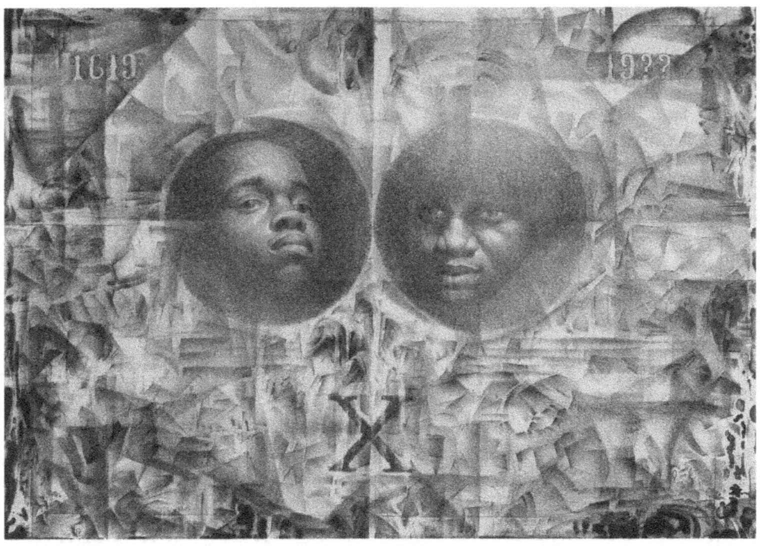

2.5   Charles Wilbert White, *Wanted Poster* (1970)

to the inherent humanity of those individuals in history who were, because of the institution of slavery, tragically deprived of their own individuality and dignity. White inserts the letter "X" at the composition's lower vertical axis, a reference to Malcolm X's powerful statement in rejecting his own surname, an action that had to do with another dehumanizing legacy of slavery: the practice of the renaming of slaves with the slave-owner's name and the resulting erasure of identity of African Americans. Again White uses his art to redress the injustice of history toward Africans and those of African descent.

The very difficult relation of African Americans to their own history of exploitation and persecution in the US, and to their identities as US citizens, was a major theme of African American art during the 1960s, the most active years of the civil-rights movement. By the mid 1960s unrest relating to how best to achieve the goals of the movement had spread, and more violent demonstrations and riots took place in the inner-city neighborhoods where American prosperity was not frequently felt, in Watts (Los Angeles) in 1965, and in Newark and Detroit in 1967. It is no coincidence that the American flag became an element in many critical artworks that sought to address the African American community's fraught relation to American history itself. Faith Ringgold's exploration of the flag as symbol of American identity is perhaps most infamous, but it should be noted that other artists, including the white artist and Fluxus impresario George Maciunas, also depicted the American flag very critically during the same years in order to make an antiwar statement. Ringgold's painting *The Flag is Bleeding* (1967) used the Stars and Stripes as a backdrop to point not only to the violence that inequality based on race would continue to evoke, but also to the fact that the inequality of women was another social concern that united women of all races with the struggle for black equality. Ringgold herself had suffered discrimination because of her gender: one might surmise that she was denied membership in the Spiral group for of this reason. Her *Flag for the Moon: Die Nigger* (1969) speaks perhaps most directly about the racial violence that underlies American history and identity. In it Ringgold manipulates the stripes of the national symbol—which had been planted on the lunar surface by the Apollo 11 crew—so that they spell out the hateful word "nigger," which was commonly used to categorize and dehumanize African Americans. The painting was part of the exhibition she helped to organize around the theme of the American flag, the *People's Flag Show* at Judson Church in New York City of 1970. As a result of that exhibition, and also her painting, Ringgold became one of the "Judson Three," along with Jean Toche and Jon Hendricks, who were arrested for "desecrating the flag."[12] Ringgold's painting of 1969 is also perhaps her most prescient, since the derogatory term she uses to render the stripes of the US flag has become a flashpoint for black musicians and artists of the rap and hip-hop era, who now regularly appropriate and thereby defuse and channel it away from its racist use.

Charles White's student David Hammons is perhaps best known for his large-scale assemblage sculptures, such as the exaggeratedly high basketball backboards of *Higher Goals* (1986), first installed in Cadman Plaza in Brooklyn, New York. But like his mentor Hammons explored the medium of graphic art to address the injustices suffered by African Americans in the US and used his work to move the black community from the margins to the center as a worthy subject of contemporary American art. In his "body prints" of 1973–4, created in Los Angeles, Hammons pressed or applied his greased body to paper, leaving an impression behind that he would then dust with charcoal or other pigments. Hammons consistently introduced an indexical mark of the African American body as an element and material that was central to his art.[13] His 1970 print *Injustice Case* (**Figure 2.6**) makes reference to the arrest of the activist Bobby Seale for conspiracy during the repressive Democratic National Convention in Chicago in 1968; Seale became one of the defendants known as the "Chicago Eight." Because of his vociferousness during his trial, the presiding judge ordered that Seale be bound and gagged. Hammons frames the body print with the edges of an American flag, thereby relating the national symbol to a vivid icon of the lack of free speech for some citizens of color. In many other assemblage works Hammons has included human hair as a material that similarly references the ethnic body of African Americans, who remain the primary subject of, and arguably the contributing material, for his art.

Glenn Ligon is an African American artist who builds upon this legacy of critical art produced in response to the civil-rights movement. A particular focus of his work is language; Ligon makes use of the textual strategies of conceptual art in order to foreground how language itself perpetuates certain social inequalities relating to race in everyday life. Like many of his other works, Ligon's etching *White #1* (1995, **Figure 2.7**) is in grisaille; it presents a sentence fragment of black letters. Cropped on each side, Ligon renders the words less legible since he has marked the background with dark drips and stains, causing the letters to blend into some of these dark areas. As viewers we do not know if the phrase is taken from any well-known source. From the words that can be discerned in their entirety in the frame of the print—"of course," "marked," "not impose," "hands," "about white," "father is not"—a speaker is implied, as is a possibly racially charged subject of discussion. It is also suggested that the sentence fragment does not intimate

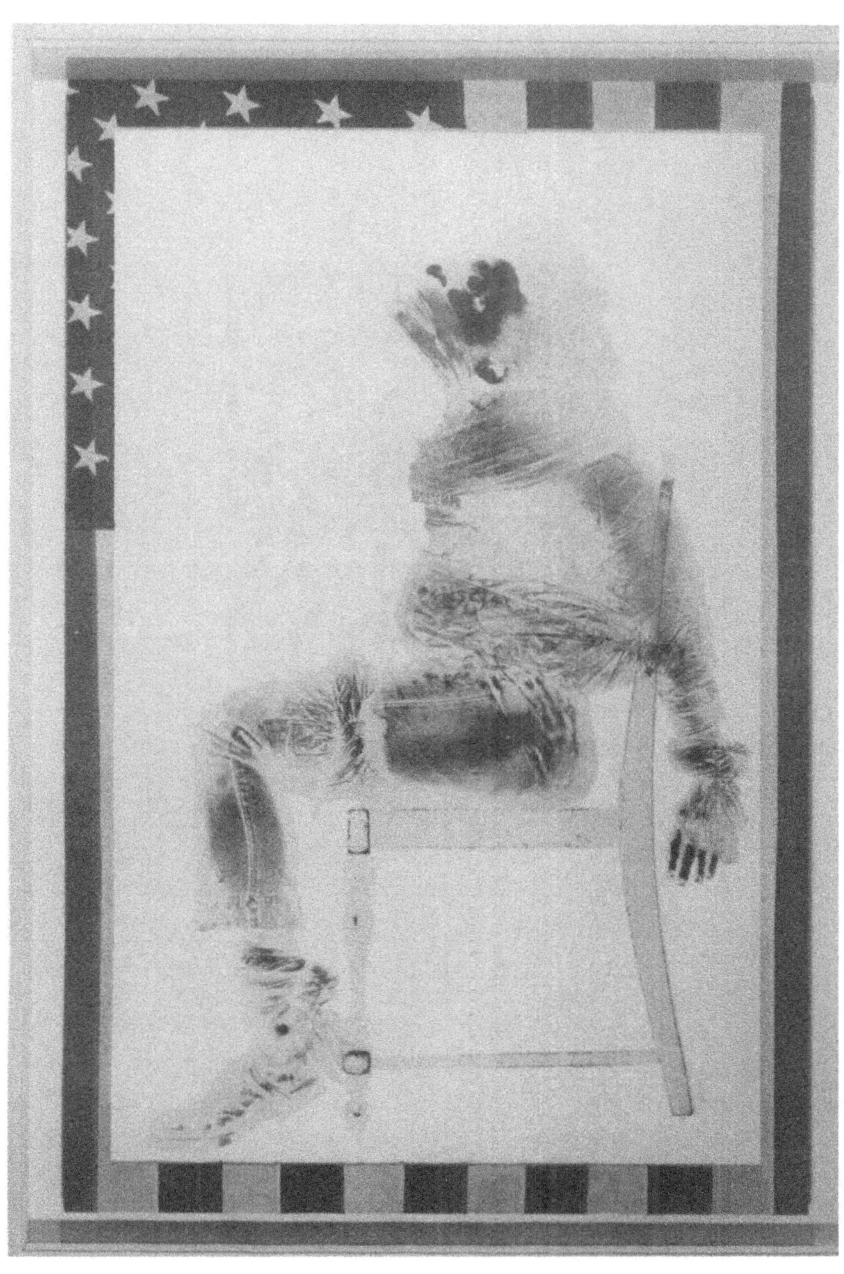

2.6   David Hammons, *Injustice Case* (1970). mixed media with body print.

2.7   Glenn Ligon, *White #1* (1995)

any issue of race, and that if the viewer makes this connection, the content of what is being "said" in the composition is neither verifiable nor certain. Ligon's language-based composition points to the imprecision of meaning that arises in language, and the difficulty of true communication taking place through it. The impossibility of communication may become even greater when those speaking do so across the gulf of racial difference. Ligon continues Ringgold's earlier exploration of the intersection of racism and language in American art.

Global Post-Colonialist Art: Creating New Languages

Where Ligon as an African American artist is interested in language as an unreliable medium impacted by the issue of race, Frédéric Bruly Bouabré sees art as a forum for his archival projects and studies that focus on visual and spoken language systems. One such project is Bouabré's mapping of the entire Bété language as a system, a quasi-anthropological and linguistic project from 1990–1 titled *Alphabet Bété*. Bouabré brings with him a utopian belief in art and language as systems that further human knowledge and that thereby grant some unity to the great diversity of human culture. Bouabré, who was born in and works in Ivory Coast, also belongs to the Bété people. He devised a long series of 449 pictograms—small-scale drawings roughly the size of an index card that combine an image with letters or monosyllabic word fragments—representing the Bété language.[14] Taken together the drawings constitute an icon-based archive, or linguistic database. Bouabré has also worked on other drawing series that further carry out his ambition to organize and categorize images and texts: the small-scale drawings of *Knowledge of the World*, a series begun in 1970 and continuing into the 1990s, gather words, statements, truisms, and images that Bouabré distinguishes for their importance. One drawing in the series, a grid with each square containing stylized eyes and mouth, is framed by the text, "*Toutes les races du monde ont droit à la liberté de la parole"* ("All races of the world have the right to freedom of speech"). Another series, *Les Grandes Figures* from 1987–8 (**Figure 2.8**), features drawings of public figures including Ronald Reagan, Leonid Brezhnev, Pope John Paul II, Senghor, and Nelson Mandela, each with a text that identifies them by name and title. Bouabré carefully dates many of the drawings, an action that underscores the diaristic quality of the series. Since he presents these elements as key components of his own knowledge system, in some sense his drawing/archives can be seen as extended self-portraits. The series maps his own relation to the images and people of the world. This relation also comprises his own subjectivity and worldview. In this artwork Bouabré presents himself as a subject most subtly, as well as with great modesty.

Like Bouabré, other contemporary African and African-diaspora artists fashion their art around material culture that they have carefully collected and assembled. They critically address the history of colonialism and conquest through these collections and materials as a type of evidence. As an artist of African descent Yinka Shonibare is interested in making "African art," but he points to the fact that

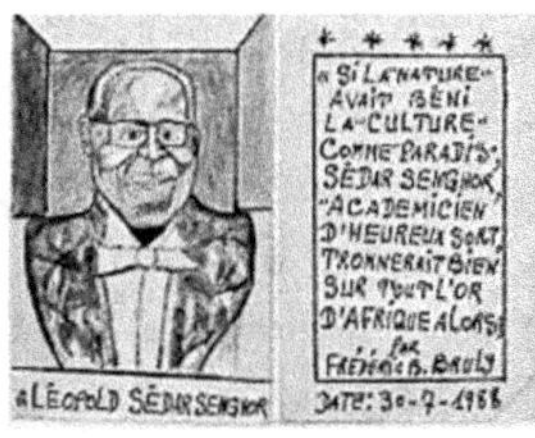

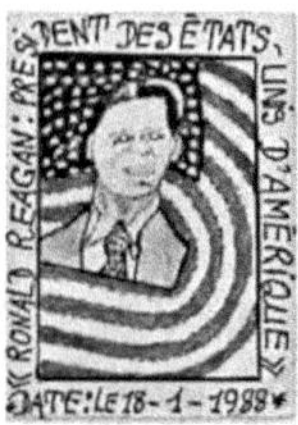
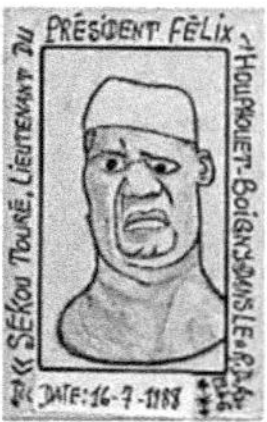
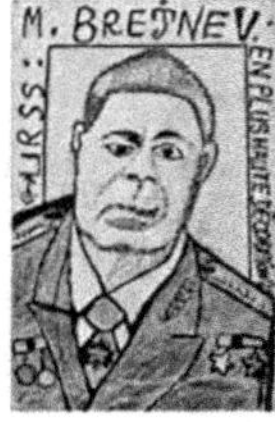
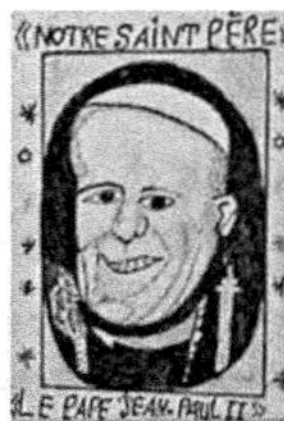
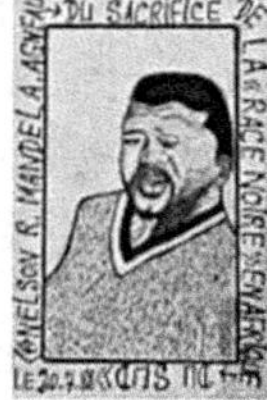

2.8   Frédéric Bruly Bouabré, *The Great Historical Figures of Our Time* (*Les Grandes Figures historiques de notre temps*, 1987–8)

African ethnicity can never be seen as a pure or stable notion but one that is always constructed and multiple. Shonibare, a British artist who was raised in Nigeria, is best known for his elaborate installations that hint at mostly European figures of the golden age of colonialism, the eighteenth and nineteenth centuries. These figures are clad in so-called Dutch wax-print textiles, the bright, patterned cloth that many identify as a marker of Africanness, but that has in actuality been manufactured in the Netherlands and exported to Africa for years. One of Shonibare's installations, *Gallantry and Criminal Conversation* (2002, **Figure 2.9**), depicts multiple figures in eighteenth-century garb such as bustles and greatcoats beneath a suspended carriage; this makes reference to the *fête galante*, or elegant outdoor gathering, a European painting genre and repeated subject matter of eighteenth-century art. Shonibare's figures are headless but carefully attired in Dutch wax-print textiles. The figures appear to be engaged in sex acts that suggest sodomy, among other things. Shonibare brings the contradictions and irony inherent to a material object, an African/Dutch textile, to his quasi-*tableau vivant* scene of European cultural history. One lesson we can take from Shonibare is that African and European cultures were already tightly entwined at the start of the early modern period, and at the beginning of colonization. Another message carried in the material object of the Dutch wax print, and that Shonibare stages in his installation, is the moral vacuum and general depravity of a European "civilization" whose ideology would give rise to the profound injustices of colonialism in Africa. Of course, both Europe and Africa continue to struggle with the effect of this racist legacy.

The Benin artist Georges Adéagbo is also an artist-archivist who works with found objects to further knowledge of the past. He groups these objects into large installations that have also been called assemblages. His installation at the Documenta exhibition in Kassel, *Explorer and Explorers Facing the History of Exploration…! The World Theatre* (2002, **Figure 2.10**), characteristically assembled a number of objects that point self-reflexively not only to the work's European site of exhibition, but also to the artist's location in Cotonou, Benin's capital. The work furthermore foregrounds the displacement that results from the transporting of his work

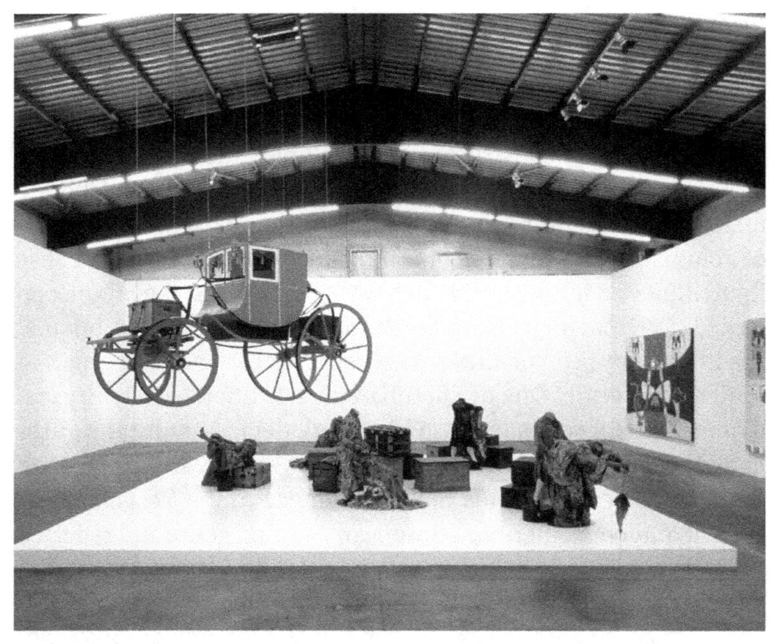

2.9 Yinka Shonibare, *Gallantry and Criminal Conversation* (2002)

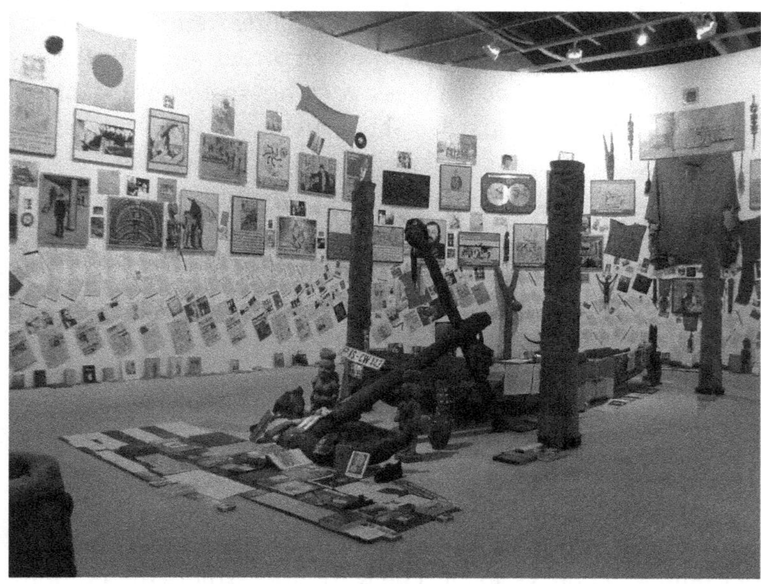

2.10 Georges Adéagbo, *Explorer and Explorers Facing the History of Exploration...! The World Theatre (L'Explorateur et les explorateurs devant l'histoire de l'exploration...! Le Théâtre du monde*, 2002)

to the exhibition. Adéagbo makes the relocation of his installation another dimension of exploration, and one that might be seen to reverse the earlier travels of imperialistic "exploration" of the underdeveloped world by the West.

Adéagbo undertook research trips to Kassel a year before his installation was to take place. During that time he collected various books, objects, and ephemera, and copied a number of images and texts from the Documenta archive. Adéagbo gave many of these images in photocopy form to local signboard painters in Cotonou who reproduced them according to their preferences for composition and size. The paintings included images of a founder of Documenta, Arnold Bode, and the artists James Lee Byars and Joseph Beuys. The artist also hired local sculptors to carve four matching wood totems, which Adéagbo finally placed at the center of his installation, surrounding a canoe that he had found on a stretch of beach near his home. These wooden objects then formed a core or base around which Adéagbo placed the painted copies and other ephemera of his collection, on the curved walls of the gallery—he stipulated that the space must have an "apse"-like structure to encourage the circular movement of visitors within the space. The core objects at the center of the installation therefore corresponded to a notion of home, or "African" objects; the explored, the results of Adéagbo's research and collecting in the US and Europe, was displayed on the walls. He also collected other objects and ephemera in Benin and elsewhere that addressed the history of Africa or cultural history more generally.[15]

Like Shonibare's art, Adéagbo's *Explorer and Explorers Facing the History of Exploration* constructs a material-culture history that relates and juxtaposes Western and African pop and high culture. In this history, Benin is at the center, and the West and Africa share the margins, in the great ocean of information and imagery that swirls about both of these world cultures. Historian and artist, Adéagbo uses art to present a history of a Western cultural site that is articulated from his position as an African, envisioned and represented from Africa. Adéagbo initiates a view of world history that is to be continued in the future; it is also a picture of the future subjects of that history.

the anti-war and peace movements

Termed the "American War" by many Vietnamese, the Vietnam War was a conflict that marked the end of colonial rule in Southeast Asia, and one that became global in scope, in large part due to the circulation of images of it. The Vietnam/American War served as the great galvanizer of anti-war visual culture in the US and globally after 1960. Art of the 1960s and 1970s that critiqued that war became the touchstone of anti-war art of the late twentieth and early twenty-first centuries, which focused on conflicts such as the Bosnian War of 1990 and those in the Middle East, including the civil war in Beirut, the first and second Gulf Wars, and the US invasion of Afghanistan. This chapter traces artists' anti-war sentiment and direct engagement with the anti-war movement during the Vietnam/American War and since. As will become clear, feminist artists were among the early initiators of anti-Vietnam War art. Nancy Spero and Martha Rosler honed the anti-war content of their art in their feminist opposition to the masculinist/patriarchal violence that is perpetuated in militarism and modern warfare.

For Vietnam, Against War

Some post-1945 anti-war art carried its critical message through a stance of artistic—or what has been called neo-avant-garde—resistance. Delivered most famously by a growing group of minimalist artists in New York by the late 1960s, this stylistically and structurally articulated position against the war resonated most strongly within the art community. Within that community, minimalism counted as highly effective political art. The "minimalist" exhibition organized by Lucy Lippard, Robert Huot, and Ron Wolin at the Paula Cooper Gallery in October 1968 was meant to raise funds for and otherwise to support the Student Mobilization Committee to End the War in Vietnam. Lippard reports that it did so quite successfully. The artists Jo Baer, Carl Andre, Sol LeWitt, Dan Flavin, and Donald Judd, among others, participated. A statement about the exhibition explained: "The artists and the individual pieces were selected to represent a particular esthetic attitude, in the conviction that a cohesive group of important works makes the most forceful statement for peace."[1] The exhibition presented the cumulative radicalism of minimalist sculpture across the work of several artists. The challenging nature of this work was mostly based, as Judd articulated it, in rejecting traditional composition by means of stacking ready-mades into "one thing after another," or serialized arrangements. But the exhibition also grouped the art and its artists as a kind of promotional entity, in terms of its advocacy of a student anti-war collective. The minimalist artworks therefore became anti-war art through their promotion of another social group. Although it proved itself to be highly effective within the art community, one might think of this as secondary-level political art. One might similarly categorize the early anti-war letter-writing campaigns, beginning in 1965 and continuing through 1968, waged by the Artists and Writers Protest, whose members included Leon Golub and Spero. Many of the group's letters were published in the *New York Times*. In contrast, the majority of the work I discuss in this chapter is not pacifist through association, but rather through its address of specific causes and effects—the contingencies, so to speak—of postwar military conflict.

Sculpture in the US had engaged directly with anti-war protest since the Artists' Protest Committee's collaborative *Peace Tower*, designed by Mark di Suvero and erected on a lot on the corner of La Cienega and Sunset boulevards in Los Angeles in February 1966.[2] Several Los Angeles-based artists completed the coordination for the tower's construction: Arnold Mesches, Judy Gerowitz (aka Judy Chicago), and Irving Petlin. The roughly 60-foot-high tower in the shape of a tetrahedron served as a scaffolding on which over 400 contributed paintings were hung and later sold; contributions were received from Frank Stella, Eva Hesse, Raphael Soyer, Robert Motherwell, Louise Nevelson, Ad Reinhardt, Philip Pearlstein, Donald Judd, and Chicago, among others. An opening ceremony included speeches by Susan Sontag, Petlin, and a former Green Beret. Attempts were made to vandalize the structure, but a volunteer security detail succeeded in protecting the artworks on view. The owner of the lot who gave his permission for this *plein-air* installation and exhibition came under intense pressure to remove the tower; the organizers initially planned that it would remain in place for the length of the military conflict. It lasted three months instead. Yet the tower has a considerable legacy: a second or "new" Peace Tower by di Suvero, Petlin, and Rirkrit Tiravanija was erected outside the museum as part of the Whitney Biennial in New York in 2006. The *New Peace Tower* had as its subject the ongoing American occupation and war in Iraq.[3] Almost 30 years after the conclusion of the Vietnam/American War, and three years into the Iraq War, several critics ruminated on whether the 2006 structure signaled US artists' return to an explicit address of global political conflicts that involved their own country.

As the *New Peace Tower* makes plain, anti-Vietnam War art remains relevant to visual artists who address contemporary military conflict. Art has also registered new forms of conflict—guerrilla violence, or terrorist attacks on the civilian population—that have developed globally since the 1972 "Black September" attack on Israeli athletes in the Olympic Village in Munich, Germany, that left 11 dead. The American sculptor David Davis completed a commission for a memorial to one of the victims of that act of terrorism, the *David Berger National Memorial* (1975), now an official national monument and located in Beachwood, Ohio **(Figure 3.1)**.[4] Berger was a wrestler and a native of the Cleveland area who emigrated to Israel, made the Israeli Olympic team, and was murdered in the Munich attacks. Made of Cor-Ten steel, Davis' repeated arc forms reference both the grace of athletic movement

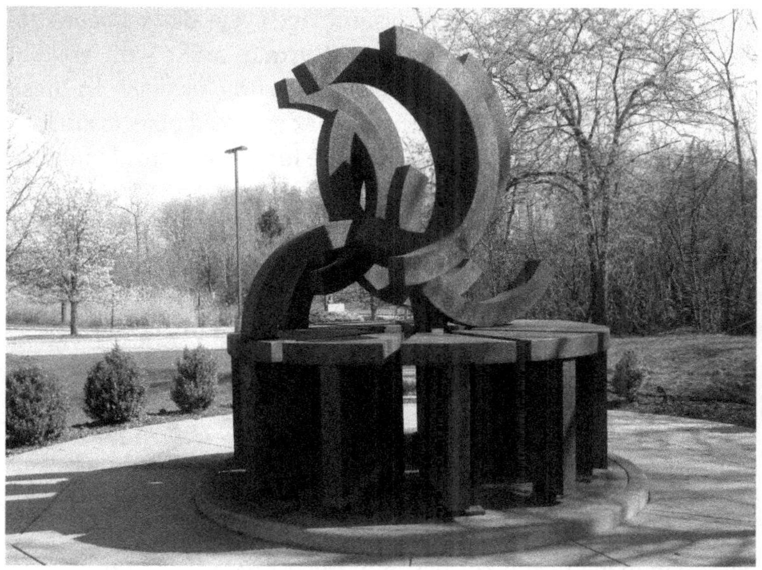

3.1   David Davis, *David Berger National Memorial* (1975)

and the fracturing and destruction of the circles of the Olympic logo. In the work Davis not only memorializes an individual, but also denounces violence against innocent victims, the hallmark of terrorism. The fictional collective the Atlas Group (in reality the artist Walid Ra'ad) has created controversial works that comment on terrorist tactics, specifically on the use of car bombs during the Lebanese-Israeli conflict of the 1980s, a terrorist technique that continues to be used globally; Ra'ad is discussed later in this chapter. Assemblages by the Colombian artist Doris Salcedo point to the absences suffered due to the phenomenon of "forced disappearance" that was practiced on the civilian population by military juntas in Latin America, in particular in the "Dirty War" waged by the Argentinian State against left-wing activists in the 1970s, and in "Operation Condor," a campaign of political repression by several states on the continent in the same period.

In the postwar period artists frequently turned to assemblages composed of found objects to address the violence and other unethical aspects of war. The assemblage cycle *Black Room*, created in the early 1960s by the West German artist Wolf Vostell, contained the works *Treblinka* and *Auschwitz Floodlight*. In these eclectic pieces Vostell uses damaged or destroyed objects such as a floodlight or a suitcase to point to the inhuman acts of violence that marked everyday life during the Holocaust. The objects in Vostell's assemblages bear the traces of an act of violence. Like his contemporary Claes Oldenburg and later artists such as Harun Farocki, Vostell implicates the use of technologies such as high-powered lights or film as tools of subjugation during wartime.

Working in the US, the American artist Ed Kienholz's major assemblage of 1968, *The Portable War Memorial* (**Figure 3.2**), resonated with two related Cold War developments: a newly globalized territory for US military involvement, and, subsequently, a lack of public interest in war as a changing succession of distant conflicts. Kienholz constructed elaborate tableaux or assemblages that suggest spatialized narratives based in the everyday life of the US or of his adopted country, West Germany, where he worked extensively, beginning in 1973. In *The Portable War Memorial* Kienholz bitterly condemns the moral apathy of the US public toward the suffering and sacrifice of war. The assemblage resembles a long altarpiece, due to the large cruciform shape that bears the work's title. Kienholz paints almost all the found objects and surfaces in this assemblage a pale silver-gray color, with the exception of the blackboard's tabular surface. This painterly aspect of the assemblage—which creates a grisaille effect—serves to flatten its elements; from a distance the work coheres into what seems to be a relief sculpture. Kienholz's uniformity of color also underscores the unity of the narrative that he presents in the artwork. Unlike Vostell's assemblages, Kienholz does not focus on the singularity and materiality of the found objects that the piece includes, but rather on the presentation of a coherent, holistic narrative.

At one end Kienholz places an approximate copy of the human forms, with only helmets for heads, of the Marine Corps War Memorial (or the Iwo Jima Memorial, located outside Arlington National Cemetery). He balances these forms with a series of picnic tables, chairs, and a soda-vending machine on the right, all

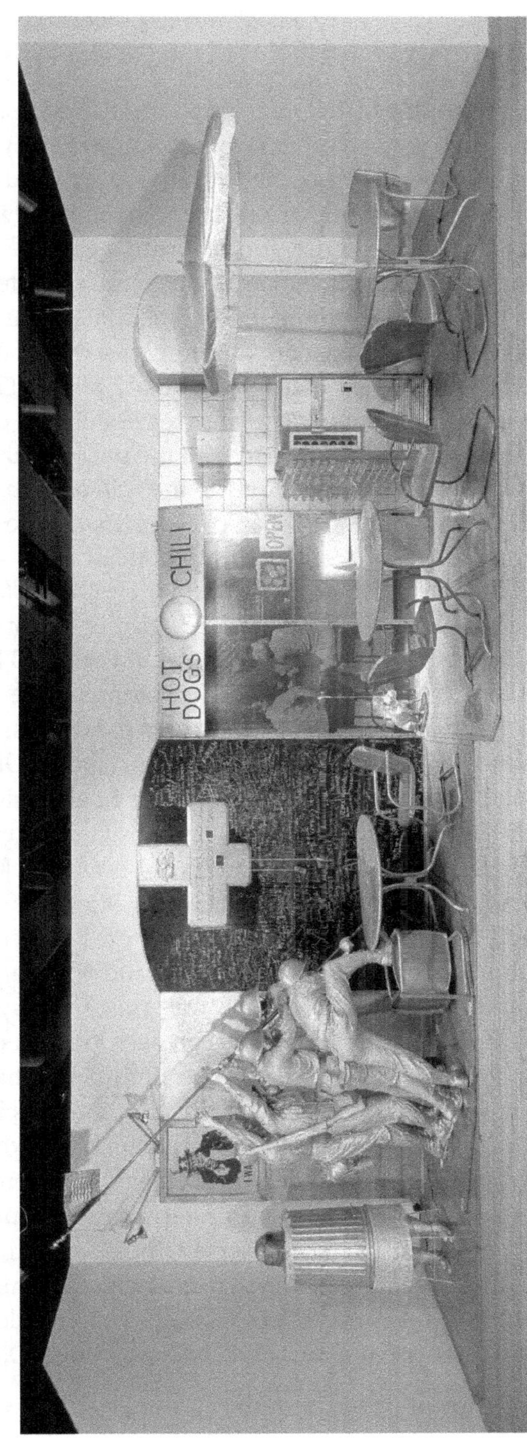

3.2 Ed Kienholz, *The Portable War Memorial* (1968)

positioned before a life-sized photograph of a couple snacking at a hot-dog stand. A chalkboard next to this image displays a list of "extinct countries," with extra chalk and an eraser placed there for additions or alterations. Functioning as the stand-in viewer of the piece, a headless female figure, formed from a garbage can with women's pumps peeking out underneath, stands isolated on the far left. This "memorial" is simultaneously dedicated to an obsolete and therefore ignorable image of heroic military sacrifice, American consumerism, and the new quasi-permanence of war. The entire tableau is taken in by Kienholz's ruthless representation of its own viewer as blind to and unconcerned with the new ordinariness of wartime sacrifice that is limited only to the military. The work is a biting indictment of the American consumer's heartlessness in relation to the subject of the Vietnam/American War.

Claes Oldenburg's *Lipstick (Ascending) on Caterpillar Tracks* from 1969 (**Figure 3.3**) encapsulates the spirit of performed and collective protest discourse of the Vietnam War era. This work has been relocated to the Yale University campus in New Haven, Connecticut. Interestingly the work appears to be an assemblage of found objects, but is actually a constructed sculpture. Oldenburg first built the piece in plywood. In giving the final version of the sculpture the look of an assemblage, perhaps Oldenburg meant to connect the work to the anti-war works of Vostell and Kienholz. *Lipstick (Ascending)* was initially installed in May 1969, outside Woolsey Hall and the Commons building on Beinecke Plaza, an area where students could congregate and voice and other-wise perform their opposition to US war policy. It stayed there until 1974, when it was installed in its present location outside a campus residential college. Oldenburg, a member of the class of 1950, commented that his design for the sculpture was intended to create a kind of stage or podium from which speakers could address public rallies. As was the case at other US university campuses at the time, such rallies and protests were frequent; Yale protests targeted the university Reserve Officers' Training Corps (ROTC) program and local armament manufacturers, among other concerns.[5] Anti-war protests often took place at Ingalls Rink, a considerable distance from the center of the campus. Oldenburg

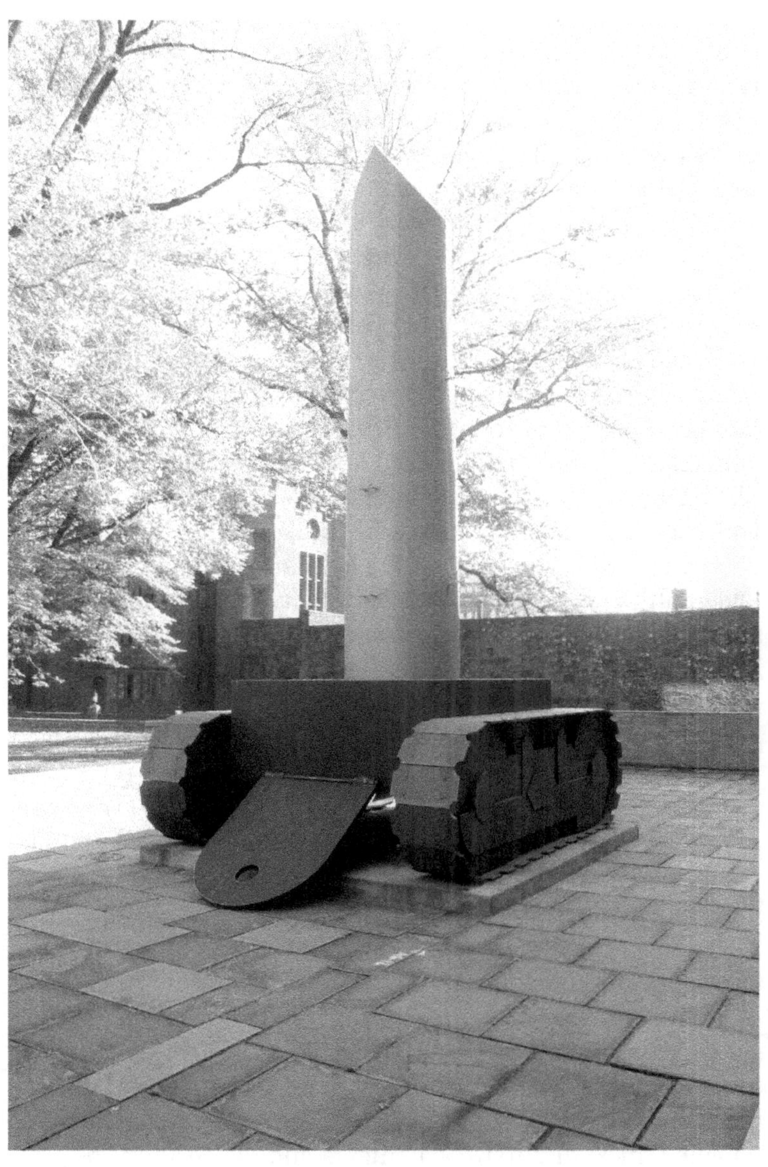

3.3 Claes Oldenburg, *Lipstick (Ascending) on Caterpillar Tracks* (1969), Cor-Ten steel, aluminum; coated with res n and painted with polyurethane enamel

was approached and commissioned to do the work by the "Colossal Keepsake Corporation of Connecticut," a group of students and faculty in the School of Architecture who admired Oldenburg's work. In part Oldenburg also used the work to reconfigure a plaza as a space for public debate and to relocate protest closer to the center of the university campus.[6]

As his maquettes for the work make clear, Oldenburg devised *Lipstick (Ascending)* as a work that could be altered at will with the use of interchangeable parts—or, as Oldenburg put it, "stages of extension"—involving its uppermost, priapic element. The pedestal-like lower portion of the work consists of a form that references the gears, base, and track of a tank. Oldenburg's military reference here is clear. The final element, a vertical column painted to resemble a tube of red lipstick, was erected on a short platform placed directly on top of the track or base of the work, which also functioned as a stage for speakers. The rigid columnar element could be replaced with a similar vertical structure that Oldenburg crowned with an inflatable, and collapsible, red balloon. The columnar element could then be completely vertical and rigid or be in various stages of flaccidity or deflation. This collapsible component of *Lipstick (Ascending)* relates to other works by Oldenburg, where he realized everyday objects as "soft sculptures" made of canvas, such as *Soft Typewriter* (1963). It is also part of the series of large-scale public sculptures Oldenburg produced in the late 1960s, which expanded everyday objects, such as a women's lipstick, into gigantic, monumental forms. One could read *Lipstick (Ascending)* as a feminist statement: in realizing an object mostly used by women as an unerect vertical or priapic form, and juxtaposing it with an arguably masculinist or military form, Oldenburg feminizes a military icon and, in the process, sarcastically emasculates it. In realizing the work as an iconic representation of emasculated US military and patriarchal power, Oldenburg literally builds and sets the stage for equally critical discursive statements and debates to take place on this sculpture. In a discussion with the critic Germano Celant, Oldenburg furthermore mentioned Vladimir Tatlin's *Monument to the Third International* of 1919–20 as a point of departure for

Lipstick (Ascending).[7] Oldenburg, then, includes in his sculpture a sly reference to the spiraling and upward movement that Tatlin had envisioned for his monument to the progressiveness of the new Soviet Union. Of the two works, only Oldenburg's critiques and literally deflates the implicit celebration of patriarchal power that was still active for Tatlin, in his iconic representation of the State.

Performance art of this period began to integrate war protest into visual culture more generally; while it originated in the realm of high art, performance also penetrated the sphere of mass culture because of ties between key media figures and the performance-art community. The anti-war performance artwork that remains the most successfully realized media event of the period is Yoko Ono and John Lennon's "bed-in," the first of which, *Bed-In for Peace*, took place at the Amsterdam Hilton Hotel in March 1969, immediately after the couple's marriage (**Figure 3.4**).[8] Both celebrities commanded enormous press attention at the time, and their idea was to stage a peace action by staying in bed for a week, an event that was to be disseminated by the mass media. During

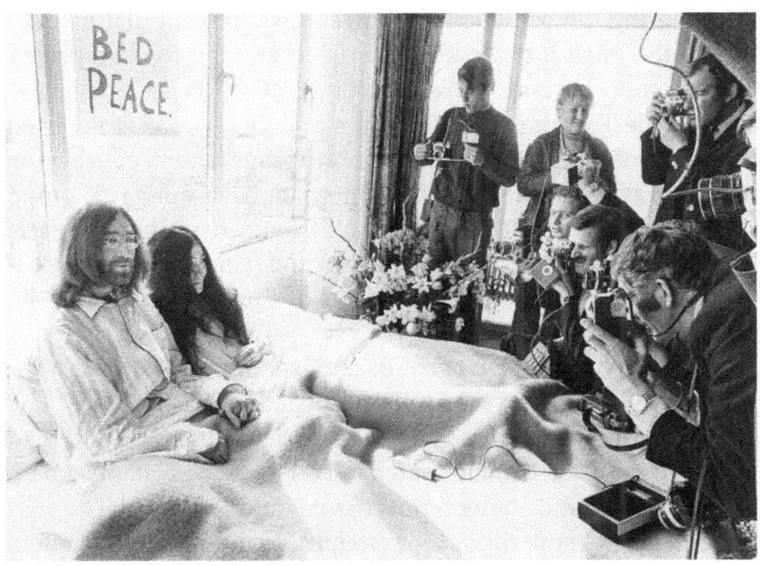

3.4   Yoko Ono and John Lennon, *Amsterdam Bed-In* (1969)

this time they discussed world peace, and hung signs reading "hair peace" and "bed peace" over their bed.[9] They followed this with a second bed-in in Montreal several months later; as part of that action they recorded the song "Give Peace a Chance" with a number of other performers including Timothy Leary and the African American comedian Dick Gregory. At an art festival the previous year in London the couple had staged a performance that they came to refer to as "bagism," where they were onstage but hidden from view in a black velvet bag for 45 minutes. Ono had already performed "bagist" works before that time. In a television interview with David Frost in 1969, Ono and Lennon explained that bagism sought to eliminate the exterior appearance of a given performer or individual so that the audience might focus solely on the substance of the message they conveyed.[10] They also deployed bagism to address gender and racial equality, which worked to underscore the seriousness of their anti-war and civil-rights activism, in spite of their celebrity as entertainers. Ironically they had clearly reached the decision that a bagist event would not have achieved the same level of media visibility and dissemination for them during the bed-ins. It is, however, significant that in addition to the Frost interview on television Lennon made repeated references to bagism in his recordings "Give Peace a Chance" and "Come Together." Therefore he and Ono successfully used the mass media to disseminate their message, and to educate the public on a global scale about the international avant-garde group known as Fluxus, in which Ono had been active since the early 1960s. Through their theory of bagism and their other work, then, the couple also foregrounded the goal of equality pursued by the civil-rights movement.

The other major icon of 1960s anti-war protest, the peace sign (☮), was more or less exclusively circulated in mass culture. The sign was originally designed by British artist Gerald Holtom for a 1958 nuclear-disarmament march in London; it was later taken up by the anti-war and student movements internationally. The sign is based on two superimposed semaphoric signals, for the letters "N" and "D," or nuclear disarmament.[11] The peace sign became especially popular on US college campuses. It has been used globally since that time to symbolize opposition to war. Recently it was used by demonstrators who assembled themselves to form the sign in Budapest in 2005 as part of their protest against the US invasion of Iraq.

Artists during the 1960s also chose to stage anti-war performances within the institutional spaces of the museum and gallery. Perhaps the best known of these actions, and in some ways the most direct and literal representation of the violence of war, was *Blood Bath (A Call for the Immediate Resignation of All the Rockefellers from the Board of Trustees of the Museum of Modern Art)*, staged by the Guerrilla Art Action Group (GAAG) in the lobby of MoMA in New York, in November 1969. Group members Jon Hendricks, Jean Toche, Poppy Johnson, and Silvianna (Silvia Goldsmith) entered each museum and threw a text of their demands, dated November 10, 1969, into the air. They began ripping at each other's own clothing, which released containers of animal blood they had concealed there, in a simulation of the horrors brought about by the violence of war. As this occurred, they screamed gibberish phrases, that included the word "rape." They then fell to the floor, lying still. After a time, they silently rose and left the museum, without speaking to museum officials.[12] One of the early interruptions or interventions into the smooth functioning of the museum, this public "guerrilla" art action—one that was unannounced and not officially welcomed by the institution—rejected the notion that the art museum should remain silent on world events. This introduction of explicit political statements within the gallery furthermore rejected the theory of autonomy for new art that had been advanced in high-modernist criticism in the US and Europe, as it was practiced by some of the art world's most powerful critics, curators, and journals of the 1950s and 1960s. The GAAG action would open the door to other artists' anti-war statements at MoMA in the next year, including Hans Haacke's *MoMA Poll* and the Art Workers' Coalition (AWC) demonstration around their poster, *Q: And babies? A: And babies*, which I discuss later in this chapter.

Jo Baer showed her abstract paintings in 1968 in order to make "the most forceful statement for peace," as she and other minimalists had stated. Anti-war sentiment was taken up in important figurative paintings as well, perhaps most prominently by the US artists Nancy Spero and Leon Golub. The latter's paintings in particular have been marginalized in many histories of painting of the 1960s in favor of the more formally radical exploration of painting pursued by pop, minimalist, and conceptual artists; Spero's art has assumed a rightful place in the history of feminist art. Their paintings are among the most powerful cultural statements against the Vietnam/American War and other military conflicts of the late twentieth century. Both are among art history's most articulate artists on the subject of the physical brutality, violence, and conflict that characterize human existence and the male gender since antiquity. Spero in fact refused to represent the male body after the mid 1970s in her art; instead it remained a condemned absence for this very reason.

As members of the New York group known as Artists and Writers Protest, Golub and Spero published letters that advocated nuclear disarmament and criticized US intervention in Vietnam and South America beginning in 1962. The two artists collaborated closely throughout their lives, working in Paris for five years from 1959.[13] They shared a lifelong concern with representations of the body and conflict that harked back to antiquity as a hallmark of cultural history. As its title suggests, Golub's *Gigantomachy* painting series of the early 1960s references the battle between the Olympian gods and the giants of the netherworld in Greek mythology, as well as the great Hellenistic structures of the Parthenon and the Pergamon Altar on which it is narrated. Painted on a large scale and with dry acrylic brushstrokes on linen, the size and medium that he favored throughout his oeuvre, Golub's work intimated the linear qualities of the most dramatic and monumental sculptural reliefs of ancient Greece, and the writhing surface of other representations of bodily conflict, such as Pollaiuolo's Renaissance engraving *Battle of Naked Men* (1465).

Upon the couple's return to the US in 1965, Spero began her *War Series: Bombs and Helicopters* on paper (see for instance *Soldiers Pushing Victims from Helicopter*, 1968, **Figure 3.5**). In these spare, gestural paintings on a white background, Spero depicts

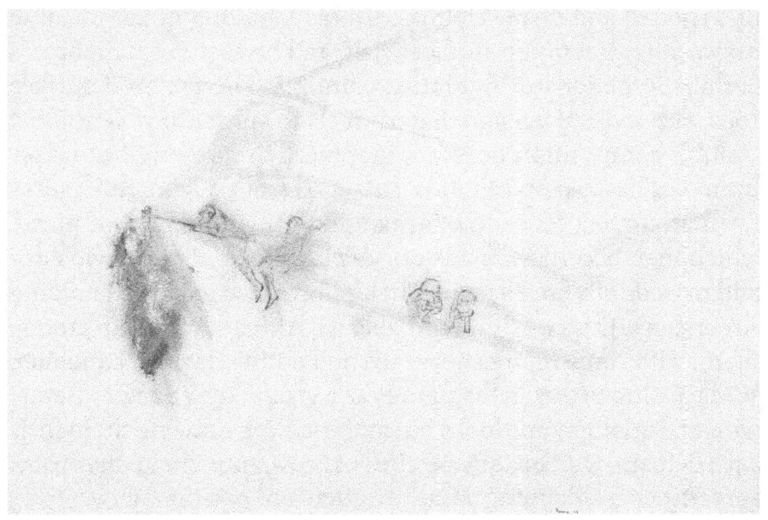

3.5   Nancy Spero, *Soldiers Pushing Victims from Helicopter* (1968)

bodies and body fragments—grotesques, severed heads, genitalia—emerging from mushroom clouds, military aircraft, and crematorium chimneys, and raining onto the ground. Explosions are rendered as rapes of the land. Of the two artists, Spero was the first to address recent conflict in her art, and condemn modern military action as patriarchal, obscene, and pathological. Her later and best-known series, *Codex Artaud* (1971–2), *Torture of Women* (1976), and *Notes in Time on Women* (1976–9), also on paper, are explicitly feminist works that address violence against women.

Perhaps in dialogue with Spero's engagement with the theme of violent conflict waged by twentieth-century humans and not the gods, Golub began his *Napalm* series in 1969, and the *Vietnam* series shortly thereafter, in 1972. While they point specifically to the Vietnam/American war, Golub's paintings after 1972 begin to address more generally the staging of masculinity by means of acts of military or paramilitary violence. Golub's male figures are typically clad in military fatigues, sometimes with crassly worded T-shirts, and toting large machine guns or handguns. Golub experiments with texture and pattern in his dry-brush rendering of wrinkled and grimy clothing. In his handling of paint Golub draws attention to the surface itself, and he thereby complicates simplistic notions of figurative painting. The textured surface roils with a visual tension that parallels the physical violence that Golub's composition does not graphically represent, but rather intimates has just passed. In *Vietnam III* (1973, **Figure 3.6**) figures form an almost fence-like formation against the picture plane, which then becomes a stage on which various rituals of violence and masculinity are enacted. The uniform of armed and standing American GIs is clearly identifiable, an African American among them, with some figures helmeted and outfitted with a bandolier. While Golub presents the figures as a group, they do not interact with one another; one looks out at the viewer, drawing them in as a participant. Odd opaque patches of brown punctuate the space, sometimes overlapping a figure; others are positioned next to or before these large areas of paint. The space of the painting does not cohere into a stable figure-ground relation. Further contributing to this inconsistent space are three foreshortened figures scattered horizontally on the ground between those standing; one is a woman, while another seems suspended near the horizon, an oddly tangled and upside-down mass. A long lintel-like form transverses the entire center of the painting, fading out on the left into indistinct brushstrokes, reminding the viewer of the constructed and fictional nature of all the forms in the composition. Are we as viewers witness to the aftermath of a massacre, or have we just missed an heroic moment of survival, male bonding and victory in war, the subject matter of many Hollywood films? Who are the victims or the victimizers here? Is this Golub's update to the older genre of history painting, with its rhetorical flourishes intact, or his condemnation of that genre's whitewashing of violence?

Golub constructs a similarly ambiguous position for the viewer in his later painting series *Mercenaries* (1980) and *White Squad* (1983). These paintings address the postwar development of para-militarism as a tool of State political power and as another stage for the performance of masculinity. In the latter series only one work—*White Squad IV (El Salvador)* of 1983—refers specifically

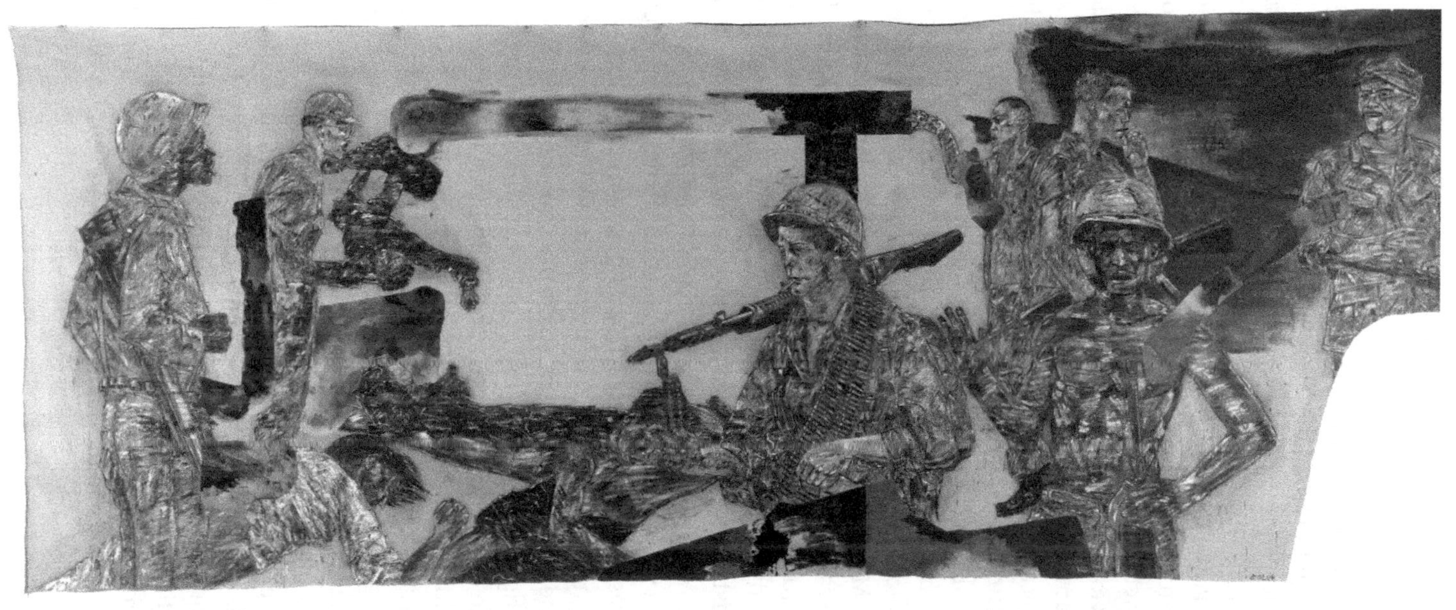

3.6 Leon Golub, *Vietnam III* (1973), acrylic on linen

to the activity of covert paramilitary groups in Central America. This would indicate that Golub considers paramilitarism to be a global development, yet one that often directly or indirectly involves US citizens. In the work *Mercenaries V* (1984) Golub again stages what may be terrifying moments before or after intense violence between the global migrants who are paid to unleash terror onto their victims in the name of vested interests, even those of the State. Golub underscores the totalitarian, anti-democratic element of paramilitarism: the victims of mercenaries and covert squads are typically activists who agitate for the opposition or who protest against ascendant military juntas or organized crime groups. Golub also relates paramilitarism to new race dynamics after the dismantling of colonialism, which opens new territories for post-colonialist power struggles where mercenaries can become active. *Mercenaries V* presents a less ambivalent performance of small-scale power and violence, presumably staged here for the camera to commemorate in a snapshot-like scene. As he did increasingly after 1980, Golub elevates the atrocity photograph, a mainstay of war photography, into the medium of painting. The titular mercenary waves jovially at the viewer, or a presumed cameraman who takes the viewer's position, all the while keeping his "charges" at gunpoint in torturous positions. Golub uses race to distinguish the victims from their white victimizer; we are left to imagine the violence that may take place momentarily. Since none of the figures are in any kind of uniform, this might otherwise be a scene of petty bullying that we could place in a schoolyard, or could imagine taking place among street thugs.

As short as the moment may be, Golub opens the medium of painting to the dynamic of physical domination and submission that the threat of violence, and the brandishing of the firearm, brings. Such moments are enacted daily, and Golub uses painting to universalize this primal and primitive moment of the creation of male power. No less disturbing is the similarity of Golub's composition to photographs of US military atrocities in Iraq, which the artist did not live to see. The dark, base quality of human suffering is Golub's subject, and in choosing it he recognizes the primitive drive to dominate through the threat and infliction of pain. In *Snake Eyes II* (1995) Golub features Nietzsche's words on the almost primal psychic pain that drives the cycle of violence, taken from *The Gay Science*. Golub abridges Nietzsche in his painting, but here is the full quote:

> I have named my pain and call it "dog"—it's just as faithful, just as obtrusive and shameless, just as entertaining, just as clever as every other dog—and I can scold it and take my bad moods out on it the way others do with their dogs, servants and wives.[14]

The philosopher of photography Susan Sontag argued for the special relation between the medium of photography and mechanized warfare, two developments of the modern era. According to Sontag war photography is a subgroup of a larger genre: images of the suffering of others.[15] In the twenty-first century we still know how influential photographic images of war can be in molding public opinion in the modern nation state. We also recognize that states have sought to control or conceal such images and thereby retain public support for military campaigns waged overseas, far from the public eye. Sontag harked back to the Weimar Republic's censoring of the brutal images of World War One that were contained in Ernst Friedrich's 1924 photo volume *War against War!* Certainly Friedrich sought to remind German citizens of the suffering and horror many of them had been spared, and therefore he encouraged anti-war sentiment in Germany. The US government went to great lengths to keep images of the flag-draped coffins of deceased US soldiers returning from Iraq in 2003–4 out of the national media, in favor of the soothing media myth that no human suffering or sacrifice was required of US citizens in that conflict. It was simply a matter of withholding from public view the photographic images of suffering and death inflicted by that war.

In the tradition of war photography that Sontag outlines—from the Crimean War and the Sepoy Rebellion of 1857 to the contested "combat" photographs of the Spanish Civil War—the Vietnam/ American War holds a special place, since in it photographers no longer staged battle as they had in the past. This change also confounded the public's ideas about what the war situation or experience entailed. Nick Ut's famous image of the then nine-year-old Phan Thị Kim Phúc fleeing a napalm attack, and Eddie Adams' 1968 shot of an execution in a Saigon street, are among the most widely known war photographs after 1945, though interestingly neither implicates US military actions directly. These images surely contributed to the US public's ultimate rejection of the human cost of that war. Vicki Goldberg has stated that Vietnam photographs were widely published not only in newspapers but also in photo-based mass-media illustrated journals like *Life* and *Look*.[16]

Like Walter Benjamin before her, Sontag recognized that the political import of any photographic image, even of violence and its aftermath, hinges on how that image is contextualized and described in language. She also notes that the position or even the "mood" of the viewer impacts how a particular photographic image is read. What is a horrifying image to one generation might be seen as heroic by another. Ethnicity or nationalism can also fundamentally alter how a viewer sees an image.

But in a kind of delayed action of understanding that the art historian Hal Foster has described for postwar art more generally,[17] this critical pivot in the reading of a photograph was revived in the postwar era by artists active in the anti-war movement of the 1960s. These figures returned to the mediums of collage and photomontage as tools to contextualize and examine the new dynamics of war photography, in order to sway the viewer toward a critical view against the war. Wolf Vostell's *Miss America* (1968) appropriates and juxtaposes the cropped Adams image with that of a presumably American fashion model; Vostell asks the viewer to link violence in Saigon with American interests and with US culture more generally. As was the case with the GAAG *Blood Bath* action, war photography was also deployed to attack the stance of autonomy of the art world and its institutions, again targeting MoMA. In 1970 the "Artists' Poster Committee" of the AWC in New York—Fraser Dougherty, Jon Hendricks, and Irving Petlin—appropriated another infamous image, Ronald L. Haeberle's color photograph of the civilian victims of US-army war crimes committed at My Lai (Haeberle had extended his permission to the group to use the photo). They framed the photograph with the words, "Q: And babies? A: And babies" (**Figure 3.7**). These words were taken from an interview with one of the perpetrators, Paul Meadlo. It is estimated that over 500 unarmed civilians were killed, and some raped and tortured before their deaths, as part of this massacre in March 1968. MoMA had first agreed to produce the poster jointly with the group, but when the design was circulated the Board of Trustees reneged on their agreement. The Artists' Poster Committee printed and distributed it anyway, and used the poster *Q: And babies? A: And babies* in their demonstration against MoMA that year, famously holding it up in front of Picasso's *Guernica*.[18] This joint action involving the poster, on the part of the AWC, the GAAG, and others, thereby suggested that the US war crime paralleled some committed by the Nazis—that is, the attack on the Basque town of Guernica, Spain, by German and Italian air forces in April 1937 that Picasso memorialized in his famous painting, which in 1970 was housed at MoMA, according to

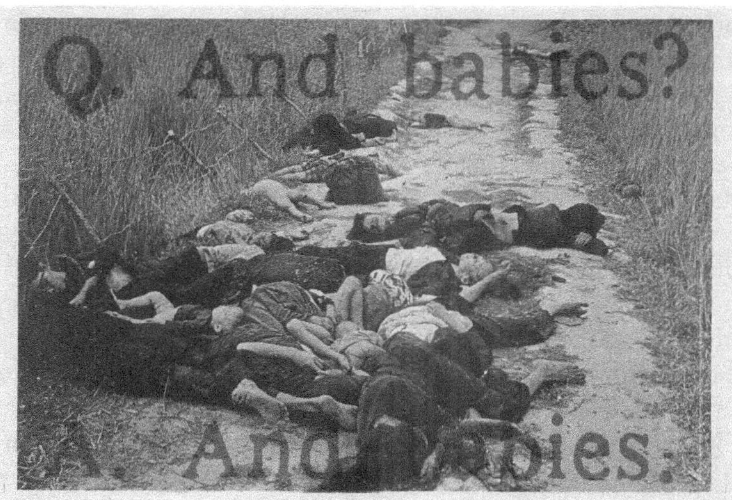

3.7   Poster Committee of the Art Workers' Coalition (Fraser Dougherty, Jon Hendricks, and Irving Petlin) and Ronald L. Haeberle, *Q: And babies? A: And babies* (1970), offset lithograph

Picasso's wishes. Jon Hendricks reports that artists had requested that Picasso remove the painting from MoMA in protest of the Vietnam/American war. *Q: And babies?* was an indictment of an unpunished war crime. The AWC demonstration widened this indictment to include the art institution, which did not have the fortitude to denounce savage violence against Vietnamese civilians. Lucy Lippard claims, however, that due to extensive informal artist and anti-war networks the poster was published widely, and arguably helped realize the turning point of popular opinion against the Vietnam War in the US.[19]

The American artist Martha Rosler also dedicated some of her art to a similar recontextualization of war photography. Rosler began her photomontage series *Bringing the War Home: House Beautiful* in 1967. Similar in spirit to Erró's 1968 *American Interiors* paintings but worked in the medium of photography, Rosler's series appropriates photographs of the chic interiors of American upper-class homes from advertisements, and refashions them as settings for fragments of appropriated war photography. In one work in the series, *Red Stripe Kitchen* (1967–72, **Figure 3.8**), Rosler brings together images of an impeccably designed white and red kitchen with one of foot soldiers in full combat gear doing what appears to be a search of an adjoining hallway. These photomontages underscore Sontag's observation that the memory of war remains local and mostly restricted to sites where it happened; they jog and shock the long-distance viewer of war with a visceral reminder of the developed world's privilege not only of wealth, but also of distance from the battlefield. She reminds viewers of how easy it is to forget even the most searing photographic images of war if one remains a distant spectator and not a (forced) local participant. Like Kienholz, Rosler attacks the US public's lack of interest and lethargy on the topic of war. In 2004 Rosler continued the series; these new works make use of recent photographs from the Gulf and Iraq Wars. Her message to specifically US viewers of these images is still powerful.

The Vietnamese-American artist Dinh Q. Lê continues this critical contextualizing of war photography. Perceptively, Lê expands the category of war photography to include fictional images that are

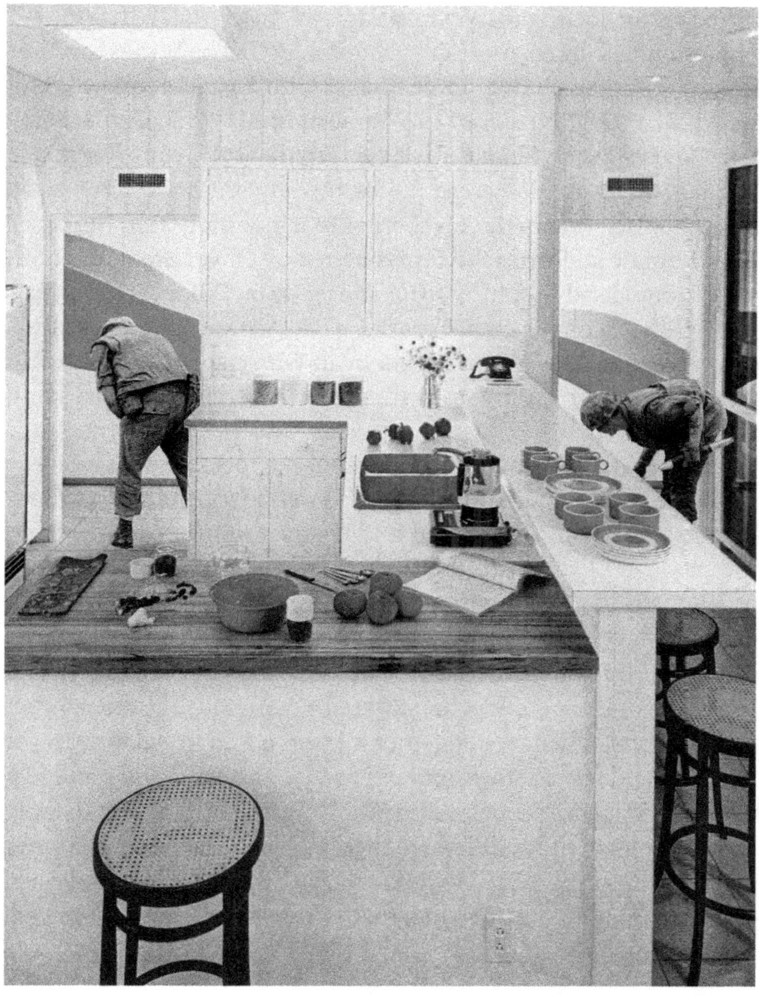

3.8   Martha Rosler, *Red Stripe Kitchen* (1967–72), photomontage

best known in the West because of their circulation in American mass culture, especially in the wave of Hollywood films of the 1980s and 1990s that had the Vietnam/American War as their subject. Some of these films and images have taken on the semblance of realism in the popular imagination, perhaps even overshadowing the powerful documentary photographs of the period. Lê has moved photomontage into a more abstract vein, in that he brings together his appropriated photographic images with the technique of grass weaving, a traditional craft in Vietnam. In his work *Untitled (My Lai/Willem Dafoe Platoon)* (2000, **Figure 3.9**), from his series *From Vietnam to Hollywood*, Lê brings together two large-scale type-C prints: one is the Haeberle My Lai photograph; the other is a dramatic still from the film directed by Oliver Stone in 1986, which depicts the culminating moment of Dafoe's character's martyr-like death. Lê combines these two American images of US involvement in the Vietnam/American War, fashioning them into the same cloth in cutting each image into thin strips and weaving them together.

In viewing the work, one must chose to focus on either one or the other of the two images in order to make it out; otherwise both images vanish into a colorful and abstract woven pattern. With the passage of time, the filmic fiction of American martyrdom in Vietnam has become as prevalent in American constructions of the history of that war as did earlier documentary images that evidenced US war crimes. In the process of this visual forgetting, the Vietnamese people who suffered greatly during the conflict disappear from history altogether. Lê uses a traditional working of material and surface to point both to Vietnamese culture and to a distinctly Vietnamese point of view that has become absent in most US accounts of the conflict. He thereby reasserts the Vietnamese subject's importance in histories of the postwar era and complicates American mass-culture myths that effectively silence this voice.

Anti-War Art Since Vietnam

Several of these photographic works about the Vietnam/American War remain a touchstone in visual art, and in artworks that examine continuing national and global conflicts in the Middle East, including the decades-long Lebanese civil war and the Gulf Wars of 1991 and 2003. Lebanese and Lebanese-diaspora artists have produced some of the most powerful of these works, making

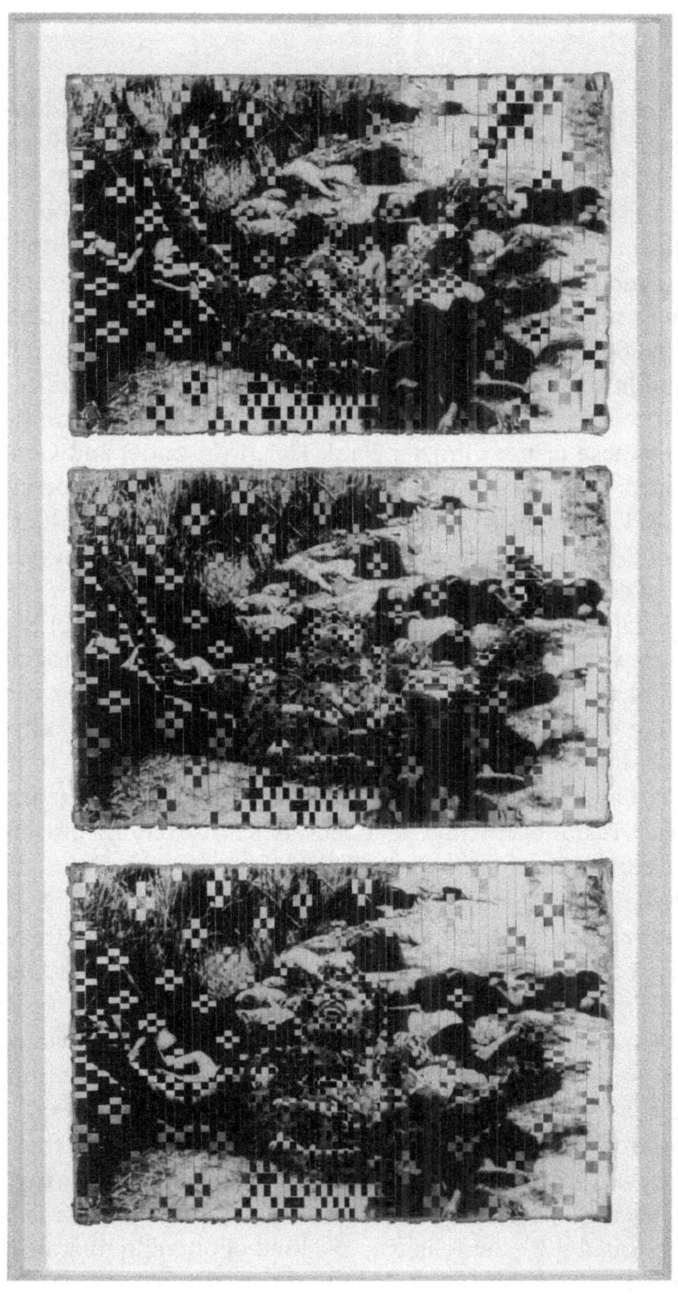

3.9   Dinh Q. Lê, *Untitled (My La./Willem Dafoe Platoon)* (2000), chromogenic print and linen tape on board

use not so much of photomontage as of appropriated and found images, sometimes arranged in collage forms. These artists also take on the concerns and conventions of conceptual art. Works by Joana Hadjithomas and Khalil Joreige and the Atlas Group take on the critical mantle of postwar anti-war art while asserting the voice and presence of the local Lebanese inhabitants who suffer under multiple military occupations and within conflicts that are fed by global concerns and interests. Much of this art points to loss of human life in Lebanon and the continuing instability and violence there, especially in Beirut, the site of the assassinations of Lebanese prime minister Rafik Hariri (in 2005) and General Wissam al-Hassan of the Lebanese Internal Security Forces (in 2012). These artists use photography to mourn the death of the city of Beirut as a cultural and intellectual center, and as a vibrant tourist destination, in the Middle East.

Hadjithomas and Joreige seek to represent the city of Beirut in film, video, and still photography. Many of their photographs present the problems inherent in the process of representing a space of destroyed fragments as a holistic or unified city, by day or night. They are furthermore concerned with charting the violence that has taken place in this city even when armed conflict is not occurring, such as the deaths that are attributed to celebratory gunfire at certain times of year. They have stated that they began work on their series *Wonder Beirut: The Story of a Pyromaniac Photographer* in 1997 and continued through 2007; one example in the series is *Wonder Beirut #20, Beirut by Night* from 1998–2007 (**Figure 3.10**). They claim that they contacted a local photographer, Abdallah Farah, who had been hired to provide images of major landmarks in Beirut, mostly of the lavish hotels and beaches of the "Lebanese Riviera," and to produce tourist postcards, during the 1960s. After the civil war began in 1975, Farah is said to have begun destroying the negatives of these images in his archive as the landmarks they represented were demolished, in a kind of ongoing mirroring of destruction.[20] In this series Hadjithomas and Joreige allege merely to reproduce Farah's destroyed images; their reworked postcards have also been distributed as multiples. These postcards bear

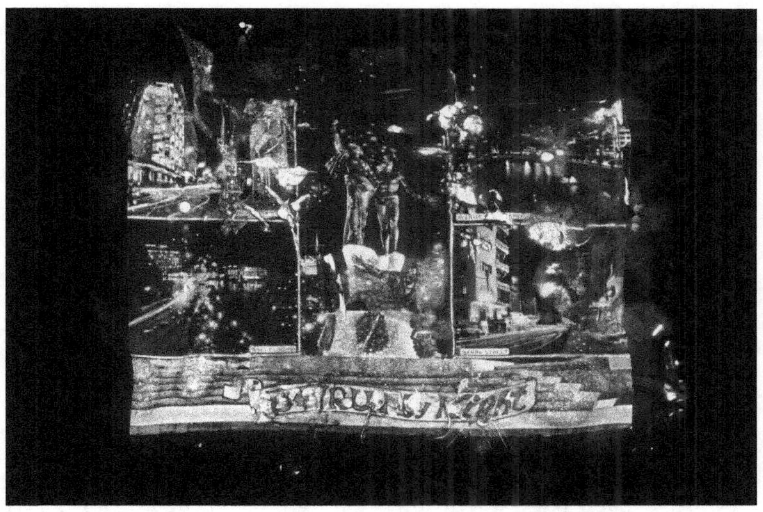

3.10   Joana Hadjithomas and Khalil Joreige, *Wonder Beirut #20, Beirut by Night* (1998–2007), lambda print mounted on aluminum

the markers of destruction, while their familiar configuration of advertising text and image are still legible: images seem to be burned off in areas or crumpled beyond recognition in others. It seems fairly certain that the photographer Abdallah Farah, along with his archive, is a fiction. The use of elaborate fictions is a strategy developed by conceptual artists, often in the guise of mock art museums or archives, in order to comment critically on the functioning of these institutions. For Hadjithomas and Joreige, Farah is a fictional alter ego; Farah's performative destruction of his own archive underscores the issue of loss in Beirut as a literally vanishing city. As is the case in Wolf Vostell's earlier assemblages, destruction is brought to bear on the material surfaces of the art object itself. *Wonder Beirut* stages the violent and self-destructive performance of forgetting by a Beirut native, which in the end is also the quasi-suicidal act of the erasure and forgetting of one's own identity.

A yet more elaborate fiction is created and staged by the Atlas Group (1989–2004), also known as the artist Walid Ra'ad, a

Lebanese émigré to New York. For the most part, the Atlas Group is another archive that consists of the papers of anonymous and named, though fictional, Lebanese intellectuals, who present eccentric kinds of documentation about the civil war. The archive also contains Ra'ad's own "real" archive with the results of his research. The archive has an elaborate website where one can download notebooks and images within any collection of papers.[21] For example, the Atlas Group's *Fadl Fakhouri File* contains notebooks, photographs, and films by this—entirely fictional—"foremost historian of the Lebanese Wars," who is said to have died in 1993. The *Fakhouri Notebook 38* is the most widely exhibited and published body of work by the Atlas Group (**Figure 3.11**). It contains numbered pages with photomontages of late-model automobiles. Captions are supplied for each in Arabic script, presumably in the hand of Fakhouri. Each page documents a single day's car bombings in Lebanon. The date, model, and make of each car is noted, along with the number of those injured or killed by each detonation.

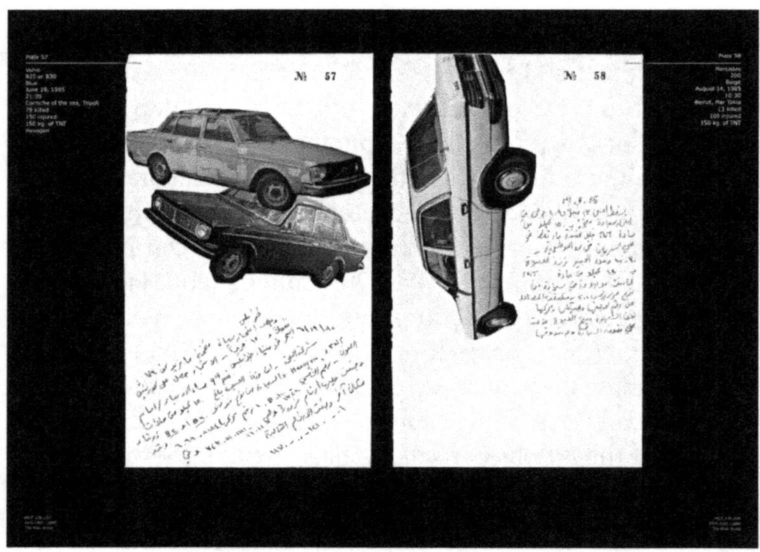

3.11   The Atlas Group/Walid Ra'ad, *Fadl Fakhouri File, Fakhouri Notebook 38*, plates 57 and 58 (1989–2004)

Another file in the Atlas Group Archives, titled *I Only Wish that I Could Weep*, contains the "found" videotapes of "Operator 17," an intelligence officer of the Lebanese army who since 1997 was assigned to eavesdrop or spy on individuals circulating on the Corniche, a boardwalk on the sea in Beirut. The tapes feature a sunset presumably shot from that boardwalk; these conventionally beautiful images of the changing colors of a sunset on the beach, then, seem not to involve the activity of the collecting of military information on the part of an army officer. In addition to these images, the tapes also present a visualization of a conscientious objector, a Lebanese citizen who rejects the evidentiary procedures of wartime in favor of another that has an aesthetic outcome and that rejects conflict entirely.

In the Atlas Group project, Fakhouri/Operator 17/Ra'ad, then, amasses the beginnings of a history of the Lebanese wars in presenting radically different kinds of visual information or data as an historical, though possibly fictional, archive. In it Ra'ad seeks to quantify and characterize this decades-long, chaotic war, which was waged by means of clandestine activity and terrorist tactics like car bombings. Both have by now become a matter of course in terrorist attacks throughout the world, and also in active war zones. Arguably Ra'ad and his Atlas Group gather and report the data from a war that the global media has turned its back on, since major industrialized nations are not directly involved in it. Ra'ad uses the format of information-based conceptual art, which presents a collection of visualized data for the viewer, instead of an aesthetically ordered composition. In his archive Ra'ad presents a new picture of how war is increasingly factionalized and makeshift, one that expands old ideas about military conflict into our present. In his latest installation, *Scratching on Things I Could Disavow: A History of Art in the Arab World*, Ra'ad distances himself from the Atlas Group. He presents that fictional collective as historical, and as a completed project. He does so in one of the installation's components, an artwork-object titled *The Atlas Group*, a miniature-scale model of past gallery installations, dating back to 1989. *Scratching* has as its subject—through an elaborate chart, lectures delivered by the artist, and newspaper and other

95

clippings—the entirety of the Arab art world. Ra'ad's installation points to a network of individuals and institutions that presently constitute it, and also to the vast monetary sums that are fueling its expansion.[22] The project is an almost manic continuation of Ra'ad's drive to collect, present, and synthesize data as a means of grasping one's place in the present.

Harun Farocki, an artist working in Germany, instead focuses on the role of nonhuman participants in warfare, which since the first Gulf War of 1991 has increasingly made use of computer technologies to keep humans of the wealthiest armed forces out of direct military confrontation. His films and video installations (also called "image installations") focus on the cultural and ideological changes to vision brought about by the "image processing"—which makes use of the computer as both prosthetic and eye—of "smart bombs" and surveillance drones. Farocki approaches the representation of war from the critical position of media theory. He examines how the technologies of representation or imaging, such as video or the combined hardware/software of the computer/camera, are tied in a complex way to cultural, social, and political contexts that in turn affect the nature of vision itself. His art urges the viewer to take a distancing and critical view of the assumptions behind certain digital technologies, and to insist that the technology continue to be answerable to humanistic values, as well as to the rule of ethics.

Eye/Machine (2000–3, **Figure 3.12**) is a cycle of three videos Farocki first developed for the short duration of television programming; all are under 30 minutes in length. In the cycle he connects to his larger concern with video and computer surveillance technologies, and with the military applications of this hardware and software.[23] As Hal Foster has noted, these technologies also mark the automation of surveillance, where the human is no longer a viewer of the image but rather the image is monitored only for unanticipated visual change.[24] This technology has also been most spectacularly developed for "image recognition" that allows for the surveillance camera/computer to compare the image with a predetermined database of other images and to search for similarity—such as in the smart bomb's seeking of a target—or

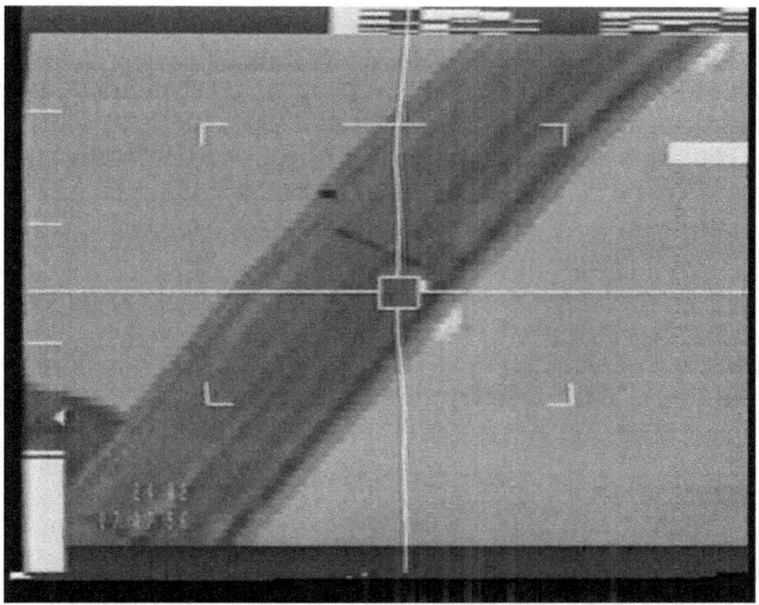

3.12   Harun Farocki, *Eye/Machine II* (2002), video still

for anomaly, such as individuals loitering around an area under surveillance.

As an installation *Eye/Machine* juxtaposes two images on two adjoining monitors or projections; the single-channel version places two images next to each other diagonally in the same frame. In doing so Farocki asks the viewer to do the work of recognition or differentiation that is usually completed by the machine. What views of physical reality are no longer taken into account, or ignored, in these instances? What happens when the database/machine coheres all of physical reality into a target, or, as Foster says, makes us enter the realm of "seeing as targeting" where no human judgment can be brought to bear? It is then a dubious matter of trust and belief in the proper functioning of this inhuman computer eye, as long as we are not within its lens but behind it. As Foster says, "we are further empowered by the destruction that we seem to direct"—since Farocki allows us to view comfortably the camera image of the target generated by the smart bomb. We also continue watching after the image turns to video snow, once the bomb and its camera have both been detonated. We survive this automated destruction as long as we remain those who control the software programming and hardware it runs on, insuring that we ourselves remain only spectators of the technology's function. We as viewers can stay out of its destroying gaze while we direct it onto others, usually far away from home. Can we trust a world where images are made and viewed only by machines, which then automatically initiate a predetermined response, without the input of any human? Farocki suggests that we cannot, and that our very humanity may be at stake in keeping human oversight over military conflict, which now can be carried out solely by computers. He calls for us to preserve a space for a humanist ethics in modern warfare, even if it is the case that war can now be conducted without humans. He points to our collective responsibility never to forget the human cost of war.

feminisms

A number of postwar artists after 1960 used their art as a means to criticize the institutions and practices that were operative in the art world. Feminist artists certainly participated in such critiques, and introduced a distinct point of view that attacked the marginalizing of women as makers of art, while also insisting on the necessary equality of women in art as well as in all other sectors of social life. Often feminist art had as its subject the representation of women in Euro-American society. It has been suggested that we have now reached a moment of "global feminisms"—that is, when the representation and status of women is discussed globally, including in societies outside of the West.[1] A critique of patriarchy, of the current situation of women, or of the stability of the category of the female gender, is generally advanced in artworks that can be termed "feminist."

As Linda Nochlin has already pointed out in her famous essay of 1971, "Why have there been no great women artists?," the "woman question" or the "woman problem" was certainly at the heart of first-wave feminism in the nineteenth century, when political philosophers like John Stuart Mill, Karl Marx, and Friedrich Engels began to analyze and question the oppression of women in modern society as ideology.[2] (Of course, the writer Mary Wollstonecraft had a century before advocated for women's rights.) This cultural and intellectual activism finally led to women's suffrage in many Western societies by the 1920s. In the US, the post-colonialist ideas that gave rise to the demand for equal rights for black Americans in the civil-rights movement of the early 1960s also prompted reconsideration of the social and political inequality women continued to face. The creation of the Presidential Commission on the Status of Women by President John F. Kennedy in 1961 and the National Organization for Women by Betty Friedan in 1966, and the drafting of a possible Equal Rights Amendment in 1967 (which would finally fail to be ratified in 1982), together illuminate a particular cultural turn of the time: that the fact of women's inequality, alongside civil rights, was being reconsidered in American society by the mid 1960s.

In the key year of 1971 feminist artists and art historians began to recognize that the ideology or "naturalness" of women's inferiority and oppression had been perpetuated throughout the entire history of modern art and was still actively constructed in contemporary visual culture. Nochlin's essay marked the epistemological shift into feminist art history, and the new awareness that the entire apparatus of high art—from the artworks themselves, to art education, to the distribution system of art galleries, to museum institutions—was complicit in marginalizing women as producers and viewers of art. In almost all instances this apparatus or system rendered female artists invisible. A call to action closes her essay:

> using as a vantage point their situation as underdogs in the realm of grandeur, and outsiders in that ideology, women can reveal institutional and intellectual weaknesses in general, and, at the same time that they destroy false consciousness, take part in the creation of institutions in which clear thought—and true greatness—are challenges open to anyone, man or woman, courageous enough to take the necessary risk, the leap into the unknown.[3]

Generational Feminisms, US and Europe

Artists responded to Nochlin's call almost immediately. In October 1971 Miriam Schapiro joined the art professor Judy Chicago at

Fresno State University in expanding Chicago's "special course for women students" in studio art and establishing it at the California Institute for the Arts. In working and training exclusively female students, Schapiro and Chicago concluded that these students found it imperative that they represent themselves, or rather their own bodies, in their art practice. Chicago stated her intention to "transfer the basis of my artmaking from the male structure in which I learned, into an art with a female core."[4] She understood this art as a process that would humanize women by means of representation, a quality that they otherwise lacked in American society. She also believed that the inherent differences between male and female "iconography" have nothing to do with essential biological differences between the sexes, but rather with cultural difference, an aspect that is learned. In terms of her beliefs, then, Chicago did not adhere to a strictly "essentialist" notion of feminism—that is, that the essence of the feminine is anchored in the biological female body—as she has been accused of in the generational conflict that emerged between second- and third-wave feminists.

Early in the next year, 1972, the team-taught CalArts class worked collaboratively on a large "environment" or installation, one that they realized in an abandoned building in Hollywood in Los Angeles: *Womanhouse*. This building also became the setting for live performances by individual artists as well as those by the Feminist Art Program Performance Group.[5] Individual students and teams renovated and reconstructed recognizable domestic interiors of a suburban home: a kitchen, a dining room, or a bathroom. Schapiro, Chicago, and the students also understood the act of collaboration and cooperation between them on this project as another aspect that contributed to its quality as a feminist artwork. Each installation critically rethought domestic space, one that modern visual culture often associated with woman as wife, mother, and nurturer, along with the role and position of woman within them. In presenting domestic space as a framework for art, *Womanhouse* thereby also rejected the male-determined space of the "white cube" gallery for the dissemination of art. It might, then, also be thought of as an early public-art project. The building and its installations were demolished in February 1972.

Some of the most compelling installations in *Womanhouse* associated domestic space with the labor and body of the mother. Many of its spaces otherwise staged the viewer's identification with the female body. Several rooms focused on the preparation and presentation of food, tasks traditionally left to women. Susan Frazier, Vicki Hodgetts, and Robin Weltsch painted the walls, appliances, and most other objects in *Nutrient Kitchen* in flesh tones. They covered the ceiling with familiar concentric-circle relief sculptures that resembled sunny-side-up eggs, but like an aberrant wallpaper pattern, as the reliefs continued down the walls, they resembled breasts. They placed kitchen utensils above the stove that further echoed these reliefs and the rounded forms of the female body. The team of artists transformed the kitchen space into the mother's body/breast, the first source of sustenance in every human life.

In comparison, the *Dining Room* installation began to distance itself from the mother body; the space was outfitted with formal window treatments, a chandelier, and an elaborately laid dinner table, covered with tablecloth and fabric "china" filled with baked-dough formations as "food." Faith Wilding's *Crocheted Environment*, another important installation in *Womanhouse*, reworked a room into a womb-like enclosure by encircling it in a web of white crochet. Wilding is said to have based this structure on ancient architecture devised by women. She also pointedly makes use of the craft of crocheting within an artwork. Usually such handiwork is associated with women, not seen as art, and is relegated to the sphere of hobby and craft. Her *Environment* also denies traditional male architectural structure in its softness and malleability. Wilding's installation is a visionary work that would influence later figures who rethink architectural space, like the Brazilian artist Ernesto Neto.

After the conclusion of this project Judy Chicago devoted years to the preparation of *The Dinner Party*, completed in 1979. The work has, with some controversy, been designated an icon of feminist art.[6] After traveling to various exhibition venues for years but without an institutional home, *The Dinner Party* was finally acquired for the Elizabeth A. Sackler Center for Feminist Art, which opened at the Brooklyn Museum of Art in 2007. A physically enormous work, it has become the permanent centerpiece of this first institution dedicated to feminist, rather than "women's," art. It is remarkable that Chicago's work—largely billed and understood by museums and the public as a piece created by one author, which it is not—has eclipsed the more experimental, cross-generational, collaborative, and ephemeral *Womanhouse* as the most important (US) feminist artwork of the 1970s. Perhaps *The Dinner Party*'s traditional qualities, including its permanence, have positioned it in this way. The work might be considered an extended rethinking of the *Dining Room* from *Womanhouse*; it is furthermore a metaphor for the entirety of women's history. While the work is certainly an achievement by a larger group or collective of women, and it is a powerful statement about women and history, its lacunae and shortcomings must also be taken into account, and not merely in terms of its "essentialism."

The Dinner Party in its current installation consists of five components; most central are the "Place Settings" and the "Heritage Floor" **(Figure 4.1)**. These settings are arranged on three 48-foot-long

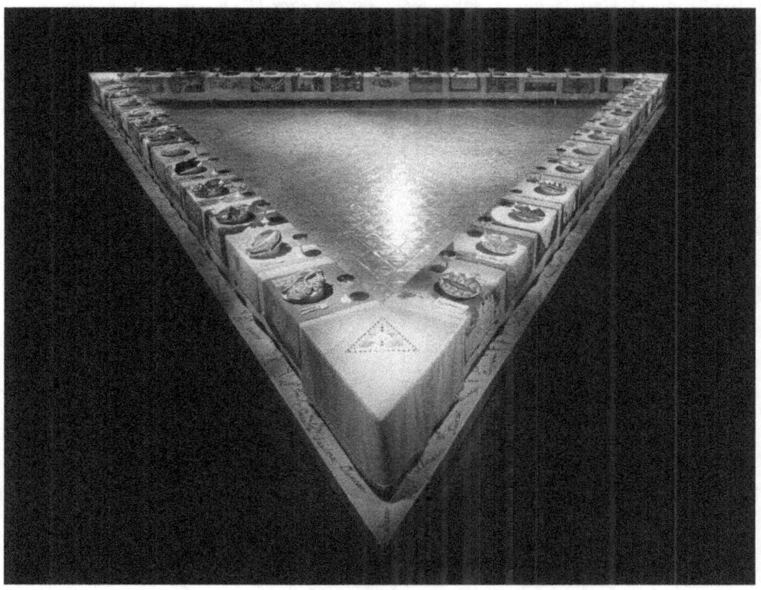

4.1   Judy Chicago, *The Dinner Party* (1979), mixed media

tables that are positioned into an open triangular form; the triangular floor covering between the tables consists of porcelain tiles inscribed in gold with the handwritten names of 999 women. These include both historical and mythical figures, from the "primordial goddess" to the American painter Georgia O'Keeffe. The place settings present 39 additional women, each with a painted china plate, a chalice, and an embroidered napkin and runner bearing the woman's name. Chicago indicated that she chose which historical figures to include in consultation with scholars.

As was the case in *Womanhouse*, Chicago rejects male-dominated art mediums like painting in favor of craft production in ceramics and fibers. The plates, with the exception of one, depict the "central core" female iconography that Chicago had advocated as a rejection of male-determined representations of women; these are clearly to be read as stylized depictions of female genitalia (a subject that not only occupied many early-1970s feminist artists in addition to Chicago, but continued to concern younger feminists like Zoe Leonard). Chicago also believed that the "central core" is a universal signifier of all women, across history and races; she therefore made it the repeated and unifying element for all of women's history. However, as some of her critics have pointed out, only one plate, that for Sojourner Truth, the American abolitionist of the nineteenth century and a woman of color, does not feature central-core imagery, but rather a depiction of an African mask. While some feminist art historians have argued that Chicago includes two other settings dedicated to women of color—for Hatshepsut, an Ancient Egyptian Pharaoh, and Sacagawea, a Native American woman who acted as guide to the Lewis and Clark expedition—and also includes famous lesbians, the Truth setting points to a kind of separatism in the work that is at odds with the feminist unity to which Chicago is otherwise devoted. The work makes several religious references—to Christianity as well as to other faiths—the central and most obvious analogy being to Leonardo's Renaissance icon, *The Last Supper*. *The Dinner Party* also includes settings dedicated to pagan "goddesses," another anti-patriarchal subject for 1960s and 1970s feminist artists; it makes numerological reference to other matriarchal theologies in including 13 settings on each of the three tables, the number of women in a coven (in witchcraft or Wicca).

To respond to the criticism that Chicago exploited her collaborators on *The Dinner Party* and took sole credit for the work, the Sackler Center installation of the work features "mural-sized" "Acknowledgment Panels" of photographs of 129 women and men working on the project at various stages with the text: "The artist gratefully acknowledges the many people who cooperated in the realization of *The Dinner Party*." Not only physical work was completed by this team; a committee of sorts also finalized the list of names to be included in the artwork. *The Dinner Party* is a successful envisioning of what a revisionist herstory might look like; it retrieves important women in history from oblivion. It furthermore urges female viewers to reclaim, as a feminist act, world history for themselves. It celebrates these women of history through "female" craft, and through a universalized image of female interiority, a transcendent essence that Chicago claims is largely metaphorical. Yet the artwork also constructs its maker as an originator of feminist art, and this originator has been institutionalized along with the work. Hopefully the feminist revisionism that is the content of *The Dinner Party* can still be discerned despite the large-scale persona and figure of Judy Chicago.

At the same time that Chicago finalized *The Dinner Party* into her universalizing vision of woman and history, other artists in California were also exploring feminist ideas, this time from the position of multiculturalism. Their art redefined feminist art in terms of ethnicities and cultures that were critical of representations of women of color in white culture, and worked to present positive and ethnically diverse images of women. The African American artist Betye Saar, working in California in the 1970s, used her art to critique the combination of sexism and racism that could be traced on objects and images that she located in daily life; her art might also be connected to the work of California assemblage artists of the 1950s and 1960s like Wallace Berman and George Herms. Her assemblage *The Liberation of Aunt Jemima* (1972, **Figure 4.2**) includes objects and images of the often-reproduced stereotype of the black "mammy" figure that is connected to the

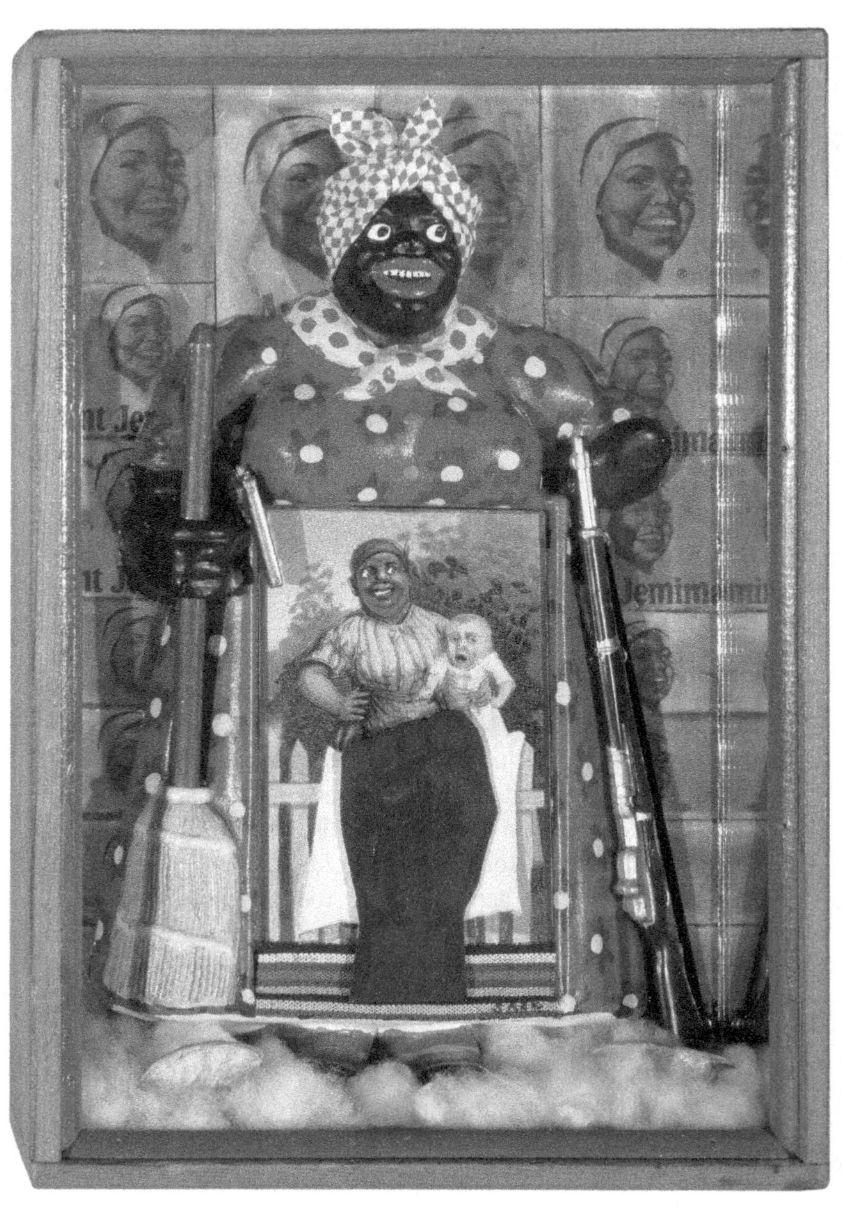

4.2 Betye Saar, *The Liberation of Aunt Jemima* (1972), mixed media assemblage

Jim Crow south. The most widely known representations of this figure in American culture remain the character played by the Hollywood actress Hattie McDaniel in *Gone with the Wind* (1939) and "Aunt Jemima," who continues to identify a brand of pancake mix. Saar encloses a large mammy figurine on a bed of cotton in a diorama box, before a backdrop of the repeated Aunt Jemima image; she holds another depiction of a mammy/black woman holding a white child. Before this found image, Saar has placed a dark-skinned fist raised in the "black power" salute; the figurine behind it holds a rifle in one hand to balance the broom she carries in the other. Saar then contrasts white culture's mythical image of the obedient black servant with signifiers of black radicalism and separatism of the 1970s. Saar's feminist artwork is a revision of history; she too "corrects" historical distortion and the invisibility of real-life black women in dismantling a dehumanizing caricature of women of color. Yolanda López's painting *Portrait of the Artist as the Virgin of Guadalupe* (1978, **Figure 4.3**) presents the familiar Catholic image of the Virgin Mary that is so ubiquitous in Mexico that it has become an icon of that nation. López presents herself as young and smiling, striding, in athletic shoes and a simple dress, toward the viewer. She crushes a small *putto* underfoot, and strangles a snake in one hand while holding on to her billowing robe in the other. As some have suggested, this self-portrait can be associated with the "goddess" subject of early-1970s feminist art, but the image is also a clear depiction of the artist as Chicana, sharing in Latino culture.[7] Instead of rejecting it as other feminists have done, López takes on the medium of painting, shifting it away from its roots in Western patriarchy. She also reinvigorates the image of the Virgin of Guadalupe, in rendering her as active and modern, and as an icon of Chicana self-determination.

In a strategy closer to Saar's empowering and radicalizing critique of cultural representations of women, an entire group of feminist artists used their work to examine filmic or photographic representations of the female body and of femininity more generally. These images often distance themselves from those of the mass media, and also from images of the female body created by male artists and filmmakers. Some feminist critics argue that these performing feminists utilize the mechanism of seduction (of the viewer) to achieve their critique of patriarchal control of the female image.[8] Not so much motivated by a desire for positive representations of a universalized female body, these feminist artists present their own often physically beautiful bodies in order to gain control over their representation in these mediums, as artists. They are

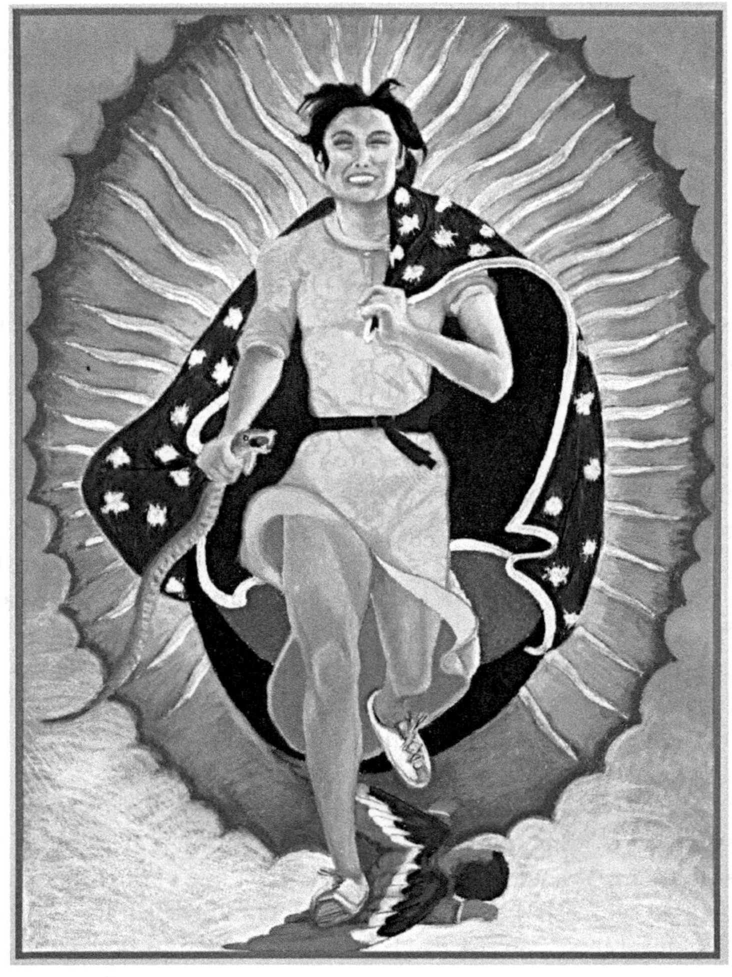

4.3   Yolanda López, *Portrait of the Artist as the Virgin of Guadalupe* (1978)

then able also to become subjects in asserting control over the photographic/filmic image (of women). For almost all of this group of feminist artists—and the most important of them include Hannah Wilke, Joan Jonas, Valie Export, and Carolee Schneemann—the medium of performance, or performing the body as the feminine subject, is equally important to their art. This practice has been termed body art. These feminist body artists were a great influence on the following generation of post-modern feminists.

The American artist Hannah Wilke created what she termed "performalist" artworks; her *S.O.S.—Starification Object Series* of 1974–9 (**Figure 4.4**) is a group of 28 black-and-white photographs of the bare-chested artist posing (or mugging) for the camera with various props such as sunglasses, hair curlers, or head coverings. In each photograph small repeated relief sculptures decorate the artist's face and body. Wilke created these small sculptural reliefs from chewing gum, forming them into vulval and phallic shapes. She understood these forms as both decorations of the body and markers of wounds that functioned like scars: "African Scarification Wounds [...] the internal wounds that we carry within us, that really hurt us."[9] She enumerated the very situation of femininity, and of female beauty, as a social and cultural construct, and as "wounds." Thus the exhibitionism and narcissism that was linked to Wilke's display of her own naked, youthful, and thus "sexy" body—for which she was criticized by a number of important feminist critics—also had the function of critically revealing female beauty not as an asset, but rather as a wound resulting from the ruthless visual objectification of women inflicted by patriarchal culture, working in tandem with the goals of capitalism. In her equally empowering final artwork, *Intra-Venus* (1992–3), completed while the artist was in the last stages of treatment for lymphoma, Wilke fearlessly continued to present her withering body to the camera, thereby maintaining her status as a female subject, as maker and creator, even as she struggled with her own mortality. Amelia Jones has argued that Wilke's art uses a procedure of psychic "feminist narcissism," along with strategies of seduction, or what she terms the "rhetoric of the pose," in order to critique the sexism inherent in Western visual culture's depictions of the female body.[10] Wilke

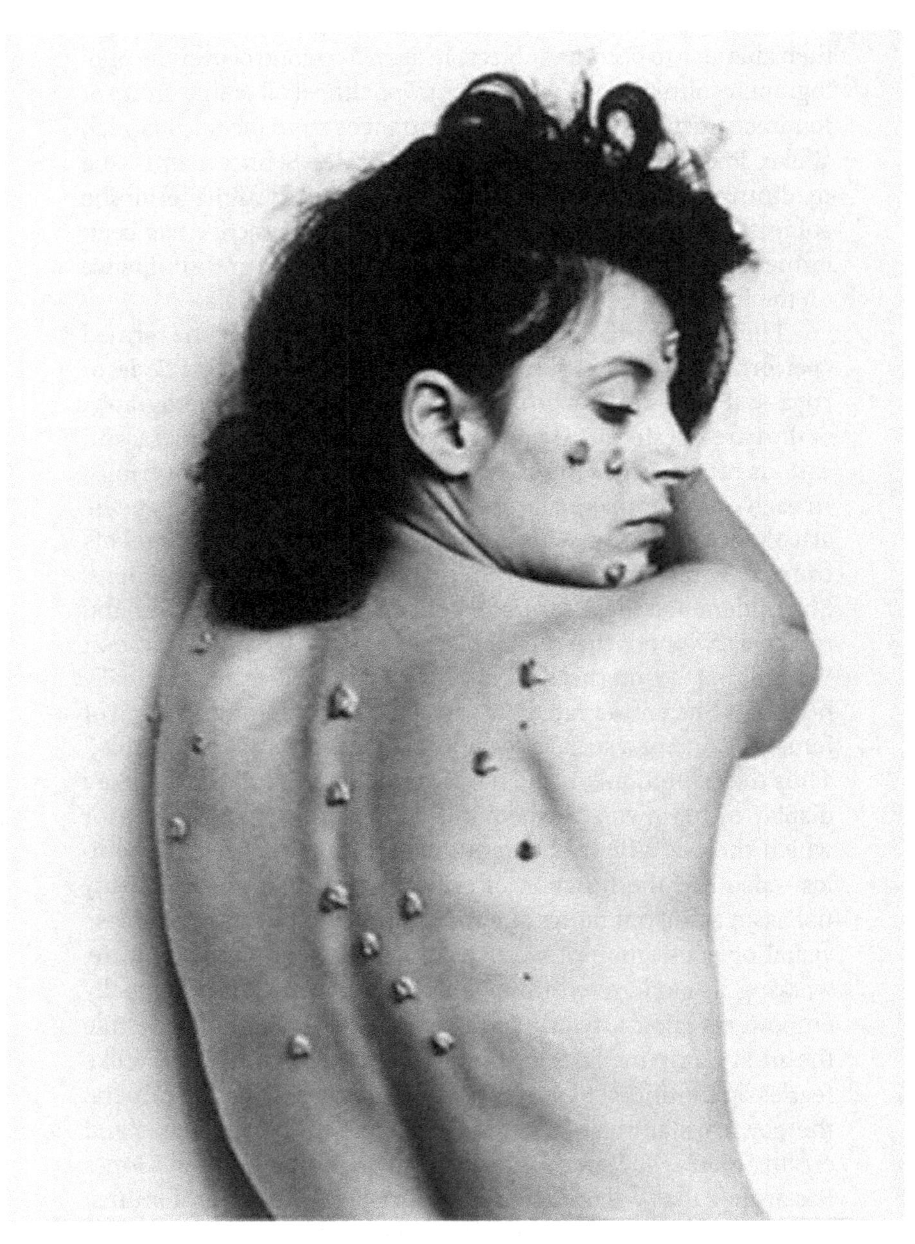

4.4 Hannah Wilke, *S.O.S.—Starification Object Series*, back (1974), black-and-white gelatin silver print

succeeds in turning the male gaze back upon itself as a means of control, and realizes the feminine subject as maker and as a mind, not just as a body/object.

Joan Jonas, another American feminist, has concentrated most of her body-art-oriented work into video practice. Her first performances made use of a mirror that she, along with other performers, used to reflect themselves and the audience. Beginning with her performances in 1972, Jonas began to integrate into her performances a closed-circuit video camera, along with its monitor, as an "ongoing mirror."[11] In these single-channel videos Jonas then examined the dynamics of the electronic image of woman usually presented in the medium of television. She took on an alter ego in her performances, whom she named "Organic Honey," and who was often masked or exotically costumed as she performed for/with the video camera in what appears to be an elaborate, slow-moving ritual. In these works, *Organic Honey's Visual Telepathy* and *Organic Honey's Vertical Roll* from 1972 **(Figure 4.5)**,

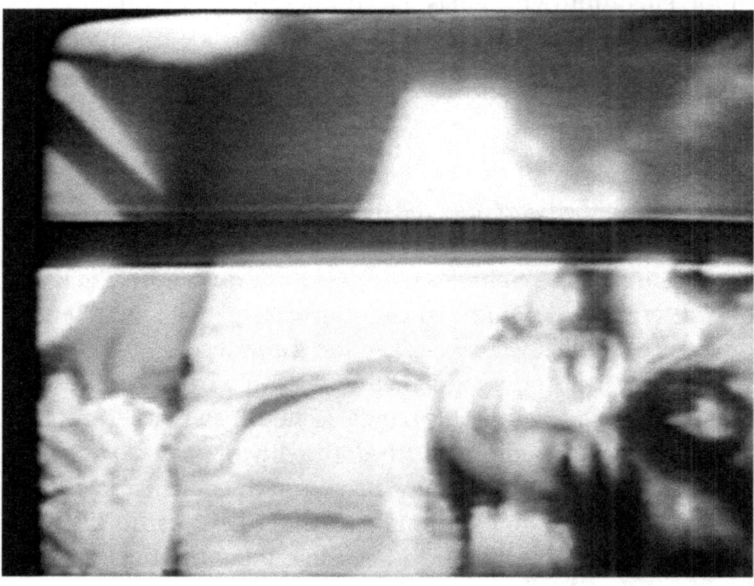

4.5   Joan Jonas, *Organic Honey's Vertical Roll* (1972), still

Jonas' video monitor functioned as an onstage mirror for the artist during the performance. In *Vertical Roll* Jonas obscures the electronic image of "Organic Honey" by various means: by using masks and a costume with veils, and by severely distorting the picture, achieved by manipulating the vertical-hold control of the video camera. The latter effect renders apparent the highly mediated aspect of video that is at work in each televised depiction of women. Jonas underscores her visual distortion of the image through the manipulation of the audio track, which is a grating and repetitive thudding or striking sound that corresponds to the black horizontal that rhythmically rolls from the bottom to the top of the video image. This jarring soundtrack further accentuates the element of distortion; this electronic image of woman is no longer pleasurable for the viewer to take in. The work is feminist in that Jonas reveals the electronic image of the female body to be a phantasm, a function of the technology itself—this is also communicated in her recuperating of an obsolete and ossified image, that of the exoticized femininity of the "vamp," which harks back to the silent-film era. Jonas' electronic image of woman is not an operative, holistic representation that points to "woman" as a stable and recognizable referent. In *Vertical Roll* Jonas takes on the critical stance of many feminists of the early 1970s who called for the destruction of the sexist visual pleasure that the technologies of film and video offered to their (male) viewers.

Two other body-art oriented feminist artists, the Austrian artist Valie Export (who is also referred to as VALIE EXPORT) and the American Carolee Schneemann, also critique representations of women by making reference to the essentialist site of female difference, or what Chicago called the "central core," in their performances. Export distinguished herself in what was otherwise the all-male body-art performance scene in Vienna, dominated by the Viennese Actionists (Rudolf Schwarzkogler, Hermann Nitsch, Otto Mühl, and Günter Brus) and the machismo of their endurance-based works. Export's assumed artist name, like Judy Chicago's, is an implicit refusal to use the surnames given to her through patriarchy—that is, by her father and through marriage. Export used street-theater tactics to criticize the cinema's standardized codes for film's objectification and rendering public of an eroticized female body, representing that body without any aspect of its own subjectivity or mind.[12] In *Touch Cinema* (1968), which was performed by the artist and one of her female colleagues in a number of European cities including Cologne and Vienna, Export enclosed her bare-breasted torso in a "theater"-like box with a curtain opening at the front; a second performer would encourage passers-by, men or women, to touch her (concealed) body, thereby fondling her breasts. Documenting photographs depict an expressionless Export staring impassively as various strangers chose to participate in this anti-visual "expanded cinema" of tactile sensation. In another cinema-critical performance, *Action Pants: Genital Panic* (1969), the artist marched between aisles in an art-film cinema in Munich with crotchless pants, physically exposing her genitalia at the viewer's eye level. Export's performance parallels the passive public consumption of the filmic female image within the apparatus of the film theater, contrasting this passivity with the artist's aggressively positioned and revealed sex/privacy toward the viewers. Export's short film *Man & Woman & Animal* (1973) presents filmed images of female genitalia (the artist's?) in menstruation or coming to orgasm, images that are taboo even in pornography, which famously prefers to focus on the so-called "money shot"—that is, the moment of male ejaculation. Export then uses performance and film to reject the singular norm of male sexual satisfaction—either hetero- or homosexual—that the cinema in almost all its genres continues to serve. She also "reveals" women's actual invisibility in cinema and its sites of distribution.

Schneemann, who was associated with the Fluxus group, also used performance to expand the female *subject*'s active or kinetic role in representation, and noted the silence that is typically foisted upon the female body when it is represented in art history. Schneemann used and preferred the term "art istory" as an alternative to and rejection of this male-defined and -determined discipline. In her performance *Interior Scroll* (1975), Schneemann first disrobed down to an apron before the audience while reading from her book (published in 1976), *Cézanne, She Was a Great Painter*.[13] At the same time she painted her body with dark brushstrokes, striking standard poses of the female model in life-drawing courses. Removing the apron and nude, she unraveled a scroll from her vagina and read from it; Schneemann recounts that this text came from one of her earlier films, a discussion with a male filmmaker addressing his misunderstanding of her art. The text also contrasts stereotypical notions of male creativity as logical and ordered or cerebral, with female creativity as intuitive and connected with the body. *Interior Scroll* refuses this clichéd polarity, along with the Enlightenment mind-body division. In the performance the meaning of the body of the (female) artist is recoded to emphasize its reasoning and logic, and it becomes the site of creativity; the female body comes to speech, breaking the discipline of art history's insistence on keeping women static and silent, on the margins of that history. Schneemann retrieves the notion of an essential aspect of femininity located in the body, but she is more concerned with breaking down the division between mind and body and elevating the latter—male or female—as an important site of action and creativity.

Feminists in the 1980s brought a new strategy to bear on their critique of the representation of the female body and subject. In tandem with the rise in importance of critical theory and psychoanalysis within art criticism, this anti-essentialist feminism rejected the notion that the female body needed to be represented at all in the crucial cultural action of resisting and dismantling sexism. Anti-essentialist feminists returned to an assertion by the philosopher Simone de Beauvoir in her 1949 book *The Second Sex*: "One is not born but becomes a woman." This new generation of feminists claimed that the female gender was constructed culturally; they also rejected the idea that there was a "natural" woman who existed outside the constructs of language. Feminist artists and critics then applied psychoanalytic theory, particularly that of Jacques Lacan, along with theories of language forwarded in structuralist and poststructuralist philosophy, to understand how this acculturation process toward gender identity worked.

Mary Kelly's 1974 work *Post-Partum Document* (**Figure 4.6**) is seen as emblematic of this shift into anti-essentialist feminism.

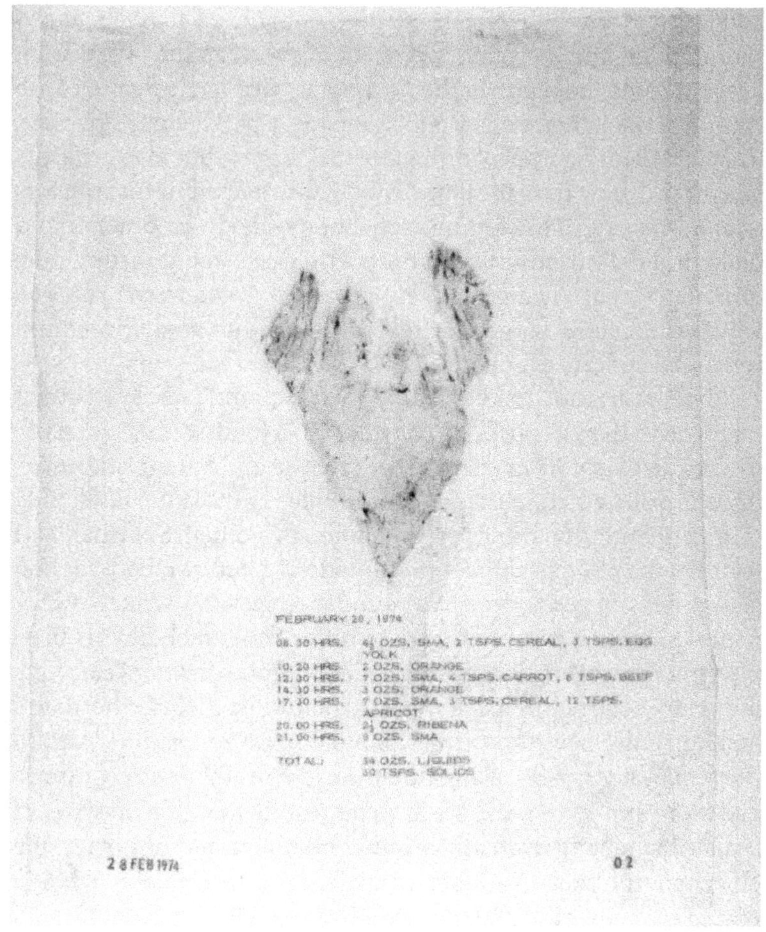

4.6   Mary Kelly, *Post-Partum Document: Documentation I, Analysed Faecal Stains and Feeding Charts* (1974), Perspex unit, white card, diaper linings, plastic, sheeting, paper, ink, detail

Kelly's large-scale installation, consisting of documentation of her young son's entry into language, included quasi-clinical observations about him and about the artist's own role as a mother; this documentation included bodily traces of the infant (fecal stains on diapers), feeding charts, diagrams, and a record of his first words, altogether 135 items.[14] The installation not only used psychoanaly-sis to understand her child's process of socialization—into what Lacan termed the realm of the "symbolic," that is, the realm of the "name of the father," of law and language, a parallel in some ways to what Freud had termed the Oedipal stage—but also critically questioned how female subjectivity is formulated in this process of child-rearing. This feminist rejection of body-art practice and biological definitions of femininity also came about through the growing importance of conceptual art in Western art centers, which considered language and text as another area or medium for contemporary art practice.

The American artists Cindy Sherman and Barbara Kruger emerged in the early 1980s as post-modern feminists who, in anti-essentialist fashion, continued the critique of the imagistic objec-tification of women in mass culture while rejecting the possibility of an authentic or natural representation of women. Sherman's art features the photographic representation of her own body; at first glance her images appear to be similar to those in Wilke's *S.O.S. Series*. However, her photographs differ fundamentally in their post-modern stance concerning codes of representation, concepts drawn from structuralist and poststructuralist theory. Sherman's breakthrough black-and-white photographic series, the *Untitled Film Stills* of 1977–80, all feature the artist in elaborate costumes, and role-playing in what seem to be readily identifiable types of female characters from any number of Hollywood B-movies: the gun moll, the cheating suburban wife, or, as in *Untitled Film Still No. 48* (1979, **Figure 4.7**), the teen runaway. Each photograph in the series presents a different "character," in different settings, and each exclusively features the artist. Sherman's titles, of the series and of each image, furthermore suggest that the images are taken from a larger filmic narrative. Therefore, she presents the viewer not with "real" women or with her "true" self/body, but with an already-in-place code or language of female types that exists and circulates in the realm of mass media. Sherman represents the female body as a visual convention, a pre-existing narrative. Many feminist critics have read a critical and feminist point of view being presented in these works, but Sherman has consistently refused

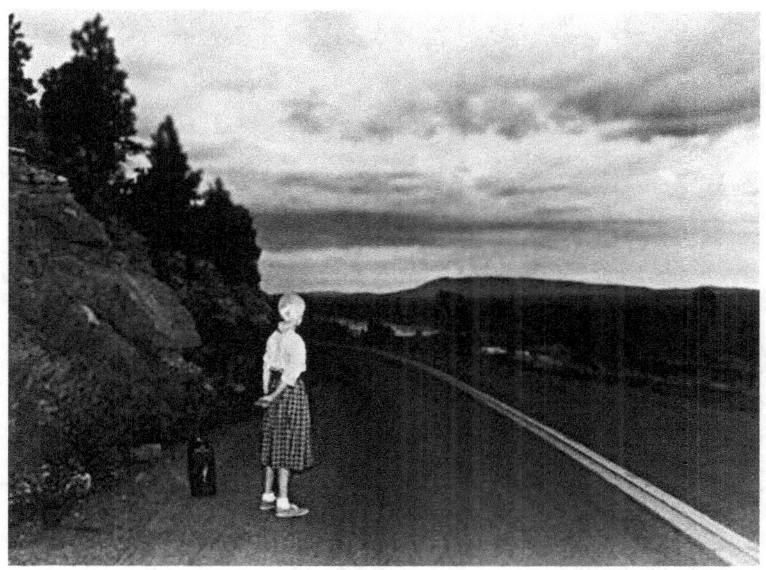

4.7   Cindy Sherman, *Untitled Film Still No. 48* (1979), black-and-white
photograph

to position them as feminist in statements and interviews. The
ambiguity of these artworks toward their subject—the question of
whether Sherman's images really critique mass culture conventions
of women, or if they just repeat these conventions uncritically—is
another aspect that renders them post-modern.

Barbara Kruger is more direct in her feminist critique of mass
culture, particularly toward the imagery of advertising. Kruger's
photomontages of images and texts are close to the slick layout of
advertisements; she makes use of found photographs and large
blocks of color and text. In that they follow the conventions of
advertising, Kruger's works seem already familiar to the viewer,
as though they could be found advertisements. In *Untitled (It's a
Small World but Not if You Have to Clean It)* from 1990 **(Figure 4.8)**,
the words making up the work's subtitle appear in white text on a
red background; this text is placed over a black-and-white found
photograph of a well-groomed, 1950s-era woman staring out at
the viewer through a magnifying glass. In a sense Kruger's found

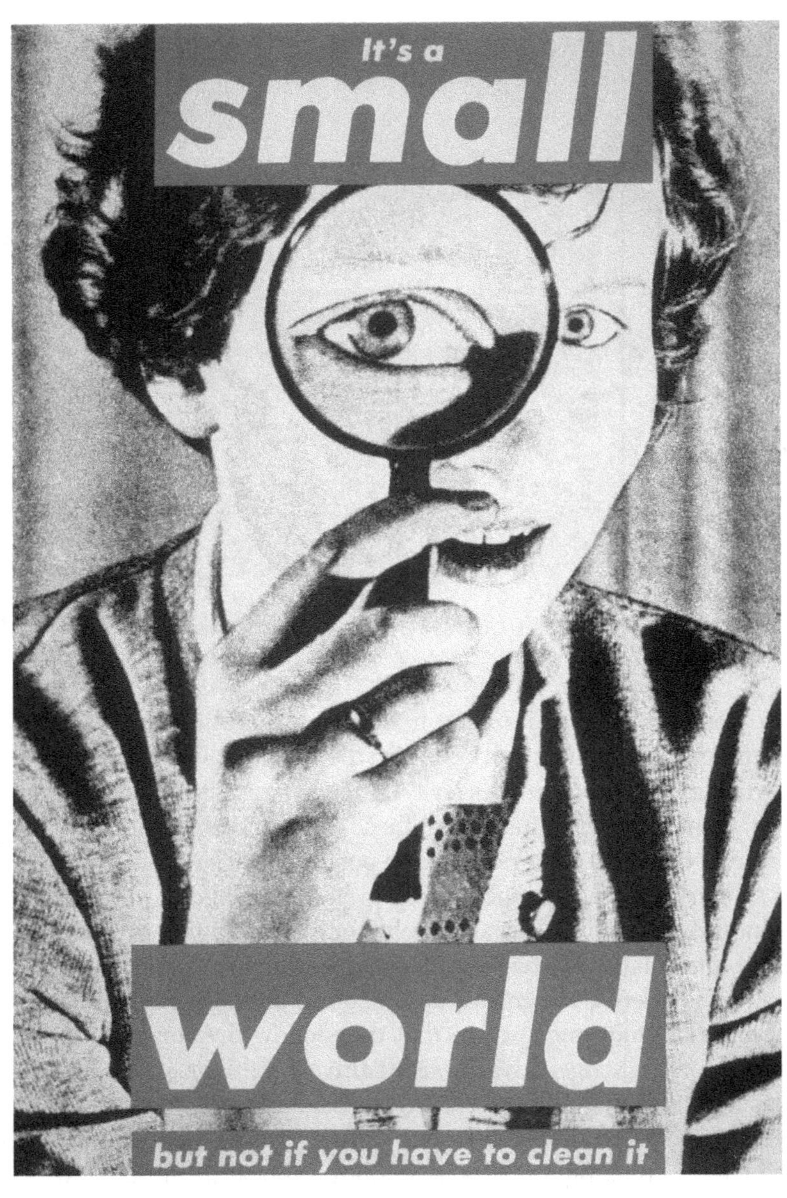

4.8   Barbara Kruger, *Untitled (It's a Small World but Not if You Have to Clean It)* (1990), photographic silkscreen/vinyl

photos are representations of representations, and thereby maintain the anti-essentialist view of feminism. The text and image together seem to condemn the cliché "it's a small world" as the voice of privilege that does not belong to women; it suggests that the traditional role of women as housekeepers imprisons them into largely invisible labor for others' sense of private space. Kruger also produced visually arresting posters to support a 1989 rally in Washington DC that marked the attempt by the US Supreme Court to overturn the Roe vs. Wade court decision of 1973 that legalized abortion. Kruger has therefore used her art to give explicit support of controversial feminist political issues.

Third-Wave/Global Feminisms

As has been discussed earlier in this chapter, as far back as the early 1970s feminist artists of color like Betye Saar and Yolanda López pointed to the assumptions and exclusions of Euro-American feminism. Alternatively the terms "post-feminism" and "third-wave feminism" have been used by feminists of color to argue for the need for feminism also to account for female *ethnic* subjectivities. The term "post-feminism" is generally rejected by feminists because of its implication that the goal of feminism to eradicate the inequality of women has been achieved and it is therefore no longer needed, or that sexism no longer exists as a source of oppression. The filmmaker and theorist Trinh T. Minh-ha, in her essay "Difference: 'a special Third World women issue'" (1989), takes up philosopher Julia Kristeva's comments in her text *About Chinese Women* (1977) on gender difference as she observed it in China.[15] Trinh does so to underscore white academic feminists' erasure of "Third World" women. Trinh notes an assumption common among feminists—that feminists must choose between their sexual identity and their ethnic identity, and that generally ethnicity cannot be at play in feminism. Kristeva points out that, in China, there is little difference between men and women in terms of their behavior in many aspects of everyday life. Trinh finds Kristeva's surface observations about the relationship between genders in Chinese society useful. Kristeva notes that Chinese society then evidences "not a simple repression of a sexual difference, but a *different* distribution of sexual difference"; Trinh agrees that this difference between genders is a matter that is constantly contested or renegotiated in Chinese society.[16] Again in agreement with Kristeva, Trinh argues that the constant challenging of difference that Kristeva observed in the "Third World" makes it impossible to set into place sexist "power-based values" supportive of patriarchal privilege there, or to solidify an "authority-based subject." Trinh's film *Surname Viet Given Name Nam* (1989) similarly attacks anthropology's idea that it can establish authentic ethnic and gender identity, an action that the discipline ties to the name of science. In Trinh's view, these actions are at work in one of anthropology's instruments, the ethnographic film. In her use of actors for the interviews presented in her film about contemporary Vietnamese women, she rejects the validity of the idea of an authentic ethnic and gender identity that is usually advanced in ethnographic film by Western anthropologists. According to Trinh, feminism must open itself to many contestations of gender difference outside the West, in Vietnam for example, and to the notion that the difference of femininity is varied, multiple, mutable, and therefore perhaps indefinable.

Shirin Neshat, an Iranian artist living in the US and working in photography, video, and film, further expands and complicates the representation of women in these mediums to consider the role of women in Muslim society, and the rigid gender differences that have come to be realized in her own country after the revolution.[17] In her installations, such as *Rapture* from 1999 (**Figure 4.9**) Neshat projects two videos simultaneously on different walls of the gallery to depict the stark differences between men and women in what has become a fundamentalist Islamic society. *Rapture* juxtaposes these gender differences in starkly lyrical black-and-white images of figures in the landscape, or in (segregated) worship in a mosque. Women are equally starkly represented in these settings in that Neshat depicts them in black burkhas, but without face veils, or niqabs. In contemplating her works the viewer must necessarily shift her gaze back and forth between these images or even worlds. Neshat then makes it difficult if not impossible to come away

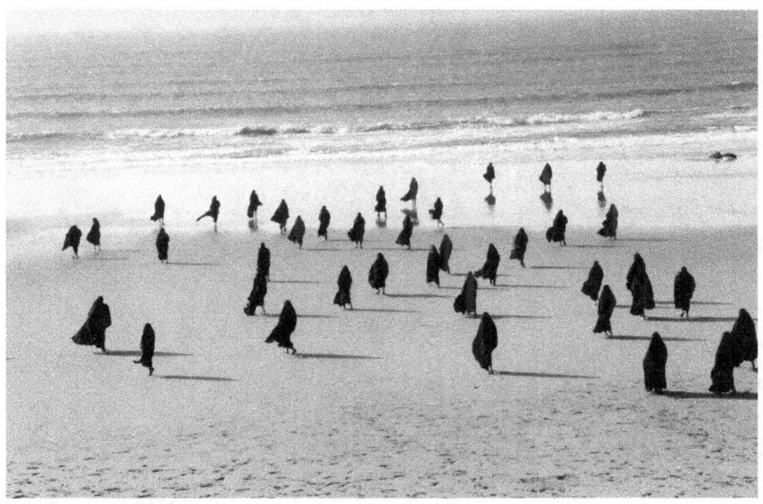

4.9   Shirin Neshat, *Rapture* (1999), production still

with a cohesive picture of women in the everyday life of Muslim society. The alienated individual figures in *Rapture*—not only women but also men—suffer from these stark gender divisions. Neshat is then critical of certain reforms that have been realized in conservative Muslim societies.

Increasingly Western museums and biennials have come to focus on contemporary African art; within these exhibitions African feminist artists also reconfigure and expand the meaning of both feminism and feminist art. Wangechi Mutu lives and works in New York and was born in Kenya. In some ways returning to essentialist roots while standing it on its head, Mutu works in large-scale collage; the human and particularly female body is the dominant form in her compositions. *A'gave You* from 2008 (**Figure 4.10**) contains a figure that is simultaneously beautiful and monstrous. It is recognizable as female and human but also animal or botanical, like marine life; growths and protrusions erupt on this body at various points. Mutu manipulates the figure-ground relation so as to fuse the two and almost make them indistinguishable, as though these formal elements were one. In *Lizard Love* (2010) the figure's right edge dissolves into particles and stains. Mutu's

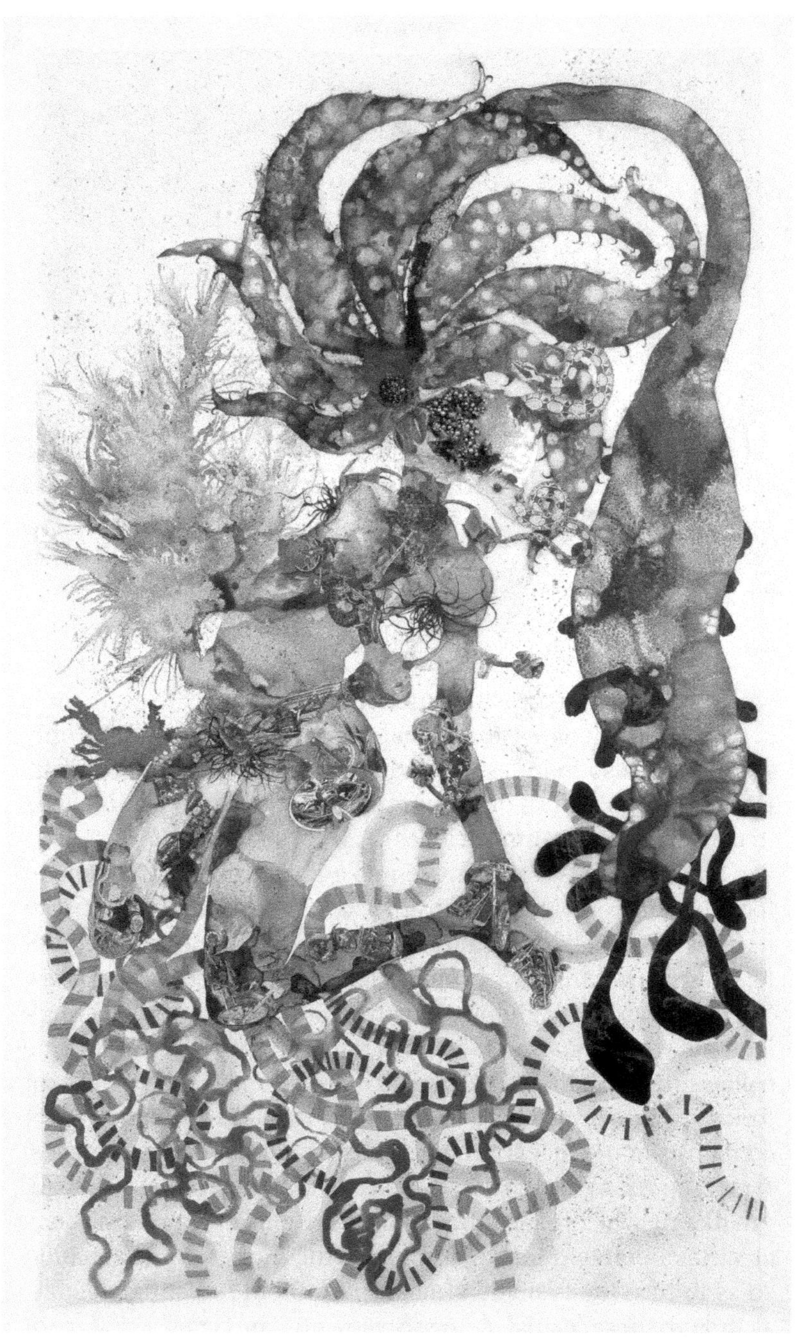

4.10 Wangechi Mutu, *A'gave you* (2008), mixed media collage on Mylar, 93 x 54 inches

women are not "real," nor do they have a "core"; the body she depicts is drawn from various printed sources, as Mutu gets the raw materials for her collages from magazine clippings. She also incorporates a further accumulation of ink, glitter, acrylic, and plant matter in her works. Her female forms are barely contained by the edges of the Mylar surfaces she works on, and, like Jackson Pollock's abstractions, these bodies seem to have the capacity to expand in all directions infinitely, spreading out into the universe with centrifugal force. Like the category of woman that Trinh described, Mutu's quasi-female forms are dynamic, mutating, and hybrid; they seem to include all ethnicities and forms of life. Perhaps not immediately identifiable as the "positive" depictions of woman second-wave feminists once desired, Mutu's fantastical, monstrous, and universalizing bodies suggest an accumulative notion of femininity as an organic force that holds within it the possibility of further mutation, but no essence. They form a picture of woman as change itself.

Le Groupe Amos is a collective of Christian-affiliated male and female intellectuals, playwrights, and activists who work in the Democratic Republic of Congo (formerly Zaire). The group formed in 1989 in Kinshasa, and its members include Thierry N'Landu Mayamba, Flory Kayembe Shamba, José Mpundu, and Jos Das. The group organizes various cultural events for the public in the DRC, including lectures, video presentations, plays, radio programs, and painting exhibitions.[18] As Okwui Enwezor has observed, Le Groupe Amos connects to the anti-object, text-oriented practices of conceptual art but refuses the latter's general lack of interest in political injustice.[19] The collective works to establish a sense of community and independent *African* subjectivity or "sovereignty" for Congolese citizens in the shifting political climate of the DRC, independent of colonialist institutions that continue to operate there and that include the Catholic Church and non-African NGOs. In an effort to include all Congolese, the group members, along with others from the public, produce many of their programs in vernacular languages such as Swahili and Lingala, in addition to French, the official national language. They also produce materials for those that are illiterate.

Many programs and materials are didactic and positive in nature, to educate the public toward the building of an African citizenry through social and political change. Thierry N'Landu has specified that women's rights and "education for life" remain a central and recurring interest of this group. Thus Le Groupe Amos produced and screened *Congolese Woman, Woman with a Thousand Arms* (1997), and the video *And Your Violence Made Me Your Woman*, in the Lingala language, in 1997. Didactic material opposing violence against women was also presented in a series of paintings and poems entitled *The Stations of the Cross of the Congolese Woman*. One theater-based project invited housekeepers to participate as actors during their free time, thereby including these individuals not only to take part, but also to become organizers of future events for the public. Public lectures on female sexuality, for example, encourage women to discuss an otherwise taboo subject; these discussions are videotaped so that they can be screened in other venues. A Groupe Amos flyer of 1994 encourages Congolese men and women to vote and to realize a "free and democratic election in Zaire" (while this election was scheduled, it never took place).[20] In this way Le Groupe Amos uses art, discussion, and other materials to raise Congolese women's consciousness about customs or laws that infringe upon their equality as citizens, and about the need for positive change to realize that equality. The group includes members of the public as collaborators within this feminist collective. Even though some members of the group don't consider themselves artists, Le Group Amos' inclusion in art criticism and in large international exhibitions like Documenta (2002) has recognized the collective as one that relates to feminist art, and also to the recent trend in "participation" in contemporary art practice. Collective and not individual, not only female but also male, counting artists and everyday citizens as its members, and focused on the specific situation of women in the DRC, Le Groupe Amos exemplifies the inclusivity and "glocal" concerns that are likely to characterize feminist art of the future. The group expands the realm of art to realize bell hooks' important notion that "feminism is for everybody."[21]

gay identity/ queer art

In the first volume of his planned four-volume study *The History of Sexuality* (1976), Michel Foucault observed a "sudden, radical condensation of sexual categories" in the West, beginning in the late nineteenth century. This meant there appeared to be a new intellectual concern, across several fields of knowledge, with distinguishing heterosexual from other sexual behaviors such as homosexuality. As was typical of Foucault's historically based works, *The History of Sexuality* traced the cultural and historical development of a social and epistemological category, here of sexuality, and the dynamics of power and ideology that hinge on the construction of that category through social institutions or intellectual disciplines. Some have argued that in this book Foucault also took aim at the theory of sexuality established by Freudian psychoanalysis: namely, the assertion that human sexuality was fundamentally repressed, and that this repression needed to be overcome before individuals could attain a kind of sexual health or balance. In their adaptation of Freud, Western Marxists from several different corners—from surrealists in France and in Latin America to, in the postwar era, Frankfurt School theorist Herbert Marcuse in his book *Eros and Civilization* (1955)—claimed that sexual repression was a negative effect of advanced capitalism in industrialized societies. For Foucault repression was simply how sexuality had been configured in these theories of sexuality.

Homosexuality took on particular if marginalized importance in theories of sexuality put forward by Western Marxism in the postwar era. Where "mainstream" or canonized surrealists such as André Breton were generally homophobes, other surrealist thinkers like César Moro in Peru considered the movement to be a vehicle that could forward notions of homosexual desire that fused with revolutionary goals—that is, with socialist and political liberation. Unlike Freud, Marcuse considers "genital sexuality," or sexual activity that has procreation as its goal, part of repression, or what he terms "sublimation." Eros, on the other hand, refuses to instrumentalize sexuality in this manner. Homosexuality, Marcuse believed, is another non-procreative "perversion" that is also part of the "Great Refusal" of the conditions of the status quo: "the perversions [...] establish libidinal relations which society must ostracize because they threaten to reverse the process of civilization which turned the organism into an instrument of work."[1] Finally Marcuse also thought that the recovery of "pregenital polymorphous sexuality" would create larger social groups that could channel their new erotic energies into political liberation as well. Marcuse, however, quickly gave up on this notion of homosexuality as a revolutionary element; by the time he wrote *An Essay on Liberation* (1969) he does not even mention it. By 1969 he understood that the potential of Eros had already been co-opted by advertising propaganda and transformed into an engine of capitalism. (In strong contrast to Marcuse's defeatist stance of the late 1960s, surrealist and post-modernist artists understood that this territory remained highly contested.) In the end homosexuals constituted only a "perverted" subgroup for Marcuse—the term was positive in his usage—but otherwise as a group they lacked any social or political specificity.

But as Eve Kosofsky Sedgwick uses it in her important book on queer theory, *Epistemology of the Closet* (1992), the term "closet" becomes a critical tool that allows for the investigation of homosexuality and heterosexuality as the most important culturally constructed categories in twentieth-century intellectual history. Sedgwick uncovers and questions the heteronormative categorization of homosexuality in her study of certain canonical authors of modern literature, along with its delineation of the "homo/heterosexual definition." She concludes that this definition is highly contradictory and unstable. The "relations of the gay closet," as she calls them—silence and/or secrecy, and even the social deception regarding the gay man's sexuality and relationships, and the threat of stigma and bias that forces the perpetuation of a cycle of secrecy about one's identity, at great psychic cost—typified homosexual daily life and culture in modern Western society until the watershed event of the Stonewall riots of 1969 in New York City's West Village, after which the gay-rights movement became much more confrontational. Sedgwick draws on key authors who contribute to the debate on the homo/heterosexual definition, including Herman Melville, Oscar Wilde, Henry James, and Marcel Proust. Since Sedgwick took up the gay closet as an issue relevant to Western culture and to queer theory, art historians such as Kenneth Silver have examined visual artworks that similarly engage with the strictures of closeted gay existence during the pre-Stonewall period. During that time, what was known as the "homophile movement" in the US gently advocated equality by assimilation—that is, through gay people's conformity with the norms of heterosexual society.

The New Queer Art

Kenneth Silver argues that key works by the US artists Jasper Johns and Andy Warhol of the late 1950s and early 1960s "began to label something—male homosexuality—that had hitherto been considered too unworthy or too dangerous to name."[2] Earlier twentieth-century American artists had also dealt with gay culture—Silver discusses Marsden Hartley and Charles Demuth as important precedents for later artists who took on homosexual life and culture as a subject, and another art historian, Richard Meyer, points to the painter Paul Cadmus. But arguably Johns and Warhol were among a younger generation of painters in New York whose art turned against dominant notions of artistic masculinity as it had been set in place by the New York School, or abstract expressionism, of the 1940s and 1950s. Johns' work most explicitly critiques the calligraphic brushstroke as a celebrated marker of the machismo of abstract expressionism. His *Painting with Two Balls* from 1960 (**Figure 5.1**) is made up of intricately placed brushstrokes, and not the bold gestures of large-scale abstraction. Johns interrupts the painting surface not only with two wooden balls wedged between the canvas sections, but also by

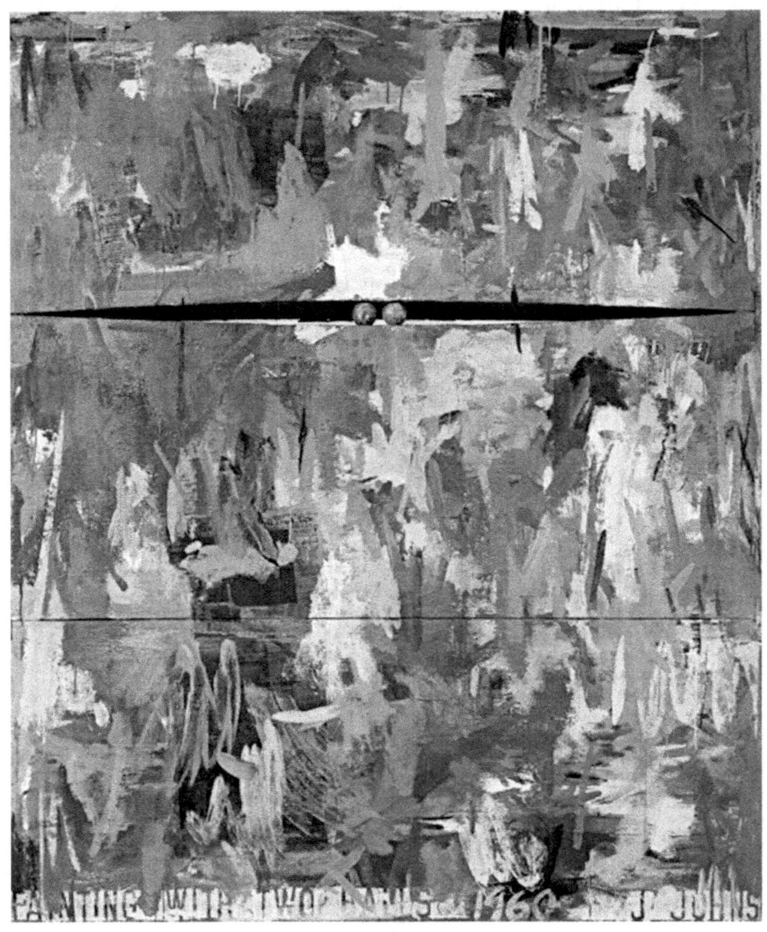

5.1   Jasper Johns, *Painting with Two Balls* (1960)

neatly stenciling the title and the artist's name across the bottom of the composition. Perhaps a visual play on words, Johns ironically presents a painting "with balls," mocking the heroics, the clichéd blue-collar heterosexuality, and the sublime aspirations, of the New York School painters. These exclusively heterosexual masculine qualities were also to be found in the language of the art criticism that championed the "forcefulness" and "directness" of earlier abstract painting in New York. Johns contests such assertions, suggesting the existence of other modes of artistic masculinity. Johns' art continues this contestation in other paintings such as *In Memory of My Feelings, Frank O'Hara* of 1961, in which Johns pays homage to a recently deceased friend, the gay poet and curator Frank O'Hara.

In Silver's reading, *In Memory* makes direct reference to the secretiveness that by necessity characterized homosexual culture in the US during the conservative 1950s. Johns' painting consists of two hinged panels positioned like a diptych; one can then close the painting upon itself and completely seal it from view. Johns takes the painting's title from one of O'Hara's poems; it can be read as marking loss, and it may suggest more intimate relationships. Perhaps an affair took place between the artist and the writer. O'Hara's poem also reflects on the loss of falling out of love. Silver notes that in the same year that this painting appeared, Johns' relationship with Robert Rauschenberg was coming to a close. The painting's multiple ambiguities and its veiled references to past and necessarily secretive love affairs underscore the qualities of indirectness and concealment that were part of homosexual relationships, and of living a closeted life, during a repressive and homophobic era. Perhaps as a result of the US debate on gay marriage, some have recently suggested that homophile-type assimilation might bring positive benefits to gay men.[3] But in the early 1960s, Johns used his art to point to the heavy cost of assimilation: a stunted and unrealizable sense of self as a gay *artist*.

It is a widely held view that in his paintings and films Andy Warhol refused the strictures of closeted homosexuality that had plagued American artists like Johns and Rauschenberg in the generation before his. He instead chose to present a commentary on gay culture and identity, albeit one that remained encoded. As one would expect of one of the most important artists of the twentieth century, the literature on Warhol is voluminous. Most often it points to his art's engagement with gay identity in the "camp" aspects of the subject matter that animates the work, and usually cites Susan Sontag's famed essay "Notes on 'camp'" (1964) as a source. While Sontag mentions, almost in passing, that camp is frequently associated with homosexual culture, the two have come to be treated as practically synonymous. More generally the outmoded, sentimental, trivial, excessive, and bad-taste qualities of what constitutes camp—cultural marginalia or detritus, of not only "serious" culture but also of pop culture—have been associated with marginalized communities, and particularly with the gay community. Camp has also become a mechanism of the margin's political resistance to the cultural status quo. Thus Warhol's long series of paintings of the film actress Marilyn Monroe, completed after her death in 1962, is associated with the camp fascination with the outmoded, since by 1962 Monroe was something of a has-been. She was then a camp figure, and, in addition, a gay icon; it is questionable whether there were any empathetic motives behind this series, or behind any of the huge number of portrait-type paintings that Warhol produced during his lifetime. Instead, as Thomas Crow has suggested, Warhol seems more interested in these icons as visual indicators or as an effect of the functions of the mass-media system, and the place of individual tragedy within it.[4]

Richard Meyer has argued that Warhol's early advertising images asserted a sense of gay community within the advertising industry in New York City. Best known among Warhol's advertising images of the 1950s are his illustrations for a campaign for the shoe store I. Miller, which ran primarily in New York newspapers. In 1956 Warhol showed his gold-leaf collages of shoes at the New York Bodley Gallery and bookstore, and at the Serendipity, a café frequented by art directors from advertising and from the theater. In another work from the same year, *Untitled ("To All My Friends")* **(Figure 5.2)**, Warhol presents an ensemble of 11 single shoes, each

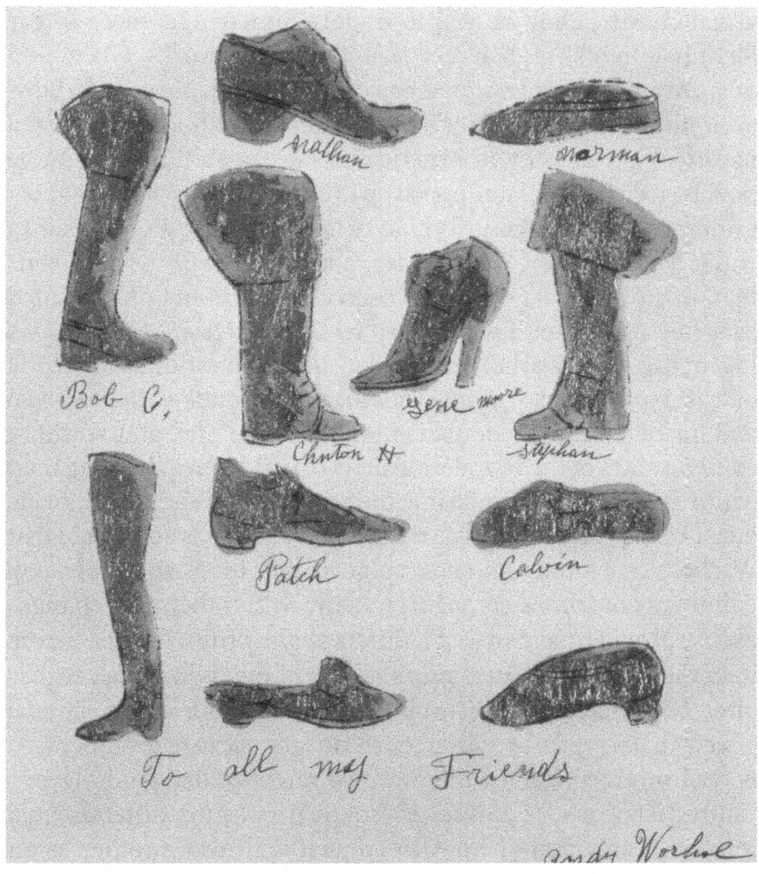

5.2   Andy Warhol, *Untitled ("To All My Friends")* (1956)

inscribed (possibly by his mother) with the handwritten name of
a close friend or business associate. Meyer relates that this was a
social circle of gay men, some of whom were dating or in relationships with each other.[5] *Untitled* underscores not only interconnected
personal affairs and relationships, but what is in today's parlance
called a support network, of like-minded professionals in a given
field, who also serve as advocates for each other.

Warhol's post-modernist refusal to separate high and low
culture, and his move to merge each into a broader category of

visual culture, allowed him to import similar references to gay identity into his "high art" or post-advertising works. His notion of a private and professional gay community in New York, however, ultimately matured into an awareness of the marginalized nature of gay identity in American society, a shift that might be read in some of his later pop art paintings. This is perhaps most evident in Warhol's contribution to the New York World's Fair in 1964, *Thirteen Most Wanted Men*, a large panel of 15 silkscreens that, in a bizarre act of double censorship, was not only painted over but also covered with a tarp by Fair officials. Meyer argues that in this work Warhol first aligned, in metaphorical fashion, the outcast figure of the criminal with that of the "outlaw" homosexual and his desires.[6] The double entendre of the title, and Warhol's configuration of the found mugshots of good-looking young men within his grid of panels so that they gazed upon each other, made quasi-veiled reference to gay desire. Moreover, it is suggested that Warhol's repetition of photographic images in his silkscreen pop paintings contains a complex strategy: within them, he changes each repeated image so that it differs slightly from the one before it, in the manner of Duchamp's notion of the *infra-mince*. As has often been noted, Warhol is able to achieve subtle compositional effects in his repeated silkscreened images because his repetition is far from identical. In this way, we might understand Meyer's claim that Warhol's *Double Elvis* (1963) presents differentiated images of two male bodies in contact with one another as an erotic possibility, and also as a flash of recognition of gay desire.[7] Finally, however, Warhol's awareness in the 1950s and 1960s of his own place within an "outlaw" gay community is difficult to reconcile with his later lack of interest, in the mid 1980s, in the harrowing situation of many gay men in New York City during the AIDS crisis.

Like Warhol, the West German artist and filmmaker Rainer Werner Fassbinder refused debilitating notions of homophile artistic assimilation. At the time of his death in 1982 Fassbinder had come to terms with his own homosexuality and was occupied with a cinematic working through of Jean Genet's notion of homosexuality and/as criminality. Fassbinder was perhaps the most important filmmaker and auteur of the West German "New German Cinema" of the 1970s and 1980s. It appears that after his death commentators did their utmost to scour Fassbinder's gayness from his films and legacy, mostly through marginalizing his queer films, which feature gay protagonists and either implicitly or explicitly address gay identity. Fassbinder famously worked across multiple films with an ensemble of actors he began to cultivate during his years at the Action Theater in Munich in the late 1960s.[8] As he began to make films he sometimes recruited non-actors, both female and male (many of whom were his lovers), to star in his films, such as Irm Hermann, Günther Kaufmann, and El Hedi ben Salem. Even in his earliest films there existed a strong connection between Fassbinder's personal life and the actors and even the narratives that animated them. He featured his real-life male lovers in his films as objects of desire; in the film *Germany in Autumn* (1977) Fassbinder appears in the nude with Armin Meier, who later committed suicide. Fassbinder also married two women in his lifetime. At the time of his sudden death in 1982 he seemed, however, to embrace gay culture and his own gay identity; his last film *Querelle* (**Figure 5.3**), made in the year of his death and adapted from Genet's novel *Querelle of Brest*, is a queer film in that it is concerned with Genet's view of (sadomasochistic) gay sexuality and otherwise more or less explicitly focuses on the gay sexual relationships that define the

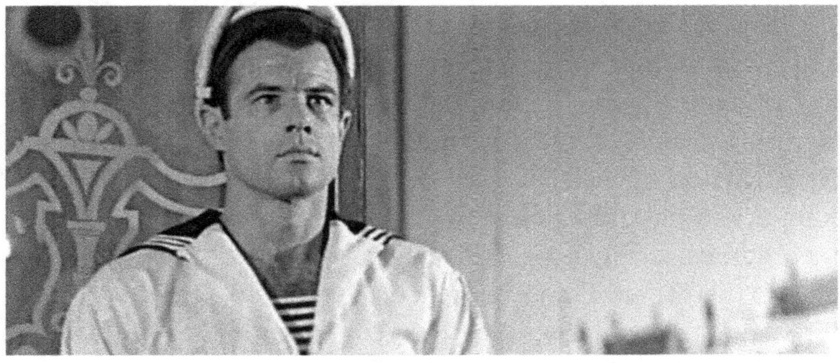

5.3   Rainer Werner Fassbinder, *Querelle* (1982), film still

lead character, a sailor who is a thief and a murderer, played by the American actor Brad Davis.

In terms of his resistance to patriarchal repression and authority, Fassbinder has been claimed for feminism: the female protagonist of his most mainstream film *The Marriage of Maria Braun* (1978), to give only one example, is a woman with phallic power who reaches success, independence, and wealth on her own terms and despite the men that surround her. Kaja Silverman has argued for the anti-patriarchal and liberating aspect of "deviant" male sexuality that is to be found in Fassbinder's films, in part based on the masochism that is the basic driving force of human interaction within them. In Silverman's view this masochism offers some measure of fulfillment of the self—she uses the Lacanian term "masochistic ecstasy."[9] However, masochism is a universal within Fassbinder's cinema; as Thomas Elsaesser has stated, "Fassbinder's second strategy was to replace the oppressor/oppressed model by the sadomasochistic double bind."[10] It therefore seems difficult to stake a claim for masochism's specific relevance, within Fassbinder's films, to *gay* identity and experience. As others have also pointed out, one implication of Fassbinder's queer films, and of his own life as an artist, is that gay desire and relationships may also bring the suffering of heterosexual ones. He therefore does not cast gay identity in a consistently positive or celebratory light. Yet Fassbinder's openness in exploring Genet's views on homosexuality in relation to his own artistic identity brought the issues of gay identity and sexuality into mainstream art cinema of the 1980s.

In (West) Berlin, a city with a history of tolerating homosexuality and gay culture, several German painters took a different approach in ruminating on their personal relationships and on their own sense of self as gay artists. Two members of the painting group "Die Neuen Wilde" ("The New Wild Ones"), as they called themselves, Rainer Fetting and Salomé (Wolfgang Cihlarz), openly accepted their homosexuality in a number of paintings that also made reference to their affair. They explored the possibility of gay self-portraiture, taking up and extending the genre of modernist portraiture as their chosen stylistic predecessors, the German expressionist group known as "Die Brücke" ("The Bridge"), first developed it.

Die Neuen Wilde organized itself as a group through the highly successful "self-help" or alternative space Galerie am Moritzplatz, in Kreuzberg, West Berlin. In addition to Fetting and Salomé, key members were Helmut Middendorf and Bernd Zimmer.[11] The "return to figuration" in painting on the part of West German neo-expressionists of the late 1970s has been lambasted in art criticism, with some claiming that this movement contained fascist elements or sympathies.[12] These dismissive statements ignore the aspects of resistance—against patriarchy and against heteronormativity as it is practiced within the medium of painting—that are to be found among these artworks.

The gay painters who made up this postwar group were likely more interested in the expressionist genre of the male nude than in a generalized shift to figuration. The homoerotic element in German expressionism, particularly in Brücke painting, is a fascinating and under-studied aspect of this direction of the avant-garde. While all of the members of the Brücke group produced portraits and woodcut prints of each other, Ernst Ludwig Kirchner's are perhaps the most well known. The portraits point to the close-knit nature and the shared camaraderie of the Brücke group. Among other works, Kirchner's painting *Bathers at Moritzburg* (1909/26) indicates the artist's interest in the male nude, which he often depicts frontally and with a clearly delineated phallus. Kirchner also posed frontally and photographed his male African model, the circus performer "Sam," in his Dresden studio, an indication of Kirchner's fascination with and eroticization of the black male body as Other. This sexual interest in the black body was also an aspect of expressionist primitivism.

Fetting and Salomé were participants in West Berlin's booming club and music scene of the late 1970s, when the British rock musicians David Bowie and Brian Eno also lived and recorded there. Like the artist and impresario Martin Kippenberger, Salomé formed his own punk band, "Geile Tiere" ("Horny Creatures"), in 1980 with Luciano Castelli. Both Fetting's and Salomé's self-portraits from these years point to the culture and dynamics of gay nightlife, of stage performances in drag and otherwise. Introducing the quasi-ritualized action of drag and other types of sexualized performance as subject matter for painting, these self-portraits also have to do with the medium-specific construction of the artist-self as a gay painter. Salomé sets many of his self-portraits of the 1970s on a kind of stage that might be read as reminiscent of a nightclub, sometimes posing before a paravent in various drag costumes, as in *Figure Before a Paravent* (1976), or, in camp fashion, in a woman's corset and stockings, in *Strip (Tryptichon)* (1977). In the latter the artist paints his own body as an object, in a doubled gesture of empowerment; he performs the act of bodily and painterly seduction that is also the basis of his artist-persona pseudonym. This construction of painting as a claustrophobic theater of seduction featuring the artist also occurs in Salomé's strongest series with this motif, *The Salomé Story* (1979).[13] In the series harshly lit, chalky, and almost nude figures, at times in the contorted poses of what might be a dance, again appear alone or

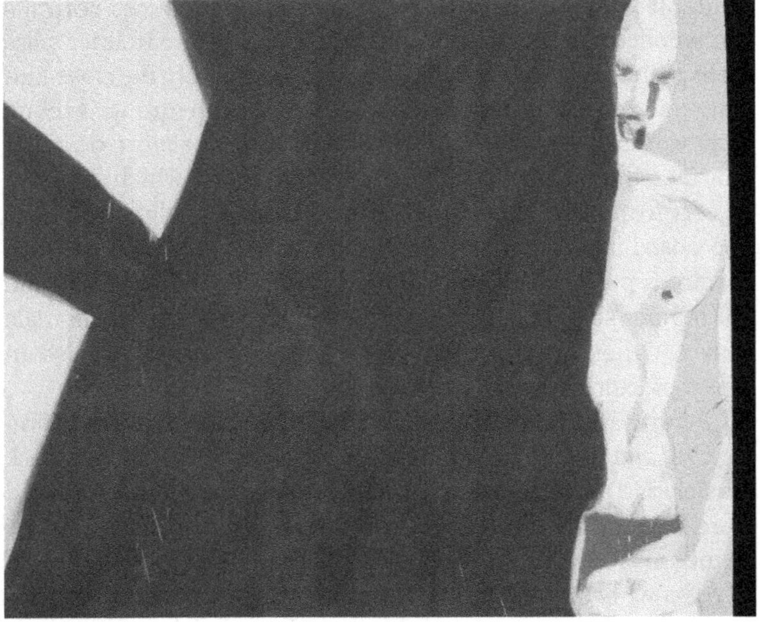

5.4   Salomé (Wolfgang Cihlarz), *Death (Der Mord)* (from the series *The Salomé Story,* 1979)

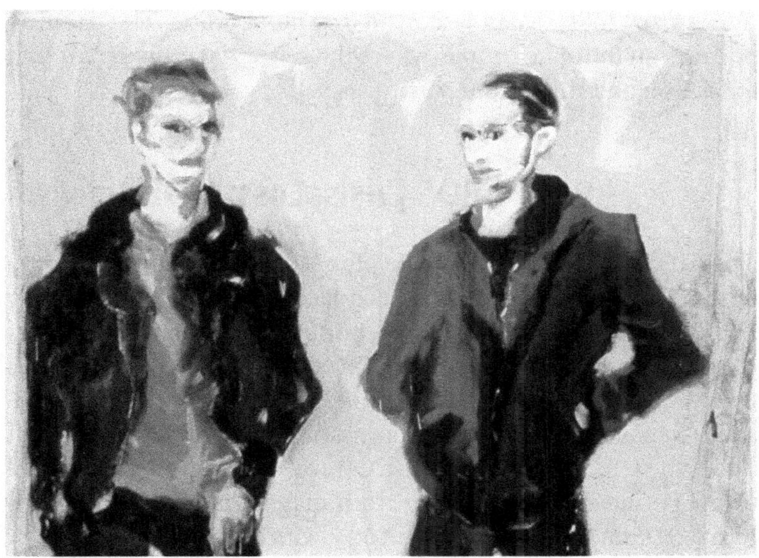

5.5   Rainer Fetting, *Self and Salomé* (*Selbst und Salomé*, 1976)

together on a raised stage. In *Death* **(Figure 5.4)**, a blue shadow eclipses a slighter figure to the right, almost forcing it out of the frame. The series arguably presents a metaphorical tracking of the bloom and eventual death of passion. The title of the series implies that this melodrama has to do with the artist himself.

Rainer Fetting's approach to painting and to the subject matter of gay relationships is less theatrical. In a longer series of self-portraits from 1977–8, Fetting depicts himself in the nude, sporting a red-lacquer manicure and matching lipstick, in drag, or with a fedora with the same rouged lips, a dramatic brushstroke of red. The artist's body is always close to the picture plane in this series, and the figure gazes directly at the viewer. These works show the artist comfortably taking on, or mixing and discarding, various signifiers of gender within the genre of the self-portrait.[14] Fetting's painting *Self and Salomé* from 1976 **(Figure 5.5)** memorializes their affair. It is almost a doubled self-portrait; it is difficult to distinguish one figure from the other. Fetting positions the two as though one were the mirror image of the other, a doubling of the self that in itself can be considered homoerotic. The painting portrays an intimate couple, where the self/artist utilizes painting to take on and mirror the partner as self.

AIDS Crisis; Loss; AIDS Activism

The AIDS epidemic of the 1980s plunged the gay community into crisis. The disease was first named (acquired immunodeficiency syndrome) in 1981, after doctors reported cases of unusual cancers (Kaposi's sarcoma) and pneumonia in otherwise healthy young men in New York and Los Angeles. The disease soon spread to transfusion recipients and to infants born to mothers with AIDS. As of 2008, the US Centers for Disease Control and Prevention recorded over 617,000 deaths resulting from diagnoses of AIDS. Deaths from AIDS in the US peaked in 1993, with the highest number of diagnoses occurring in the state of New York. Because of the wider availability of "active" antiretroviral therapy and drugs by the mid 1990s, AIDS deaths had declined by 40 percent by 1997; as of 2006, more than one million people were living with HIV infection in the US. As of today there is still no cure for HIV. However, before these drugs were developed and made available, HIV progressed to full-blown AIDS quickly, in just a few years, and was fatal. In the US large numbers of gay men contracted and died of it in the 1980s; these deaths greatly affected the art community in New York.[15]

The US government did not respond promptly to the rise of AIDS, nor did it make the crucial effort to educate the public and at-risk communities (including intravenous drug users) in a timely manner about the measures they might take to avoid contracting HIV. The first educational mailing on AIDS issued by the US Surgeon General reached the general public only in 1988, seven years after the disease had been identified. The Gay Men's Health Crisis, formed in 1981 by Larry Kramer to raise awareness and funds for research into the disease, was instead one of the first organizations to issue pamphlets that emphasized prevention. Unfortunately social conservatives condemned such necessarily explicit explanation. Due to the successful efforts of conservative politicians like Senator Jesse Helms (Republican, North Carolina) to ban any educational materials that "encouraged homosexual activities"—and this "Helms Amendment" is still in effect—the US government declined to educate its public about AIDS promptly. It is fairly certain that the State's inaction led to the further spread of the disease in New York and elsewhere, thereby indirectly allowing more citizens to contract it.

One goal of the organization AIDS Coalition to Unleash Power (ACT UP), also founded by Kramer in 1987, was directly to counter the fear, speculation, and homophobia that had arisen in this vacuum of information about AIDS. Douglas Crimp, an art critic and member of ACT UP, stated in that founding year: "If we recognize that AIDS exists only in and through its representations, culture, and politics, then the hope is that we can also recognize the imperative to know them, analyze them, and wrest control of them."[16] A second collective, Gran Fury, was formed in 1988. ACT UP has pitted itself against the elegiac tone taken not only by the media, but also by artists, in representing gay men with AIDS. The AIDS quilt, a project first begun in San Francisco as an act of private mourning of individual friends and lovers, was shown publically in Washington DC for the first time in 1987. The quilt has more recently been seen as a project that "became a public consolation, and part of what it consoled the public for was its failure to care in time."[17] Instead of constructing memorials to the dead, ACT UP staged protests and designed highly effective counter-media imagery in posters, T-shirts, buttons, stickers, and placards, which were disseminated in public spaces. ACT UP and Gran Fury posters most often combined, in post-modernist fashion, a simple text and an amended appropriated image that together urged the public to take action, by means of protest, against the governmental neglect of the spread of AIDS. Perhaps their best-known poster is *Silence=Death* from 1986 (**Figure 5.6**), which features text and a realigned pink triangle; this symbol was first used by the Nazis to identify "sexual offenders" (mostly homosexuals). All elements are positioned on a stark black background. Even post-modern appropriationist art was reappropriated for ACT UP signage, as in Adam Rolston's retooling of Barbara

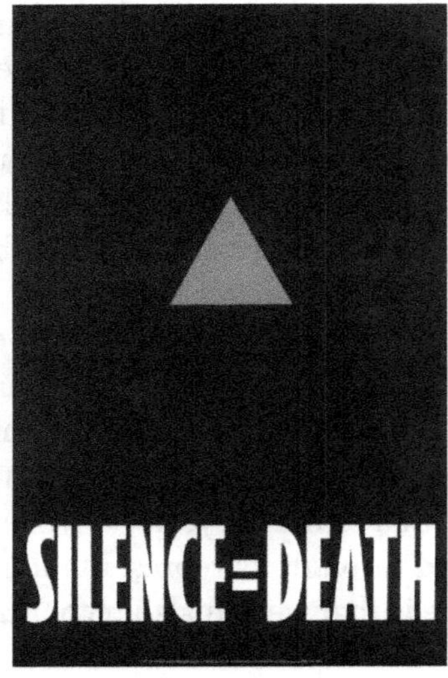

5.6 ACT UP, *Silence=Death* (1986)

Kruger in *I Am Out, Therefore I Am* (1989). ACT UP works are highly legible agitprop that resemble effective advertising, but their visual elements often resonate with high-art imagery by Warhol and others. The organization remains active and has begun the "ACT UP Oral History Project" to chronicle its history and the involvement of its members; it is available online.[18]

The art press severely criticized Crimp for advocating ACT UP's merely "political art," also accusing him of "hating" art. In response Crimp has noted that to argue for art that advocates for or avows politics is also to claim that there is art that "is beyond politics rather than art that simply disavows its politics."[19] The general inclusion of AIDS-activist goals in visual art in the 1990s, as ACT UP and Gran Fury practiced it, marked perhaps the most concerted postwar rejection of high-modernist definitions of art as autonomous, separate from the doings of society and the world. This is then another instance when the debate regarding the nature of the connection between art and politics has continued in art discourse.

As I have already mentioned, certain American artists pursued a personalized, memorializing and mournful tone in their art, which some AIDS activists did not find productive in terms of producing legislative and ideological change to improve the situation of those living with HIV and AIDS. For example, in the Cuban-born American artist Félix González-Torres' "candy spill" installations like *Untitled (Revenge)* (1991), wrapped hard candies are spread across the floor, or piled in a corner; in these works the number of candies corresponds to González-Torres' and his partner's body weight (both died of AIDS). These works serve as an abstracted memorial to the artist's partner, Ross. Viewers are welcome to take candies with them, and the depletion of the candies and their weight metaphorically references the slow ebb of mortality. Ross Bleckner's dark oil paintings at first took on explicitly memorializing content in the references implied by their titles—in *Memory of Larry* (1984) or *Memoriam* (1985). Many of Bleckner's paintings of the 1980s and 1990s, such as *In Sickness and in Health* from 1997 (**Figure 5.7**), feature ghostly and evocative forms on a dark background—sometimes birds, or possibly cellular or platelet-like shapes—and titles that suggest referents. The paintings seem to have as their subject the mourning process itself, and the struggle to recuperate from great loss after illness and death.

In their art both David Wojnarowicz and Glenn Ligon investigate the issue of the representation of homosexuality within American culture. Ligon (who is also discussed in Chapter 2) uses his text-based conceptual paintings to track the conjoined problems of racism and homophobia as they are to be found in language and visual culture. His photo- and text-based installation *Notes on the Margin of the Black Book* (1991–3) re-presents selected images from the photographer Robert Mapplethorpe's *Black Book* of 1986. Mapplethorpe's work contains highly eroticized and stereotypical images of black men, which Ligon juxtaposes with framed quotations and texts from various intellectuals. Ligon's examination of Mapplethorpe's problematic artwork directly interrogates and rejects the power relation that is realized in white artists' eroticizing and objectifying of the black male body, an old and even foundational principle of modernism.

David Wojnarowicz remains, with Robert Mapplethorpe, the most controversial artist who engaged with gay rights of the 1980s, and one of the most important artists of the late twentieth century. Almost 20 years after his death from AIDS in 1992, Wojnarowicz still generates controversy: in December 2010 his film *A Fire in My Belly* (1986–7) was removed from the exhibition *Hide/Seek: Difference and Desire in American Portraiture*, held at the National Portrait Gallery in Washington DC. This act of censorship, a decision by the secretary of the Smithsonian Institution, took place after the Smithsonian had received complaints about one image in the film, of a crucifix with ants on it, from the Catholic League and

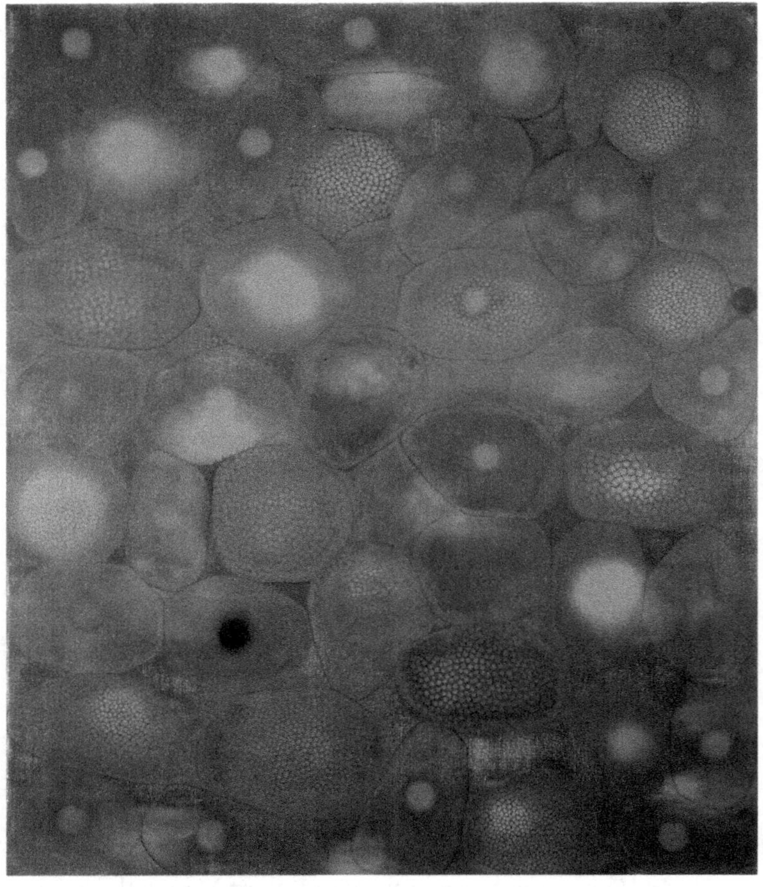

5.7   Ross Bleckner, *In Sickness and in Health* (1997), oil/linen

from the speaker of the House of Representatives, John Boehner (Republican, Ohio). Both had stated that this image or sequence was offensive to Catholics. During his lifetime Wojnarowicz fought attempts to censor or to misrepresent his art. One of its primary concerns, as Wojnarowicz himself articulated, is to make plain the pervasive censorship and marginalization practiced in American visual culture against representations of sexuality that do not conform to the normative fantasies of white male heterosexuality. A victim of child abuse and neglect, Wojnarowicz was left to live on the streets in New York on his own as a young teenager, where he became a hustler and drug addict. Like one of his cultural icons, Genet, Wojnarowicz was an outsider to almost every community.[20]

Wojnarowicz worked across many mediums including performance, but his most powerful works are in collage and photography. In his ode to Genet, the Xerox collage *Untitled (Genet)* (1979), he frames Genet's photomontage likeness with recognizable Christian iconography of sainthood, suffering, and sacrifice: Genet's face is surrounded by a halo; Renaissance-era angels, the interior of a cathedral-like space, and an image of Jesus Christ with a crown of thorns and a syringe in his arm, can all be seen in the immediate background. The work is also remarkable in that Wojnarowicz comments on the situation of addiction, something that he knew personally, as one of tribulation. The collage can then be read as deeply religious and, indeed, Christian. In it, Wojnarowicz as an addict identifies not only with Genet, but also with the figure of Jesus as the one who suffered most, and who as a deity was able to transcend misery.

Wojnarowicz's *Sex Series* of 1988–9 marks a high point in his oeuvre; the works in the series consist of photomontage silver gelatin prints. In each of these works one photographic image takes up most of the picture plane and is printed in the reversed tones of a photographic negative. Most often these primary images are of a landscape. Some images in the series feature a text, and all have at least one vignette photographic image, also printed in negative, and cropped into a circular shape; they resemble the small circular images taken through a microscope. The small vignettes are found images, possibly from pornography, of either gay or heterosexual sex acts. These smaller images seem to have no relation to the larger landscapes into which they are inserted. The work *Sex Series (for Marion Scemama), Bridge* from 1988 (**Figure 5.8**), is perhaps the best-known work in this series, because it was used in an attempt to condemn and censor Wojnarowicz's art. The image's references to scientific imagery—to microscopic views but also to the reversed tones of an X-ray image of the body—imply the penetration of surface reality and appearance to get at something concealed beneath it. The primary subject of this series is sexuality, though the artist is also interested in formal composition and the relation of visual elements. He sets up careful links between forms in his juxtaposition of photographic images. Wojnarowicz clearly considered sexuality to be part of daily life, one aspect of the landscape and world that surrounded him. As a gay man, homosexuality was also part of his world, even though it was not recognized as "normal," or conforming to the dominant modes of heterosexuality. His *Sex Series*, then, focuses on representing what dominant American culture and ideology requires remain hidden, repressed, and marginalized. Yet the artist refused to allow his own experience to be erased from visual culture. Wojnarowicz heightens the revelatory aspect of this series in using the medium of photography, which is most closely associated with its "documentary" or indexical properties and with representing the "real" world around us.

Because of the power of Wojnarowicz's photomontages and collages, they became targets of social conservatives, particularly the American Family Association (AFA). Wojnarowicz finally initiated a lawsuit against the AFA for copyright infringement and defamation of character, and won on one complaint. In order to raise funds to counter or eliminate the National Endowment for the Arts (NEA), the AFA reprinted sections or excerpts from Wojnarowicz's work and represented them as artworks funded by the NEA, the US governmental agency that had given grant funding for an exhibition and catalog of Wojnarowicz's work at Illinois State University in 1990. The AFA pamphlet had reproduced only one vignette from the *Sex Series*, a sexual image, and represented it as Wojnarowicz's "artwork," with a text entitled

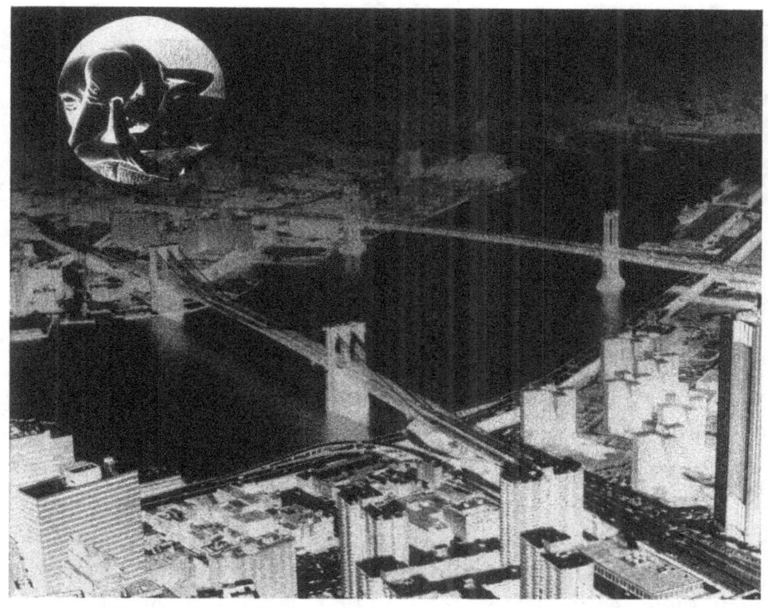

5.8   David Wojnarowicz, *Sex Series (for Marion Scemama)*, *Bridge*
(1988), gelatin silver print

"Your tax dollars helped pay for these 'works of art.'" The court
issued an injunction against further printing and distribution of
the AFA's fund-raising brochure, and awarded Wojnarowicz a
nominal sum of $1.[21] Despite the fact that the AFA's cropping and
copying of Wojnarowicz's artworks was deemed to constitute fair
use, the decision was a victory for artists' rights more generally,
since the artist was able to stop the censoring and misrepresentation of his art in court.

  While it may be something that has a stronger resonance
with feminism, another dimension of gay rights is raised and
advocated by lesbian artists. Facing greater difficulty and marginalization in the intensely patriarchal art world—which gay male
artists have not had to face—lesbian artists in modernism have
mostly remained closeted, with some exceptions. New research
on previously lesser-known lesbian gallerists and artists of the
twentieth century, including the French surrealist photographer

Claude Cahun, the New York gallerist Betty Parsons, and the painter Agnes Martin, was an outcome of what has been called the New Art History. This revisionism in the discipline began in the 1970s with art-historical studies that demanded that the discipline acknowledge the assumptions at work in how it bestowed aesthetic value on some artists and not on others. The New Art History encouraged a new interest in marginalized cultures and artists within modernism. Many art historians and critics now see the openly lesbian Gertrude Stein, in her roles as art collector and as avant-garde poet, as an important figure for modernism more generally, and have constructed counter-histories of modernism and post-modernism with Stein as the "mother" of each.

Photography remains an important medium for several artists who examine aspects of lesbian identity. Catherine Opie's best-known artworks center on aspects of the patriarchal structure that continue to shore up the dynamics of inequality and marginalization as they are applied to certain bodies—for example, the lesbian body. Opie became known for a studio-portrait series of her friends in the sadomasochistic leather scene in San Francisco, and for several provocative self-portraits. Working in color photography, Opie poses the subjects of her images before brightly colored backdrops. In her series *Being and Having* of 1991, her subjects are sometimes inches from the camera lens, and some of them, as in *Bo* (**Figure 5.9**), shown sporting a mustache. Lesbian drag kings or others wearing the accouterments of the S&M scene are represented in rich detail in these portraits. At the time of these works in the 1990s, during the AIDS crisis and when homosexuals continued to be outcast, Opie was uninterested in the notion of the assimilating lesbian. Her art intends to lend dignity to women who, like herself, pursue alternative sexual preferences. Like the photographers Robert Mapplethorpe and Nan Goldin, Opie uses photography to underscore the performance of gender, a feminist philosophical position articulated by Judith Butler as an aspect of individual autonomy and freedom. Departing from these subjects, Opie more recently has focused on children, and on the banal aspects of the domestic lives of lesbian couples. In one work from her 2006 series of color portraits, she pictures herself nude,

Madonna-like, nursing her young son; others depict children of varying ages who are also the offspring of artists and gay couples. Opie's art anticipated and cleared the way for the debate on gay marriage in the US, which has since become a central social and political issue. She upends and diversifies the whole notion of family values, opening it to her vision of a diverse and inclusive way of American life.

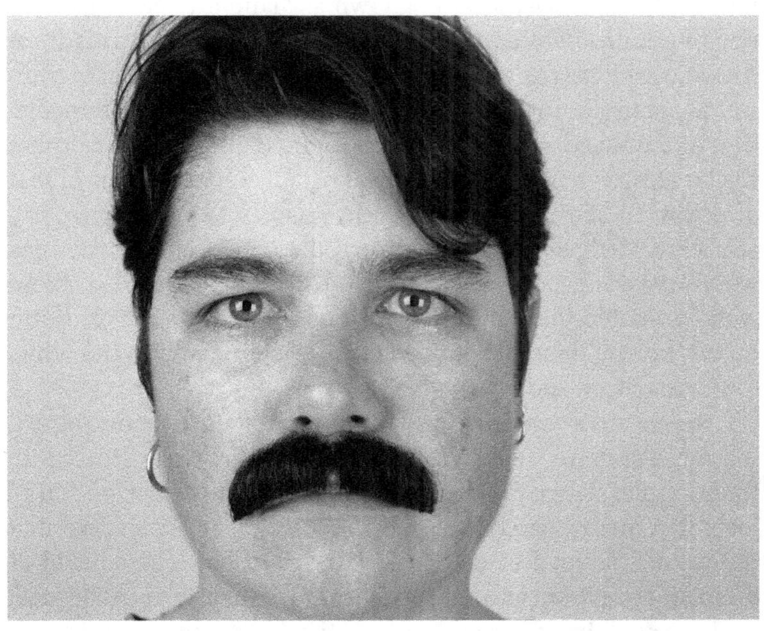

5.9   Catherine Opie, *Bo* (1991) (from the series *Being and Having*), chromogenic print

environmental art

The rise of environmental art in the US and Europe during the late 1960s and into the 1970s was part a larger shift toward activist engagement with what earlier generations had called "conservation." In some ways, what is known as "land art" facilitated the rise of a radical environmentalism that traveled outwards from the art world, first as an ideology and then later as a form of community activism involving reclamation projects for the remediation of damaged, local ecosystems. This is despite the fact that the large-scale land-art projects that usually serve as icons of that direction in art, such as Robert Smithson's *Spiral Jetty* (1970), are acknowledged to have disrupted the ecosystems of the sites where they are located. As Rirkrit Tiravanija has noted, these works initiated the "old model of land art and the artist's quest to, on the one hand, be outside of the system, and on the other, to shape nature and landscape."[1]

Newer environmental art takes on public education regarding these systems, including new technologies and research in, for example, alternative fuel sources. Frequently there is a "DIY" logic that artists attach to the technologies they explore, so that the public, instead of corporate concerns, can take control of them and use them as a means to improve their immediate local environment. In one example, the artist Amy Franceschini of the artists' collective Futurefarmers has collaborated with the biologist Jonathan Meuser in *DIY Algae/Hydrogen Bioreactor* (2004), a work that presents an "open-source backyard model" for algal-hydrogen production as "performative research" in the art gallery. As Meuser has noted, such work makes rather inaccessible scientific knowledge more readily available for public scrutiny.[2] These DIY-based environmental works tend to look more like a laboratory than a traditional artwork.

Generally environmental art emerged in the US in two centers: New York City and in the deserts of the American southwest. Ecologically aware art generally grew from formalist directions in art in New York such as minimalism and was part of the new interest, articulated by Jack Burnham in 1968, in a "systems"-oriented aesthetic less concerned with producing an object than with examining the workings of various social, cultural, or natural/environmental systems.[3] Land and environmental artwork as pursued by Robert Smithson and other American artists like Betty Beaumont struck a dialectical and shifting relation to the usual system of dissemination from studio to the gallery space—and by extension began to question the institutional functioning of the postwar gallery system in New York. Already some early artworks like Alan Sonfist's *Time Landscape*, proposed in 1965, had both a memorializing and a reclamationist slant. The latter tendency would gain currency—and greater sophistication in its grasp of geological and environmental science—in the coming decades in the work of artists such as Kathryn Miller and Mel Chin. European artists Joseph Beuys and Agnes Denes had also followed this thread and introduced the process of reforestation in their respective projects.

Early proto-environmental artworks shared a melancholic view of urban space and modernization, as well as a sense of loss in regard to the vast American landscape located beyond the boundaries of the city. Often these same artists gradually shifted away from nostalgic notions of "nature"—arguably a legacy of the American transcendentalists like Henry David Thoreau—in order to connect with the concerns of the growing environmental movement. Artists and environmental activists have gone on to engage with issues of human rights such as Wangari Maathai of Kenya, founder of the Green Belt Movement, or, like American artist Mark Dion in his work about the Amazon rainforest, to mount institutional critiques of the dynamics of power at play in the representation of endangered ecosystems. Some, like Amy Balkin, represent the land as public domain within a capitalist system grounded in the notion of private property. The British group known as Platform has coordinated public-education/public-relations campaigns regarding local ecosystems. Beatriz da Costa made use of digital technologies for unique forms of environmental-data collection; Ines Doujak's art criticizes the ecological damage inflicted by multinational corporations in their coordination of biopiracy in emerging countries, with a resulting decline in global biodiversity.

Origins; Reclamation Art

In his famed *A Sand County Almanac* the nature writer and environmentalist Aldo Leopold described the landscape of the American southwest that he had first come to know around 1909, during his early years working in the US Forest Service in the Arizona Territory. His book, published after his death in 1949, at times speaks nostalgically of old trappers' tales of life on the trails of the high country before native animals like the wolf were rendered almost extinct. Leopold condemns his own behavior as a young and flippant hunter of wolves, and realizes that because of his actions in hastening the imbalance of the local ecosystem, other wildlife and flora had disappeared from the area. In advocating a "land ethic" Leopold urged a new conception of land—or nature—as a community. He writes, "the land ethic changes the role of *Homo sapiens* from conqueror of the land-community to plain member and citizen of it. It implies respect for his fellow members, and also respect for the community as such."[4] Leopold insisted that the postwar enthusiasm in the US for the modernization and industrialization of the land be tempered by a grasp of this land ethic, an ideology that he thought must lead to revision not only of scientific or agricultural knowledge, but also to shifts within other fields of human knowledge such as philosophy and religion.

Leopold's argument for an epistemological shift toward a land ethic, or the position of environmentalism, had been taken up by artists within the sphere of visual culture by the 1960s. One reason for the interest in this discourse in the US at the time was the figure of Rachel Carson, author of *Silent Spring*, who almost single-handedly ignited modern environmental activism and made ecology a concern for a generation of American artists. Carson's book was a media event because of the confluence of several events: the publication of the book itself in 1962 as well its serialization in the *New Yorker*; a CBS televised discussion about it in April 1963; and the its selection by the mail-order book club the Book of the Month Club. *Silent Spring* and the debate around Carson's claims were surely known to many artists at the time, including Alan Sonfist and Robert Smithson. US corporations in the chemistry industry, including DuPont, Velsicol, and American Cyanamid, mounted campaigns attacking Carson's conclusions. When it was distributed as a Book of the Month selection, the publisher Houghton Mifflin included a strong defense of the book by Supreme Court justice William O. Douglas. The book's title refers to the absence of songbirds in wide areas treated with the insecticide DDT by the US Department of Agriculture in an effort to eradicate fire ants, beginning in 1957.[5] It describes mysterious human illnesses and deaths that became frequent in these areas in the years after spraying began, although this was not Carson's central claim (DDT would be proven to be a carcinogen only later). The author also described the disappearance of other kinds of wildlife and the significant withering of plant life.

Although Carson herself died in 1964, the media focus on her book introduced environmentalism to ordinary Americans outside the science community, including artists working in New York. This group included the West German artist Hans Haacke, whose early systems-oriented works *Grass Grows* (1969) and *Rhinewater Purification Plant* (1972) strove to set in place an artwork that was beyond objects, since because of its defining tie to the mutability of the environment, it could itself be "something which experiences."[6] But these organically based works also pointed to the fragility of ecological systems. In his *Rhinewater* piece, Haacke implicitly criticized the public's incorrect assumption that these systems could be sustained indefinitely without human intervention. Working in collaboration, the artists Helen Mayer Harrison and Newton Harrison would raise this issue of sustainability more explicitly in their installations of the 1970s and 1980s.

Earlier studies of land art or "earth art" have established the best-known or canonical southwest-based land artworks: *Spiral Jetty* (1970) at Rozel Point, Utah, by Robert Smithson; Michael Heizer's *Double Negative* (1969) in Overton, Nevada; and Walter de Maria's *Lightning Field* (1977) near Quemado, New Mexico. These art histories generally understood these works to be sculptural projects on a grand scale that generated much of their meaning from artists' shunning of the type of industrial, gallery-based installations that minimalism had established in New York. Smithson's famous opposition of sites and non-sites, first generated in his 1966 proposals for the Dallas/Fort Worth airport—that related sculptural works were to be simultaneously installed outdoors between runways and inside the terminal—pointed to the sites and the land that was located outside the gallery space, and the urban grid of New York. In post-modern fashion Smithson also understood his essays as works in their own right, equally concerned with representing or constructing notions of the land. Illustrated with Instamatic photographs he took on site, Smithson's essays began to explore points in the landscape most familiar to him, such as the polluted industrial sites and streams around his hometown of Passaic, New Jersey.[7] Passaic and other places that Smithson featured in his art—Pine Barrens in the same state, and the more remote Rozel Point on the Great Salt Lake outside Salt Lake City—Smithson called "sites." He kept these places, some industrial and toxic, others less spoiled by modern industry, very distinct from the texts, maps, objects, and films he presented in galleries and the pages of art journals. Smithson called these latter materials or representations "non-sites," or informational representations of the land.

In the case of even the most degraded landscapes such as Passaic, Smithson appeared to want to limit this destruction by means of his own representation of it—even as he recognized the pollution itself as though it were a kind of sublime force or an empirical fact, and thus irreversible. Even if it is not always explicitly stated, Smithson's essays have an aspect of dawning ecological consciousness to them. Recent reconsiderations of Smithson's art have pointed to unpublished plans Smithson developed around 1972 for an artwork in southern Ohio on land the Hanna Coal Company intended to redevelop.[8] Smithson stated that he meant for this artwork to encourage "a concrete consciousness of the present as it really exists."[9] Certainly environmentalism would have been part of this proposal, one that sought to contribute to a larger reclamation project. This unrealized project also indicates that Smithson was likely not as resigned or pessimistic about the possibility of stemming the forces of industrial decay on the land as has been claimed for him. His embryonic engagement with ecology calls into question earlier art-historical categories that distinguished land art as engaged neither with changing consciousness about the land nor with reclamation or ecological activism.

Artists by the early 1970s were constructing "nature" by incorporating the landscape into art in a different fashion. Large-scale outdoor sculptures such as Smithson's *Spiral Jetty* break with modern sculpture in their exploration of an "expanded field" at the limits of the notion of sculptural scale, as the art historian Rosalind Krauss discussed in an influential essay, "Sculpture in the expanded field" (1979). These post-modern sculptures, she claimed, became sites that renegotiated a relation to architecture or landscape or both. However, artists also worked on a large scale to posit other relations to the land that were not exclusively aesthetic experiments or modernist investigations of medium; these artworks ruminated on the relation of industrialization to the land. Betty Beaumont, for example, realized her work *Cable Piece* (1977) in a field in Macomb, Illinois, by recycling a long steel cable of the variety otherwise used to construct suspension bridges. Beaumont created a 100-foot-diameter circle directly on the ground with the cable. Because the shape is so large, the viewer of the work cannot take in the entire circular structure at once; in following the cable one loses sight of the object as any kind of whole and focuses instead on the landscape around it.

The scale of her abstract geometrical sculpture encourages an understanding of the land as an element of the work in its own right. Beaumont has commented that the aging of this piece is also central to its design. Like Alan Sonfist's work, it deals with the passing of time: after years grass slowly covered the cable or it broke and wore out at various points. Beaumont planned that the work would effectively be reclaimed by the prairie. At the same time the form of the circle points to the continuing and almost irresolvable conflict between the land and the material, or the very notion of industrialization.

Smithson knew other artists in and around New York City who worked with soil and land in the 1960s. Alan Sonfist's controversial projects, which are ongoing, strive to recreate or revive an earlier state of a given site before its degradation, particularly in the city. He has also called these works "public monuments" that memorialize historical aspects of our ecosystem: "Natural phenomena, natural events and the living creatures on the planet should be honored and celebrated along with human beings and events."[10] In his canonical *Time Landscape* (proposed 1965; realized 1978), an early reclamationist environmental work, Sonfist chose a vacant and rubble-strewn lot at the intersection of West Houston Street and LaGuardia Place in New York City. In this project Sonfist seeks to undo or even erase the effect of urbanization and industrialization on the land. To do so he researched the plant life that was indigenous to the island and initiated a project that aimed to re-establish a primeval Manhattan forest on a blighted plot on the city grid. Sonfist's view then is that there is a "natural" past of local forests, soils, and animal life that might not only be memorialized and celebrated, but also reconstructed and recovered as a corrective to the materials and effect of modernization. Another work, *Pool of Virgin Earth* (1975), neither involves the systems of botanical life nor realizes the process of reclamation and resuscitation of a site. In it Sonfist established a circle of pure or rich soil in a polluted field, protected by means of a high lip he created around the circumference. The circle was to catch the seedlings and other plant life that blew into it. Sonfist puts forward a view of "nature" in this work that exists as a memorial to its own disappearance. He also communicates that urbanization is a process that is generally undesirable; it can be argued that he presents an anti-modern scenario where "nature" simply cannot co-exist with urban space as a major outcome of modernization.

Agnes Denes' work took a very different view of the goals of environmental reclamation in the highly developed urban space of Manhattan. In her work *Wheatfield—A Confrontation*, Denes planted and harvested two acres of wheat on a landfill in Manhattan's financial district in the summer of 1982, in what is now Battery Park City. This site was adjacent to the former World Trade Center complex and in view of the Statue of Liberty in New York Harbor. To make planting possible, Denes coordinated the tractors that leveled the landfill; 200 truckloads of soil were brought to the site, and an irrigation system was installed, in order to create the necessary conditions for successful planting by May. Furrows were dug into the topsoil and further clearing of rocks and trash took place by hand. After a battle with a wheat smut infection in the field, Denes arranged for the wheat to be harvested in August. She donated the hay to the horses that served in the New York Police Department, and arranged for the harvested grain to be exhibited and planted internationally.

Denes' *Wheatfield* functioned as a short-term intervention, a symbolic reminder of the mutability of even the world's most highly commodified land. It also served as a reminder to its Manhattan audience of the still possible environmental qualities of urban space as land, soil, and nature. Other artists took on an educational or didactic role in relation to the abuse and poor condition of the land and environment in particular cities and states. The artist team of Helen Mayer Harrison and Newton Harrison began collaborating on their *Survival Pieces* series of 1970–2, including *Portable Fish Farm* and *Portable Orchard*, which related farming activity to the populations of urban centers. These works literally transplanted fish-farming operations, and the tending of citrus and avocado trees, into gallery spaces. *Portable Orchard*, for example, installed fruit trees in the university gallery of California State University at Fullerton. At the time, Orange County was being heavily developed for real estate, which replaced the orchards that had once marked the land. The Harrisons' installation reminded viewers of the loss of citrus trees around them and urged their preservation in the city and county. As was the case with their *Portable Fish Farm*, the *Orchard* installation culminated with a ritual public event, a "citrus feast" where the trees' harvest was consumed by the public in the gallery. Through the most visceral act of food consumption, this meal demonstrated the continuing link between the citrus trees and the survival and health of those who lived in Fullerton, uniting both as part of a closely connected ecosystem, even if it was in decline. The artist Clare Patey has returned to the Harrisons' strategy of the feast as a mechanism both to unify the community and to raise environmental consciousness and support of the "food cycle" generally. First realized as part of the Mayor's Thames Festival on London's Southwark Bridge as *Feast on the Bridge* in 2007, the annual event limits the bridge to foot traffic only. The banquet that is shared there on long tables is also accompanied by music, workshops, games, and other festival activities that highlight the centrality of the Thames to life in London.[11]

In activist fashion the Harrisons continue to use their artwork as a means to link local populations with their surrounding ecosystems, and also to prompt public responses to local environmental issues. In this focus the Harrisons distinguish their work from that of other systems-related artists, such as Haacke, who do not always target specific ecological problems in their work, but rather examine systems per se as a generative structure for art-making. It is not clear whether the Harrisons' works always result in the reclamation of a particular ecological site. They have worked in different regions of the US, from Baltimore to Santa Fe, and in Europe, from Zagreb, Croatia (*Breathing Space for the Sava River*, 1989–90) to Holland (*A Vision for the Green Heart of Holland*, 1995).

Many of these activist projects concern water use and watersheds in particular areas. Their 1977 work *Sacramento Meditations* (**Figure 6.1**) questioned the increasing industrialization of agriculture in inland California during the 1970s. The work, first shown at the San Francisco Museum of Contemporary Art, and later in other galleries and publications, included an installation of texts,

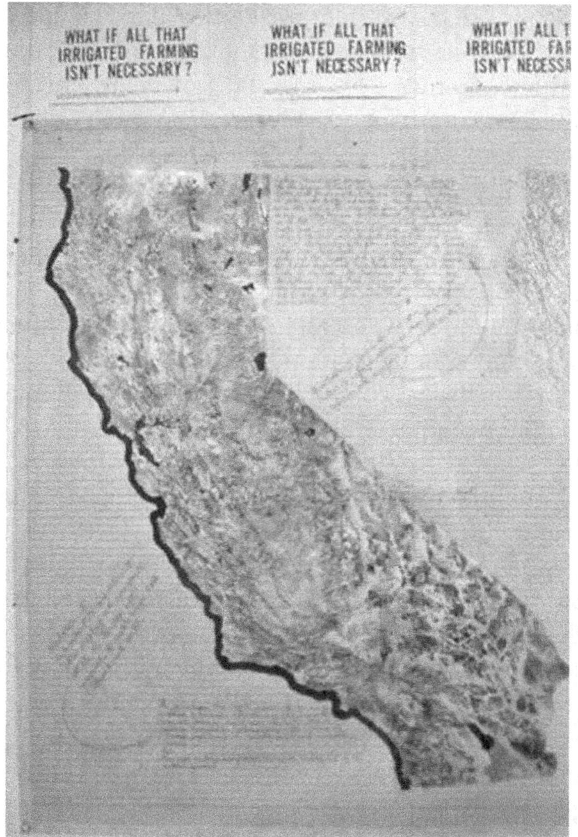

6.1   Helen Mayer Harrison and Newton Harrison, *Sacramento Meditations* (1977)

signage, and nine maps of the state that charted water resources and irrigable land. The Harrisons had gathered much of this data from the Berkeley Water Resources Library; their work was intended to raise grave doubt in the community regarding the level of industrial agriculture and to point to possible negative and long-term consequences of irrigation around Sacramento. The Harrisons also deployed related billboards and street posters as well as street graffiti outside the museum to broaden their audience. Signs in the exhibition asked, "What if all that irrigated farming isn't necessary?" and street graffiti stated, "Somebody's crazy, they're draining the swamps and growing rice in the desert." Their nine texts comment lyrically on irrigation in California as a general environmental problem. One verse reads,

> If
> The paradigms that inform the present use and energy
> practices of culture (exploitation, consumption,
> transformation into possession, transformation into profit)
> do not undergo modification by social forces
> either voluntarily (through legal means) or involuntarily
> (through revolutionary means)
> Then
> They will undergo modification through the working out of
> the natural forces (read entropy)

In the *Sacramento* project the Harrisons also pointed to the possibility that massive irrigation would paradoxically lead to a decline in the biodiversity of the land. Since periods of major drought have continued to grow more severe in California and elsewhere since 1977 (perhaps due to the effects of climate change), the Harrisons' *Sacramento Meditations*, along with their numerous other projects that target the balance between water use and watersheds in various geographical areas and regions, seems pioneering if not prescient in its understanding of the fundamental impact of industrialization upon water use, water conservation, and biodiversity.[12]

Artists also began to develop longer-term reclamation projects that responded to specific urban sites, to localized loss of biodiversity, or to local contamination of soil due to pollutants. In the same year as Denes' *Wheatfield*, Joseph Beuys began to realize his multi-year project *7000 Oaks* as his contribution to the 1982 Documenta exhibition. The first extensive reforestation project carried out by an artist—the project was subtitled *City Forestation Instead of City Administration*—the work was officially concluded in Kassel with the posthumous planting of the 7,000th tree there by Beuys' son Wenzel. Beuys had planned to continue the planting indefinitely, as well as in other cities, and after his death in 1986 the *7000 Oaks* project was expanded, with plantings in Oslo, New York City, Minneapolis, and Middlebury, Vermont.[13]

The coordination work for the project had begun well before 1982: Beuys arranged for a *7000 Oaks* office to open in Kassel, run by himself and members of Free International University (FIU), an organization he had established in 1977. This office conducted fund-raising; it coordinated the approvals process between the *7000 Oaks* office and the city of Kassel, and between the office and local residents, who had to approve the placement of the trees. It also documented the project, and managed the logistics of purchase, transport, and planting of the basalt columns and trees. Beuys secured initial funding for the project from the Dia Art Foundation in New York, but the project was intended to involve the citizens of Kassel. To do so it allowed individuals to purchase a multiple consisting of a basalt stone and a tree for 500 Deutschmarks. These collectors would receive a certificate and could select the stone that would be placed where their tree was located.

Beuys had 7,000 basalt stones arranged in a large triangular pile at the Friedrichsplatz in Kassel, the plaza in front of the Fridericianum museum, and planted the first oak at its apex in March 1982. The estimated cost of the project was set at over 3 million Deutschmarks. When funding sources fell short, Beuys contributed additional money himself, some raised by the sale of his works and those of contributing artists, who included Andy Warhol, Sandro Chia, and Jannis Kounellis; he recorded a television commercial for Nikka whiskey in Japan and arranged for a tie-in with the Holiday Inn hotel chain to raise further funds.[14]

As Lynne Cooke has noted, Beuys envisioned *7000 Oaks* as a monumental sculpture involving a number of different multiples (certificates, posters, postcards) but one primary one: a planted tree and, next to it, a short vertical column composed of basalt. As each tree grew, the proportions between this living organism and the fixed stone would be altered constantly. The fixed and unchanging state of the basalt rock in each multiple contrasts with the organic and mutable tree trunk next to it; this contrast recalls Beuys' definition of the "warmth principle" within social sculpture. This idea had to do with the "passage from chaotic material to ordered form through sculptural movement." This transformation of matter from cold to heat, or even the contrast of the material of rock to a living tree, points to the central notion of change and agency within social sculpture. In *7000 Oaks* Beuys points out that even a living tree possesses a degree of agency in realizing change. The oaks of the project certainly transformed the cityscape of Kassel. Today, years later, the trees continue to alter Kassel in photosynthetic as well as in less technical ways. They are slowly changing components of the city itself. In 1982 Beuys stated:

> I think the tree is an element of regeneration which in itself is a concept of time. The oak is especially so because it is a slowly growing tree with a kind of really solid heart-wood. It has always been a form of sculpture, a symbol for this planet.[15]

Each multiple also contains past, present, and future markers of time in natural materials. The unchanging past is referenced in the geological formation of the rock, and in the rings of the tree; the present is underscored in the current relation of tree to rock. A future is implied in the continued growth of the tree. Like Aldo Leopold's mountain and his phrase "thinking like a mountain," Beuys suggests that the tree (or nature itself) embodies the passage of time and points to the future. His tree multiples are ecological "symbols for the planet," and for human survival.

Thirty planters hired by the *7000 Oaks* office began the plantings on a schedule, but citizens could join them in the action of planting. As photos verify, many citizens became involved in realizing the artwork (**Figure 6.2**). Different varieties of oak tree were planted throughout Kassel including swamp oak, English oak, and northern red oak, and 36 other varieties of trees including ginkgo, maple ash, locust tree, and one yellow poplar. The project had its detractors who complained that parking spaces would be lost due to the new trees. A Kassel motorist died when his car drove

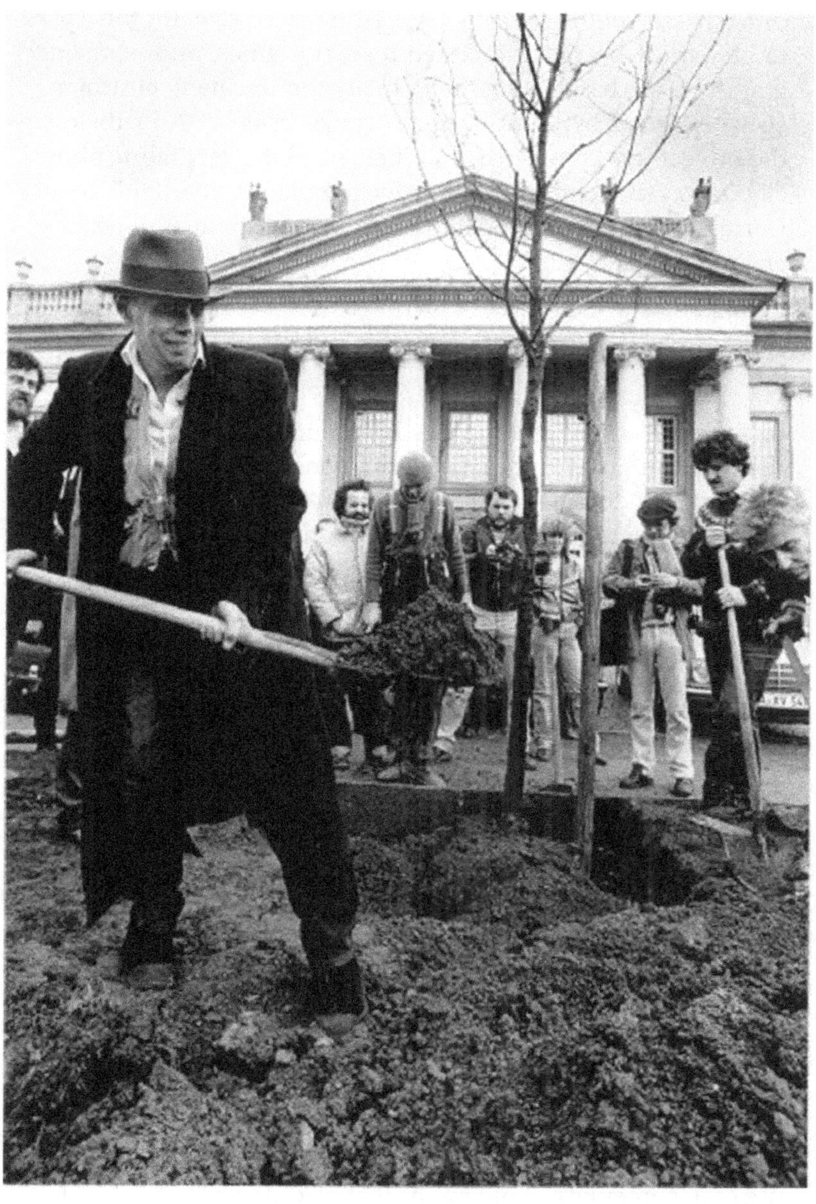

6.2 Planting team with Joseph Beuys in Kassel, Germany, *7000 Oaks*
(1982–7, continuing)

into a basalt column, which inspired renewed calls for the work to be removed; vandals attacked it several times, once spraying graffiti on the basalt stones and, in another incident, destroying 56 young trees by breaking their trunks in two.[16] Nonetheless, the project was completed, and it changed the very fabric of the city. *7000 Oaks* continues to transform the landscape of this small German city as a monument to the future possibilities of positive environmental change.

New Environmentalism

In a similar spirit, other artists have pursued reclamation and remediation goals. Like Denes, the American artist Mel Chin targeted a landfill in the US, this time in St. Paul, Minnesota, for his work *Revival Field* (1990–3); the soil in the landfill had been contaminated with toxic metals. With a scientific adviser Chin made use of phytoremediation, also called "green clean," as his remediation method: he introduced a number of plants known as efficient accumulators of metals in the soil in a small circular pattern within the large landfill area. Over the course of several years these plants could be harvested, and the crop disposed of as a toxic material as the soil was slowly returned to a more neutral state. Kathryn Miller reintroduced native plants to neglected or bare plots of land in Santa Barbara, California, by means of her *Seed Bombs* (1992). Her 1997 work *Russian Thistle Crisis* (**Figure 6.3**), completed with Michael Honer, examined a chapter of botanical history in the US—the introduction of a non-native plant species to the American West, more specifically to South Dakota, during the nineteenth century by means of flax seed imported from Ukraine. Otherwise known as the source of the tumbleweed that has become an icon of the Western American frontier, the Russian thistle is an invasive weed that flourishes on barren stretches of land denuded of other vegetation and most wildlife. Through the use of documentary photographs that placed tumbleweed in this context for viewers, Miller's work resituates the tumbleweed and uses it to debunk a sentimental icon of the West: the Russian

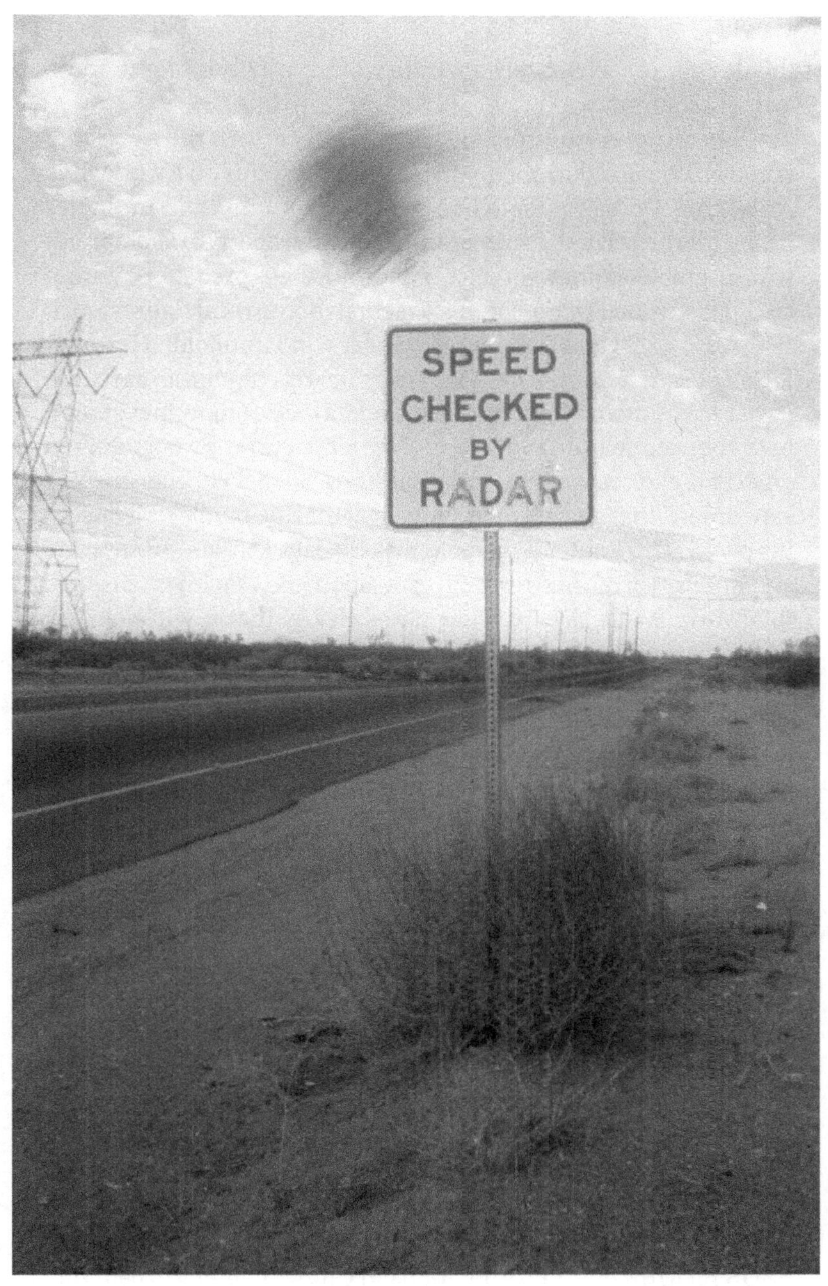

6.3 Kathryn Miller (with Michael Honer), *Russian Thistle Crisis* series (1997)

thistle is more accurately a century-old symbol of blight and a lack of biodiversity.

Emerging environmental artists contend with the new landscape of globalization and to threats to ecosystems on a worldwide scale. Ines Doujak's photo collages, photographs, and multiples deal with the related issues of intellectual property and biopiracy within globalization; she also points to their prehistory within colonialism and their relation to celebrated historical figures, such as the naturalist and explorer Alexander von Humboldt. Her work *J. Craig Venter, Master of the Gene* (2007) targets Venter, an executive in the Institute for Genomic Research, a corporation that sought to sequence the human genome. Venter is currently engaging in an ocean-exploration genome project or "global ocean-sampling expedition" that charts microbiological marine biodiversity using his own yacht. Venter has stated that Charles Darwin's *Beagle* and another British marine research expedition, the *Challenger*, inspired this work. While the Institute states clearly that it will not seek intellectual property rights over data collected as part of this global sampling and that that data will be made available "publically to any scientist," Doujak approaches this work with suspicion and implies that samples have been brought illegally into the US. She suggests there is a biocolonialist, if not racist, basis to Venter's project.[17] In this way, she connects Venter's work to the global sampling projects carried out in the era of colonialism during the eighteenth and nineteenth centuries, by von Humboldt in Latin America in particular, and which served to expand and buttress European control of scientific knowledge.

Doujak's gallery-based work *Victory Gardens* (2007) is a long, raised flower bed punctuated with 70 multiples or printed seed packages (these could also be purchased as carrying totes). Using photo collages and texts on the seed packages' recto and verso, Doujak's multiples critique key biological and scientific developments of globalization as new forms of exploitation. Her seed-packet texts interrogate a number of subjects: biocolonialism and biopiracy; current criteria for patents; DNA collection undertaken by US pharmaceutical corporations in China; Venter's expedition; and Peruvian legislation of 2002 that protects and classifies as "cultural heritage" indigenous knowledge as it relates to biological diversity. One multiple, *The Pig*, describes the Monsanto Company's efforts in 2005 to obtain patents with global reach—in more than 160 countries—that relate to widely used procedures in the cross-breeding and selection of pigs. The patent would enforce a monopoly for the company in that not only the procedures, but also the livestock itself would be categorized as a Monsanto product or patent. This would force pig farmers globally who use these procedures to pay royalties to Monsanto to continue raising their pigs or face penalties, a development which would negatively impact local food production and local economies in these countries. The critique Doujak mounts in her work—the title *Victory Gardens* also refers to the gardens the Cuban government established during the waning years of the USSR to address its food shortages—encourages viewers to be aware that, even on the microbiological level, biodiversity is under attack by those global interests seeking to own and profit from it.

Taking up the memorializing tone of Sonfist's art, commemorative projects have returned in new environmental art. Of particular note is the "living memorial" that has been dedicated to the memory of Ken Saro-Wiwa, a Nigerian environmental activist who was executed, along with eight other protesters dubbed the "Ogoni Nine," by the Nigerian government in November 1995.[18] Saro-Wiwa led activist protests against Shell Oil's development of the reserves of the Niger Delta in the 1990s, which also involved contamination of the land in the area. He coordinated a demonstration in 1993 with 300,000 Ogoni people, a minority ethnic group that lives in the Delta, to demand Shell's sharing of oil revenues, more political autonomy for the Ogoni, environmental remediation, and reparations for past damages.

Remember Saro-Wiwa, a coalition of groups that included the art and activist organization Platform, commissioned a memorial. Sokari Douglas Camp, a Nigerian-born British artist, won the commission (**Figure 6.4**). Her design, a bus, recalled the Nigerian vehicles that carried supplies, goods, or even medicine men to places like her home village in the Delta. Douglas Camp connects the remedies Saro-Wiwa sought for the Ogoni to the

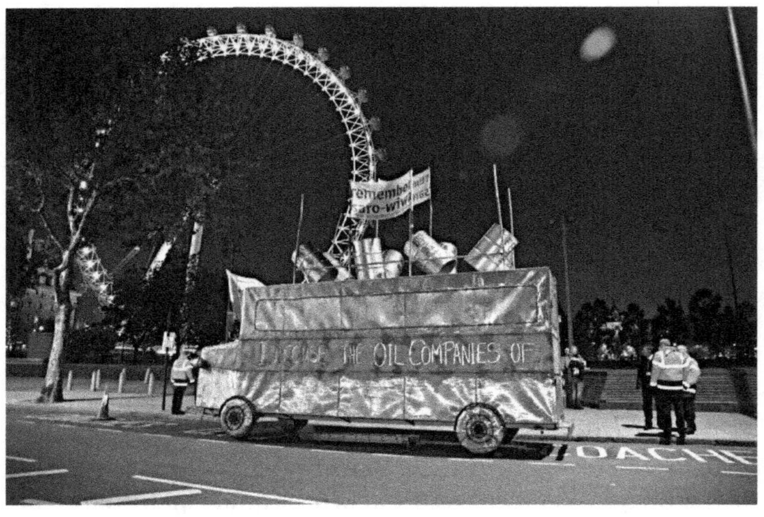

6.4   Sokari Douglas Camp, *Memorial to Ken Saro-Wiwa* (2006)

cures and hope offered by medicine men. The bus is covered with a stainless-steel shell—a monument in silver instead of bronze—and is emblazoned with a quote from Saro-Wiwa: "I accuse the oil companies of practicing genocide against the Ogoni." Douglas Camp arranged numerous oil drums on top of the vehicle, each inscribed with the name of one of the Ogoni Nine. The bus is a mobile memorial that has toured nine sites since 2006; public talks and workshops are conducted alongside it. The coalition is searching for a permanent site for the Saro-Wiwa memorial so that it might serve as a continuing reminder of both the human cost of oil production and the need for corporate responsibility.

Ecology-focused art often crosses boundaries: along with its related development, conceptual art, environmental art often concerns itself, as does environmental science, with the collection of data and information from various ecosystems. This data, gathered and "crunched" by artists, is not always visual: an example is Alan Hovhaness' *And God Created Great Whales* (1970), an orchestral piece that is interwoven with recorded whale song.

While this musical composition certainly does not arrive at any scientific conclusions about the whale population, Hovhaness' use of sound makes the listener conscious of the ecosystemic tie that we as humans have to these other beings that share our environment, as well as our reliance upon them as a continuing and stable component that maintains our ecosystem and us. In drawing artistic material from various entities that make up our environment, artists also transcend traditional boundaries of "art" and "science" to engage with both disciplines creatively. In her essay "The studio, the laboratory, and the vexations of art" art historian Svetlana Alpers points out that (scientific) investigation has been pursued for centuries within the artist's studio.[19] She understands the traditional studio as an instrument of "experimental knowledge" that historically paralleled another space, the laboratory, where other types of instruments were deployed in the pursuit of knowledge. This quality of transdisciplinarity, of the collection of data and material from the land and its ecosystems for inclusion within the work of "art" as a critical or analytical instrument, has marked the history of art since the seventeenth century. It returns—as it did in the work of the Harrisons—as a new frontier of environmental or sustainability-conscious art.

The artist and researcher Beatriz da Costa constructs prototypes for various forms of environmental-data collection. Da Costa is one of the founding members of the artists' group Preemptive Media (with Jamie Schulte and Brooke Singer). The group's mission is for artists to determine how and what data is recorded, and also by whom. This mission then contests the quasi-absolute corporate control of computer technology. Of course, this control extends to the "criteria and methods" for the application of digital technology, or, for the setting of the goals, uses and subjects of that same technology. An earlier project by da Costa and Preemptive Media, *AIR (Area's Immediate Reading)* (2006), developed a small and portable air-quality-reading device that enables pedestrians to monitor pollution levels as they move through a city. These participants are also able to chart or visualize the data that they have collected. As da Costa describes it, this device enables "grassroots scientific data gathering."[20] The artwork is therefore collaborative or community based, and empowers citizens of a city to participate in its production. Moreover, it presents evidence of where pollution is most concentrated in participants' own neighborhoods. The environmental problem is identified, and then might be addressed by these same citizens through social and political channels. *AIR* is an artwork that gently compels its participants to become activists for possible ecological changes to their immediate environment.

Da Costa's *PigeonBlog* (2006), created in collaboration with Cina Hazegh and Kevin Ponto, similarly deployed a portable air-pollution-measuring device, but involved a different species, urban homing pigeons, in the collecting of data. This project took place in August 2006 in San Jose, California, as part of the ZeroOne city-wide festival. Da Costa and her collaborators fitted trained homing pigeons with GPS-enabled air-pollution-sensing devices that could transmit, to an online mapping/blogging environment, real-time data tied to specific locations (**Figure 6.5**). In this transmission, data on carbon monoxide and nitrous oxide was "called in" by the pigeon on a cell phone-like component to a Google-powered online map. The pigeons were then in a sense "blogging" about the air pollution they flew over. Through the maps and other charts, the pollution levels were visualized for the public via a real-time website (**Figure 6.6**). The goals of da Costa's data collection differed from similar readings taken by the Environmental Protection Agency (EPA) in that the latter are taken from fixed locations. The pigeons, as mobile and roving data collectors, also gathered information from specific locations that are often neglected by the EPA, such as the lower-income neighborhoods that are frequently situated around industrial sites.

On her website, da Costa also made available the schematic and code for the board and sensors she and her team used to assemble the pigeon devices. This information would make it possible for anyone with the proper technical knowledge to construct these devices themselves, a "DIY" approach to air-quality-data collection. This kind of small and portable device might also be used to collect data or monitor air quality via people who might otherwise be difficult to access. Air-pollution researcher Rufus

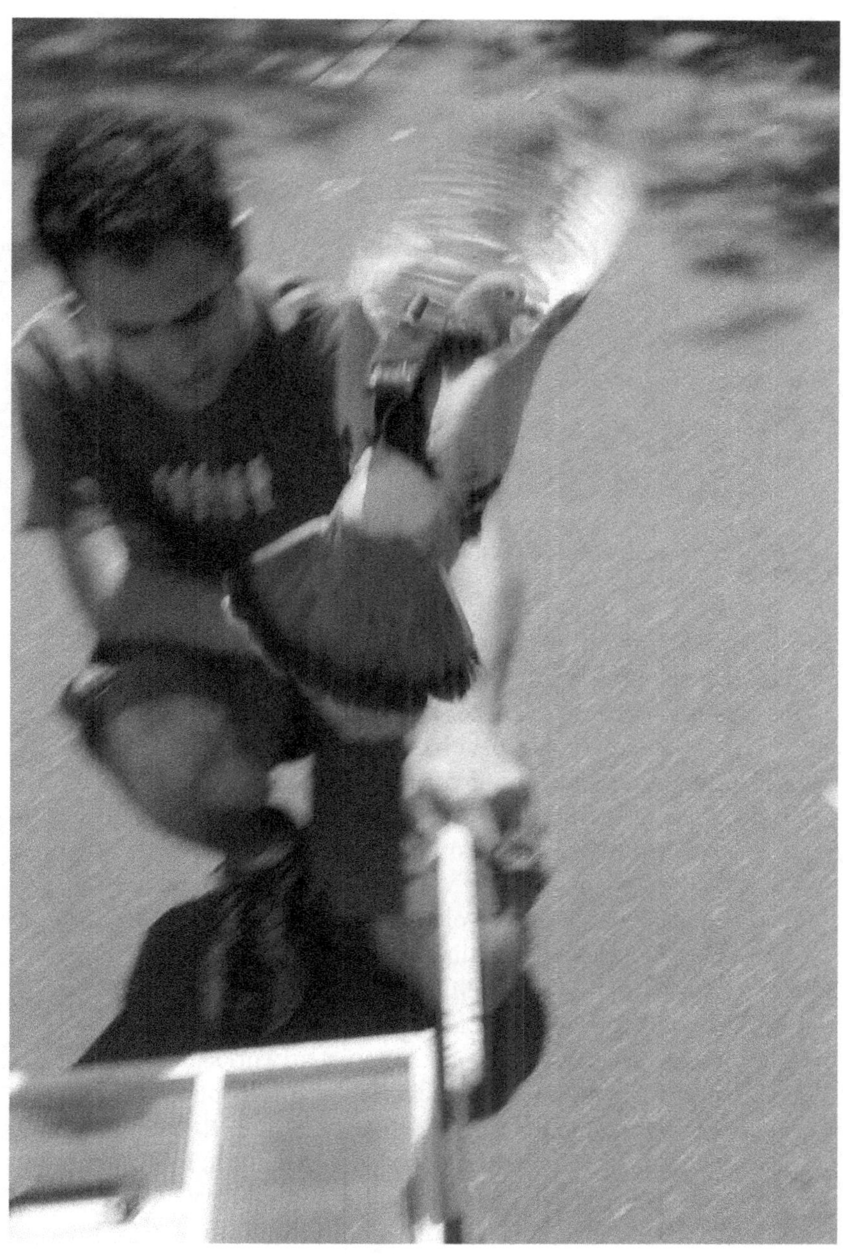

6.5   Beatriz da Costa (with Cina Hazegh and Kevin Ponto), *PigeonBlog* (2006)

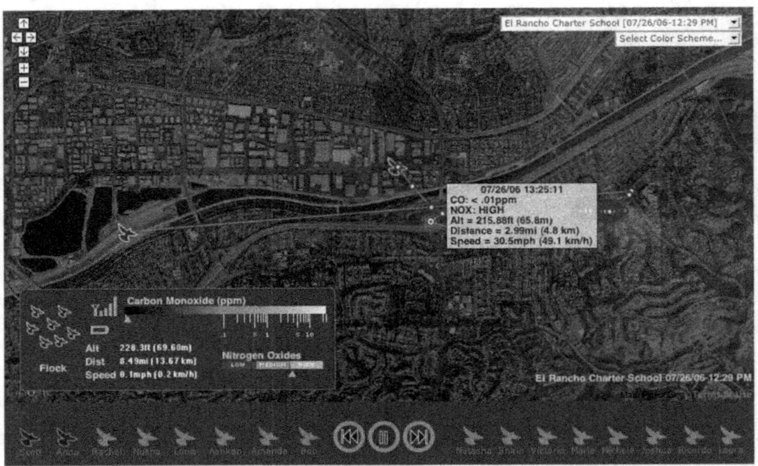

6.6   Beatriz da Costa (with Cina Hazegh and Kevin Ponto), *PigeonBlog* (2006)

Edwards points out that indoor stoves and related indoor pollution in developing countries could be more effectively monitored by means of a small, inexpensive, and reliable data-recording device of the variety da Costa has developed.[21] Within the realm of art the *Pigeon Blog* therefore introduces a new technology and approach to gathering and documenting air pollution data that is, as the artist has said, "a way of building our own circuits," from the grassroots up.

In the wake of the bad ecological news we have received over the past two decades, including the major disasters in Bhopal, Chernobyl, and the Gulf of Mexico, and the mounting evidence of climate change, some critics have pointed out that even well-intentioned early land and reclamationist artworks took a toll on the environment in terms of their violent interruption of extant ecosystems, and their liberal use of fossil fuel and other raw materials. A kind of parallel critique has emerged around the shift to "paperless" offices or bureaucracies, made possible when almost all business and other documents are electronic and stored on a hard drive. While our computer-driven society possibly uses less paper, it has also been acknowledged—by artist collectives like

Futurefarmers, among others—that the manufacture and disposal of computers involves highly toxic substances. It is no coincidence that Silicon Valley is a major Superfund site.[22]

It has been suggested that artists instead look to less invasive, or less resource- and fuel-dependent, environmental strategies. For example, environmentalists understand that found materials are a preferable source of art material—inspired by Duchamp's ready-made, but simultaneously self-conscious about the wastefulness and toxicity of industry. Artists Julie Anand and Richard Lerman in the US southwest continue the legacy of environmental art in working with various found or "recycled" materials, from images to recorded sound.

Anand takes up the alternate working process of the recycling or repurposing of materials once used for another function. Her large-scale inkjet prints present objects that she has gathered, like an archeologist, from various neighborhoods in Phoenix, Arizona. Anand photographs her fossil-like finds and assembles them into orderly grids of visual data that echo the topographical grid that orders most American cities. Her grids have a crystalline, almost clinical quality, since her photographed objects are all arranged on a solid white background. Their visual effect is closer to the quasi-medical examination of X-ray images on a light table. Through the collection and examination of its most banal trash, each of her works presents the material diversity and cultural significance of Phoenix's different neighborhoods. Her work then returns to the data-collecting direction of environmental art.

Anand's 2009 work *7th Avenue, McDowell to Glenrosa (4.6 miles, 12/31/08) Phoenix, AZ* (**Figure 6.7**) presents a grid of photo-graphed objects that both stand on their own and coagulate into a loose composition; some objects begin to form a graceful arc of subtle tones of greenish-brown across a stark white background. Metal reflections repeat across the surface. They point to a block of urban space that teems with intersecting human lives that have left a wake of voracious consumption behind them. We examine, with Anand, the accouterment of several individuals' automobiles, lost or casually tossed onto the ground; photographs that afford us a suddenly intimate and voyeuristic view into someone's life;

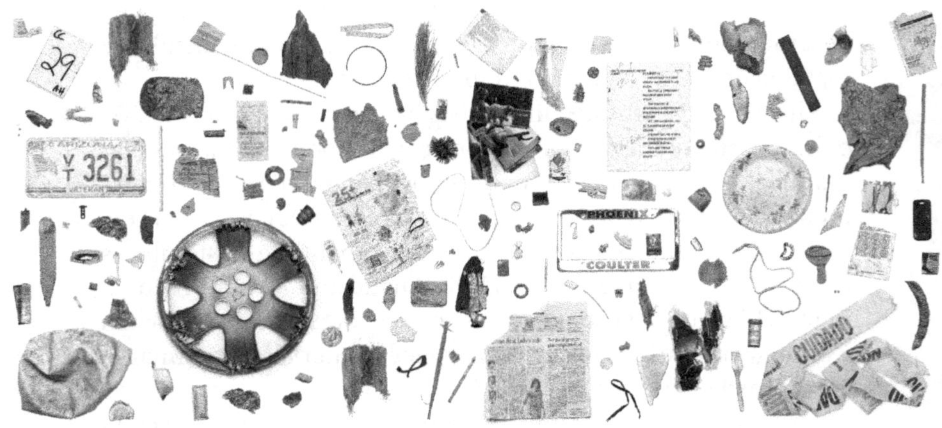

6.7   Julie Anand, *7th Avenue, McDowell to Glenrosa (4.6 miles, 12/31/08) Phoenix, AZ* (2009), archival inkjet print on bamboo paper

a vial of prescription meds that reveals someone's maladies; a decorated Styrofoam plate that displays a child's creativity; and a grimy bandana that offers traces of someone else's physical toil. One realizes that many of these objects would continue to mark these sites for years and decades to come, since many would decay only very slowly. While she offers no unifying narrative to frame these traces of humanity, Anand assumes that the objects she has gathered together constitute a material culture of urban life that is both banal and deeply historical. The land or soil continues to support the human histories that ferry back and forth across it; many of these human histories go undetected, moldering under layers of other objects and material in a landfill. Perhaps Anand makes a plea for us as viewers to consider making more conscious commitments to the objects that flow through our lives and that possibly contain the meaning of our existences, which should not merely be a function of how much of this stuff we can channel. It is a plea for a slower and more deliberate way of living with the objects we have around us.

Richard Lerman's deeply ambivalent installation *Hoover: Water/Power* of 2009 (**Figure 6.8**) both celebrates and laments the Hoover Dam (near Boulder City, Nevada) as a major site and icon of the American southwest and of US achievement in engineering and technology. The Hoover Dam, a WPA construction project completed during the Depression under the Roosevelt administration in 1936, made it possible to utilize the Colorado River as a major water source for the deserts of the southwest. This greatly accelerated the population growth and development of the region. A new-media artist and composer, Lerman works extensively with applications of piezoelectricity for sound recording. His works utilize tiny transducers or microphone disks he constructs to detect and record sound. Lerman's work connects with other data-collecting artists and scholars working in acoustic ecology, such as the anthropologist Steven Feld, who gather sonic data from the environment in the study of ecological and social systems across various disciplines.

The installation *Hoover: Water/Power* brings together audio, video, and mixed media components to represent and reflect upon the Hoover Dam as an energy- and water-generating facility that continues to displace and marginalize the fragile flora and fauna of

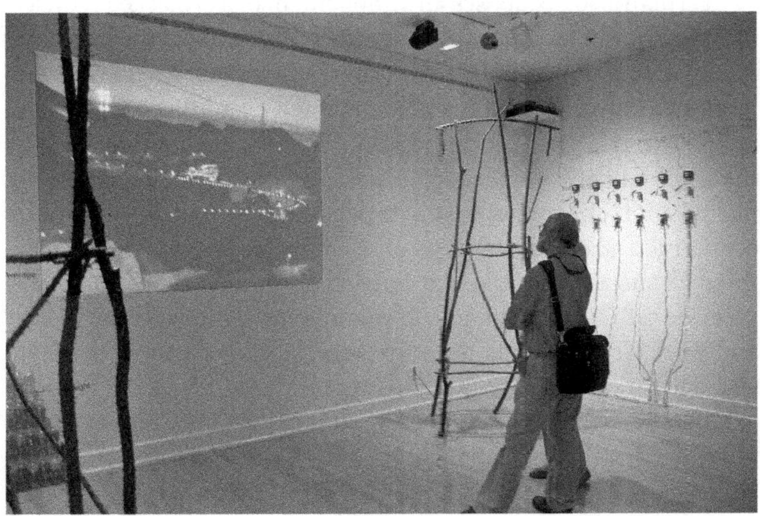

6.8   Richard Lerman, *Hoover: Water/Power* (2009)

the Black Canyon. A single-channel video projection in the installation presents the familiar contours of the dam's transmission towers while offering additional views of the scrappy plants that continue to survive around them. In front of his projection Lerman has assembled a series of sculptures made from these same plants found around the dam: brittlebush, ocotillo, and creosote. The ocotillo sculptures take on the general vertical forms of a transmission tower; ceiling wires connect these "towers" to dried brittlebushes and creosote that are suspended from the ceiling. Quiet sounds of wind-rustled branches and leaves emanate from these overhead plants in the gallery; Lerman has repurposed them as loudspeakers. In this way Lerman reimagines the Hoover Dam as a site that, in addition to putting out electrical energy, serves as a home to the plant life that is a source of the ecological diversity or eco-power of the desert, despite the fact that it is usually seen as a nuisance or as "brush" to be removed. The piezoelectric-produced hum of Lerman's recordings from the dam displaces the more familiar sound many of us know from utility power stations and electrical posts. He thereby represents and analyzes this site of engineering by using a far less environmentally harmful or invasive technology.

Lerman also juxtaposes an arrangement of 437 stacked recycled plastic water bottles next to his video projection of the dam. The bottles create a quantitative graph or chart of the fluctuating water levels at Hoover Dam since it was opened over 70 years ago. The results are not particularly encouraging, since the water levels at the Dam and at Lake Mead continue to plummet. Lerman poses the question of whether, given its declining output, the enormous economic and ecological costs of keeping the Hoover Dam online are at all sustainable. Like the Harrisons before him, Lerman suggests we rethink the situation of water in the regions where we live and work. It is perhaps time for Arizonans and others to pause and deliberate whether this great modern icon is perhaps more of an historical monument than we might currently care to admit.

anti-globalization

It has been said that with two historical milestones, the end of the Cold War in 1989 and the terrorist attacks of September 11, 2001, almost all world cultures have found themselves in a situation or condition of "permanent aftermath." This phrase, coined by the art historian Terry Smith, points to the critical and philosophical acknowledgment that even post-modernism, once understood as the most "contemporary" aspect of culture, has lapsed, as a result of the redefining of national borders and of nationalism itself that occurred after 1991.[1] This year marked the dissolution of the Soviet Union, the former world "superpower." The cultural globalizing of contemporary life parallels a neoliberal view of economics, and also has to do with a shift away from a foundation in national economies—a major element of the Cold War nationalism—toward one of emerging, investor-driven markets that spread beyond national borders and beyond the control or oversight of any single national or even global entity.

The neoliberal idea of the free and open markets of a global economy is seen as central to the phenomenon of globalization. Two key technologies have enabled the development of this post-nationalism: unlimited, quick air travel between international airports, the new transportation hubs of the globalized world; and instantaneous worldwide communication and asset-transfer enabled by a global internet. Major organizations and intellectuals of the anti-globalization movement have critically denounced neoliberal economics and its effects. Anti-globalism or "alter-globalization" protests against hyper-consumerism, world financial institutions like the World Bank, the International Monetary Fund, and the World Trade Organization, and the dealings of international corporations. Key intellectuals involved in articulating anti-global arguments include Noam Chomsky, George Soros, David Graeber, and Naomi Klein.

Up until now, this book has discussed the numerous alternative modernisms that sprang up after 1945 and that were driven by various subpopulations' seizing of the modernist notion of freedom and autonomy for themselves, as was the case with postcolonialism, gay rights, and feminism. Several chapters have also been devoted to the refusal in art of earlier aspects of modern life: the rejection of war and violence as an instrument of nation- or empire-building, or, environmental art's rejection of capitalism's "development" or destruction of the landscape and of animal life. This chapter considers artworks that critique aspects of homogenizing, globalized market- and media-driven culture, often with a view to a more equitable future use and control of the key globalizing technologies of travel and communication. Many of these artists urge the continued expansion of art's producers, viewers, and participants, in order to realize a truly inclusive globalism of a post-nationalist "cosmopolitan citizenship."

Modeling Globalism

The Swiss artist Thomas Hirschhorn has established himself as a kind of artistic modeler of the new dynamics of the global economy. His installations are studiously yet hastily constructed of the most ephemeral of materials, constructions made of brown tape and cardboard or tinfoil and plastic wrap, temporary plywood tables, found magazine clippings, and photocopies. His 1999 work *World Airport* (**Figure 7.1**) features a crudely rendered miniature fleet of jet airliners, each emblazoned with a national-airline logo such as British Airways or El Al, positioned on a makeshift tabletop tarmac. A snaking tinfoil branch or artery connects these objects

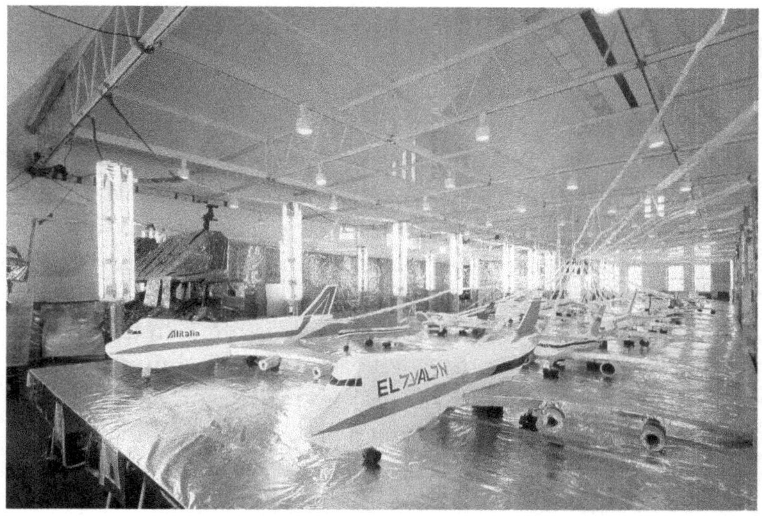

7.1   Thomas Hirschhorn, *World Airport* (1999)

with the "altars"—one is "sporting," crowned with an enormous pair of Nike high-tops; others are dedicated to the philosophers Georges Bataille and Gilles Deleuze—and air-route maps posted around the rest of the exhibition space. Information on regional conflicts in Kosovo or Rwanda, and additional texts written in various languages about the installation by different art critics, are taped to walls or left on chairs for viewers to "take away."

Hirschhorn sees these knots of models, altars, and textual information as representative of global networks that continue to mutate and otherwise grow unchecked in the pursuit of profit. He writes:

> profit, which wants to create for itself a model on one hand, and which differentiates itself on the other, separates itself, stakes claims, branches out [...] There's no confrontation or reinforcement; what happens is simply an interbreeding without confrontation [...] One's head spins, one's consciousness goes to sleep and the force dies away; it's the mergers of the multinationals on the one hand, and regional wars on the other![2]

This situation of increasing interconnection through travel for all, even those who "do not live in modern times," along with increased access for all to information via instant internet communications, has led to a situation where for the first time all, even those at the most remote locations, are contemporaneous. This is to say that everyone conceivably has access to modern centers, even if they themselves do not live a modern lifestyle. For the first time one can say that with the funds needed for access to the technologies of air travel and the internet, traditionally marginalized populations can no longer be excluded from the centers, in the West or elsewhere. This population mobility and globally shifting sense of culture was not yet achieved during the era of post-modernist art in the 1980s; it is a cultural situation new to the twenty-first century.

Hirschhorn is not the first artist to examine the dynamics of globalism; arguably the issue was anticipated by the Italian conceptual artist Alighiero Boetti (or Alighiero e Boetti as he began calling himself in 1973). After he made his reputation showing his art with the Arte Povera artists in Turin and Genoa, Boetti became a world traveler in the 1970s, and journeyed to Afghanistan, Pakistan, Ethiopia, and Guatemala, among other destinations. Perhaps in conjunction with his encounters during his travels and due to his involvement with conceptual art, he increasingly distanced himself from the idea of a singular producer of an artwork. He entered into numerous collaborations, particularly in Kabul, Afghanistan. One such collaboration was his acquisition and opening of the One Hotel there in 1971, with the help of a local assistant, Gholam Dastaghir; the agreement was that Boetti could have the best room there whenever he traveled to Kabul. Boetti considered the hotel an artwork.[3] His longer-term project the *Mappa* (**Figure 7.2**) was carried out between 1971 and 1994 with a group of artisanal women embroiderers in Kabul. These women ultimately fled to Pakistan during the Soviet invasion of Afghanistan in 1979, and only later returned. However, over 20 years they continued to produce colored maps of the world in embroidery, following a basic schoolroom map that Boetti had given them, and filling in the various countries with images taken from their flags. Boetti specified colors that were to be used,

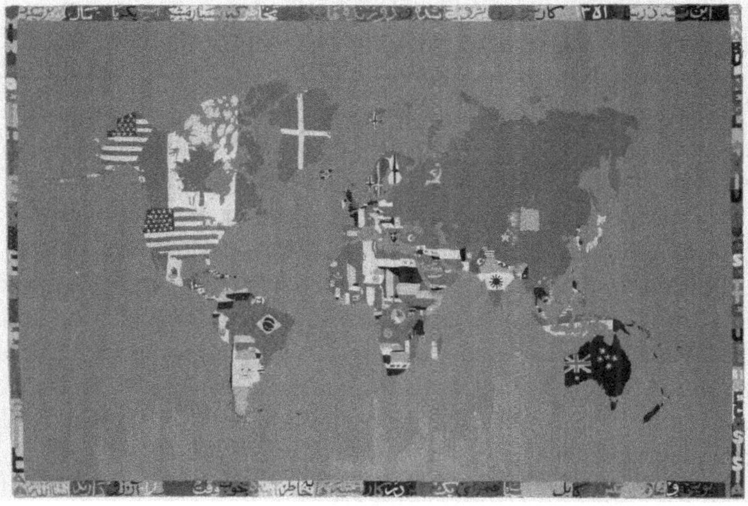

7.2   Alighiero Boetti, *Map* (*Mappa*, 1972–3), embroidery on cloth

with "mistakes" that the embroiderers made enhancing the final product (like pink-toned seas and oceans). The maps are framed with a square border of Italian and Farsi text that sometimes cites Sufi poetry, Boetti himself, or texts that the embroiderers inserted about their own lives. The *Mappa* series changed with social and political situations across the world. It is a set of works that features the craftsmanship of Caucasian weaving and embroidery of Afghanistan, merging it with the tendencies of Western conceptual art, in a transnational collaboration. Boetti considered the series very beautiful because he himself did nothing to create it. The *Mappa* is an early artwork that deals with globalism.

Migrants' and Workers' Rights

By the 1970s many artists questioned the traditional aspect of labor that was expected in the production of an artwork. This self-consciousness about a set ideology of artistic labor was most likely brought about in conjunction with the wider appreciation of Marcel Duchamp's work, and by the development of conceptual art, which I have already noted in relation to Alighiero Boetti's practice. Duchamp's notion of the ready-made is exemplified in his *Fountain* of 1917, a mass-produced object that he is purported to have purchased in a New York City plumbing store. Duchamp therefore viewed art not as a sanctified and highly skilled form of inspired craftsmanship, but rather as another mode of manufacture of an object. With *Fountain* Duchamp posited that a mass-produced, industrialized object could be art if the artist declared it so. He therefore challenged the notion that physical labor and craft were essential to the making of art, though the legitimacy of his challenge was not really recognized or registered in the art world until the 1960s. Hal Foster has coined this art-historical time lag "deferred action."

Drawing in part on Duchamp's labor-critical notion of art, and also from conceptual art, the New York artist Mierle Laderman Ukeles completed her "Maintenance art manifesto" in 1969. In this document Ukeles delineates her two "basic systems" of creation: development and maintenance. The former sounds much like a traditional view of the creative process ("pure individual creation," "progress," "change"), while the other "keeps the dust off" individual creation, "sustains" and "preserves" the new. Thus her notion of maintenance has to do with the servicing of objects and spaces that already exist in the world; she rejects the capitalist cycle of continual obsolescence and replacement of objects. Ukeles instead accepts as part of the creative process the labor that preserves and cleans that which already exists, and that keeps it in service. Ukeles has pursued the path of "maintenance art" since that time. This is despite the fact that, as she has stated, "maintenance is a drag; it takes all the fucking time [...] The culture confers lousy status on maintenance jobs = minimum wages, housewives = no pay."[4] Her later "Sanitation manifesto!" (1984) makes further claims for the importance of the work of maintenance or sanitation for the existence of large urban centers, and as a form of human labor that cements democracy itself, in that it serves everyone and furthermore "accepts that *everyone must be served in a democracy*."[5]

Some critics have categorized Ukeles as a feminist artist, but her work goes beyond an exclusive concern with women's undervalued labor. Her performance-based work *Touch Sanitation* from 1979–80 (**Figure 7.3**) involved the artist's performance and photographic documentation of the "handshake ritual"—that is, her meeting and shaking of hands with every sanitation worker employed by the New York City Department of Sanitation at the time. The ritual comprised both a gesture of appreciation and thanks on the part of the artist, but also the desire to recognize the individuals whose labor is not only devalued but also marginalized as unclean. Ukeles understands this marginalization as being related to cultural notions about garbage as something abject. Garbage in a sense becomes those who process and remove it; it is no longer "ours" as we are clean, and they are not, or we remain clean because they are not.[6] *Touch Sanitation* therefore sought to reverse this cultural casting out of sanitation workers, and of an entire type of human labor, in one of the world's largest cities. As

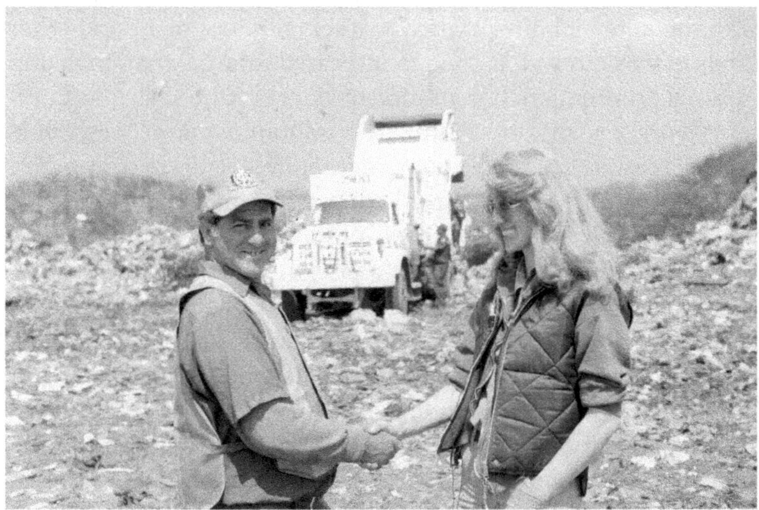

was the case in her earlier work *Hartford Wash: Washing Tracks, Maintenance* (1973)—in which Ukeles washed floors and dusted furniture inside the Wadsworth Atheneum Museum of Art but otherwise created no object—Ukeles' artworks render visible a kind of labor that is fundamental to art and its institutions. In refusing the ideology of the privileging of object-creation over other types of labor, Ukeles recognizes and brings into representation an entire social sector. In some ways Ukeles initiates a kind of "service"-based art practice: art that offers a particular service. This trend has been linked to the wider global shift from goods- to service-based economies. Other artists' works that have followed this strategy include Minerva Cuevas' *Mejor Vida Corporation* (1997) or Christine Hill's *Volksboutique* (1997).

Since these artworks were realized, another characteristic of the new global network of post-national economies and their new markets has emerged: its vacillating need for labor power. As markets quickly expand, the need for labor becomes intense and often exceeds the local, regional, or even national population of workers. The sudden demand for a labor force, combined with the new mobility of many workers because of air and other kinds of world travel, has led to increased internal (national) and external (international) migration of workers who seek this short-term work. In 1990 the number of migrant workers worldwide had increased to the point where a United Nations convention was drafted, the "International convention on the protection of the rights of all migrant workers and members of their families." It defined a migrant worker as "a person who is engaged or has been engaged in a remunerated activity in a State of which he or she is not a national."[7] While some countries have ratified this convention, the biggest economies that depend on external migration—the US, Germany, and Japan—have not.

As a result of the migration of workers responding to the sudden fluctuations of labor supply and demand, borders between states have become overly charged spaces of surveillance and quasi-militarized conflict. One of the largest and most problematic spaces is the border between Mexico and the US. It is not a coincidence that artists and artist collectives have been drawn to this border area as a geographical frame for their work, as it impacts a large work-ing population in both countries and particularly migrant workers from Mexico who seek work in the US. Chantal Akerman's single-channel video *From the Other Side* (2002)—the title also used for a related multi-channel video installation piece at Documenta in that year—is categorized as a documentary, but it is one that stretches the genre through the use of structuralist film techniques, as pio-neered by Michael Snow and others, such as the manipulation of long tracking shots, which move either left or right of the frame (the camera moves to the left in sequences shot in Mexico, and to the right in the US), or, the use of equally long static shots that similarly break the flow of narrative that the video presents. She layers these formalist elements on top of a documentary-type narrative and thereby complicates the presumed "realism" of what is presented.[8] Akerman shot the film at both sides of the border, in the towns of Agua Prieta, Mexico, and Douglas, Arizona. The long static shots of sites on both sides impress the viewer with the harsh desert land-scape that unifies the two places. As Akerman presents it, even the basics of daily life seem similar on both sides of the border.

The video features several interviews Akerman completed with individuals from both countries, but her sympathy seems to lie with those who recount harrowing or tragic stories of their own or their family's experiences in migrating to the US. One young man states matter-of-factly that he does not know his birthdate or age, due to his almost lifelong displacement and migration between the two countries **(Figure 7.4)**. These subjects speak directly to the camera, with Akerman positioned behind it, posing questions. She films an interview with a migration lawyer in Arizona who struggles to represent and assist these workers, but also an anti-immigration hardliner in Douglas whose lack of human empathy with the migrants, in addition to his considerable paranoia, is remarkable. That sentiment is echoed in a sequence of (found) border-surveillance video that Akerman includes in the film near its conclusion. *From the Other Side* presents this border as a hostile purgatory, where those on one side are victims and those on the other see a blind and impossible militarization as some kind of answer. The walls Akerman films that mark this

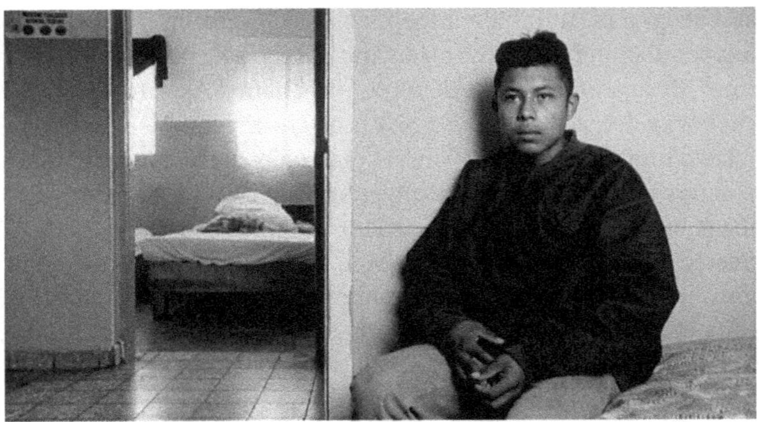

7.4   Chantal Akerman, *From the Other Side* (*De l'autre côté*, 2002), film still

border are attempts to keep the Other out, but she shows that they imprison those "on the other side" as well.

The Border Film Project (BFP) takes a differing approach to the documenting and representation of migrant workers on this international border, loosening itself away from singular authorial control in allowing migrants and others to represent themselves. Using a technique devised by anthropologists, a collective of three individuals, Brett Huneycutt, Victoria Criado, and Rudy Adler, organized the distribution of disposable cameras to two groups: migrants from Mexico and members of the national "Minuteman Civil Defense Corps Project." This second group is a self-appointed "National Citizens Neighborhood Watch" whose mission is to secure the US border "against the unlawful and unauthorized entry of all individuals, contraband, and foreign military."[9] The cameras were distributed at migrant shelters in Mexican border areas, and at Minutemen "observation sites" in California, Arizona, New Mexico, and Texas, along with instructions on how to use a camera for those who had not previously used them (**Figure 7.5**). In 2007 the BFP staged several exhibitions, culled from a pool of 2,000 received photographs and various videotaped interviews with participants, at art venues that included the Scottsdale Museum of

Contemporary Art in Arizona. None of the photographs or videos were captioned in the space, but images from each group were arranged together and isolated from the other. The Minutemen depict themselves as heroic—if overweight—outdoorsmen positioned in the landscape near their campers, sporting military-style clothing and gazing at the dusty horizon; the migrants, mostly young men in jeans and sweatshirts, sometimes smile and joke under the shade of bushes, or lie exhausted in a hotel room or shelter, recovering from their journey.

As the critic Chris Kraus has noted, the BFP reinforces the separateness of these groups, and even their installation does not point to the groups' interdependence.[10] The prosperity of the US Minutemen appears not to be connected to one of its principle sources, the migrants who answer the US markets' demand for labor. The BFP presents conceptual-art-style documentation with little or no interpretation or argument; this strategy seems to work against its effectiveness in arguing for border-policy reform. For all its strengths and good intentions the BFP echoes the state of current discourse on US border policy, since it too presents

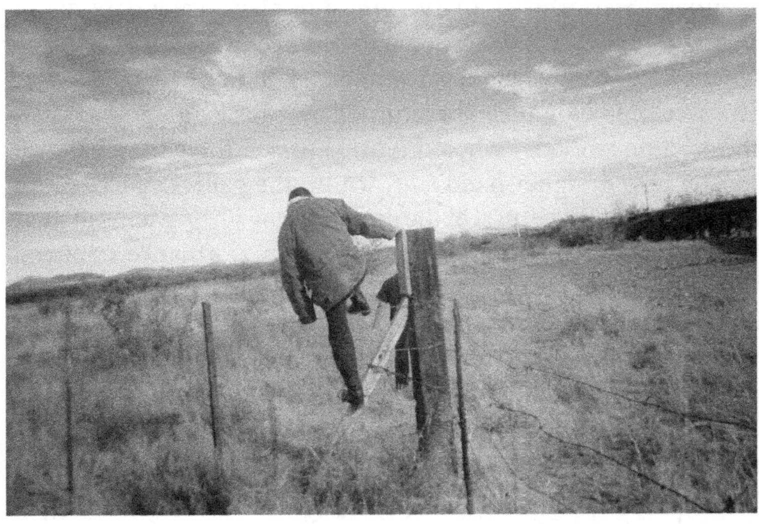

7.5   The Border Film Project, *Migrant photos* (2006–7)

localized migration problems as a stalemate that pits one population against the other, rather than revealing it as a stage where, to use Hirschhorn's words, global markets entwine and mutate.

Santiago Sierra has perhaps addressed the issue of migrant labor more controversially than anyone else. A Spanish artist working in Mexico City, Sierra's performance-based art considers the relation of migrants to the hermetic art community and its institutional network of galleries and museums. Sierra's installations are ethically problematic, and are difficult for viewers to witness or contemplate. His art has been praised by the art press on the one hand—in one instance he is claimed as a primary example of "relational antagonism," a new direction in art production—and on the other denounced as unethical.[11] For the work completed in New York City, *Nine Forms of 100 x 100 x 600 cm Each, Constructed to Be Supported Perpendicular to a Wall* (2002), Sierra hired several Mexican and Central American immigrant workers to build aluminum sculptures to specifications he supplied. He then asked that they support these forms on their shoulders in the gallery space during exhibition hours. In *133 Persons Paid to Have Their Hair Dyed Blonde* from 2001 (**Figure 7.6**), realized at the Venice Biennale, Sierra hired a large group of specifically dark-haired migrant workers, most of whom he recruited in the street in Venice where they worked as illegal vendors, to have their hair dyed a straw-colored blond. He then turned over his exhibition space to these same workers, who continued to sell their merchandise, mostly fake designer handbags, within the gallery spaces of the Biennale. A quick perusal of the documenting photographs of these works, particularly from the 2001 Venice performance, confirms that many of these workers were dark-haired and people of color, of African or Bangladeshi ethnicity. The difficulty these images and performances pose to the viewer is their stark staging, within the confines of art, of the labor of lower-salary and minority workers.[12]

As many critics have observed, Sierra's position on the matter of the exploitation of migrant labor is ambiguous or "amoral," though one has the general sense that Sierra believes that capitalist exploitation of the immigrant working poor—who are often ethnic minorities—is a bad thing. Nevertheless, he introduces

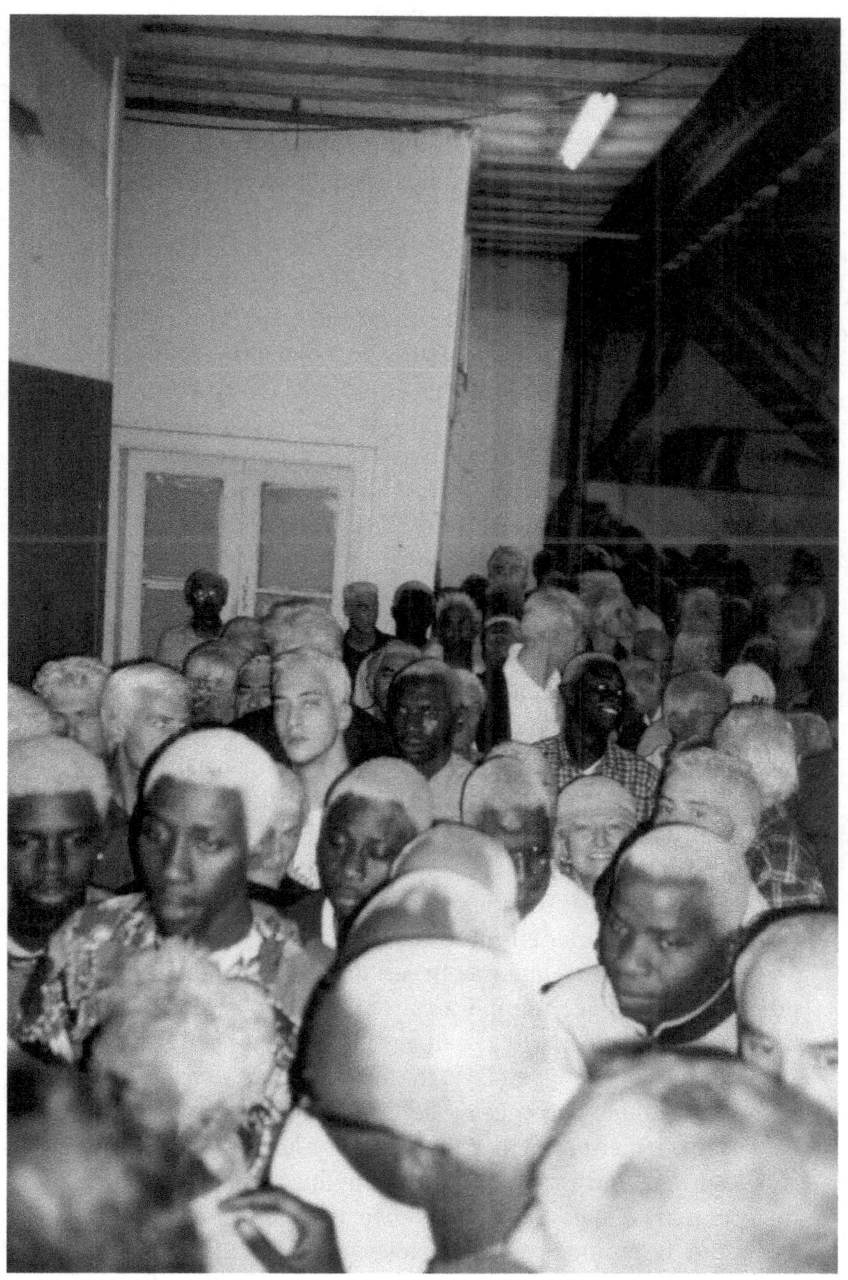

7.6 Santiago Sierra, *133 Persons Paid to Have Their Hair Dyed Blonde* (2001)

the dynamics of capitalist exploitation into the "civilized" spaces of the art gallery without comment. Thus it is unclear whether he abhors such practices or in fact promotes and condones them. However, as the critic Claire Bishop notes, his art directly addresses the exclusivity of the art community and its general exclusion of working-class people, along with the working poor. This exclusion is all the more glaring as the art world has recently charted the phenomenon of "participation" under the art-critical rubric of a "relational aesthetics" that is to provide a metaphor for the workings of democracy in gallery-staged moments of togetherness and community-building. A number of artists have been celebrated, largely uncritically, under this moniker in art discourse. Sierra is an artist who fully displays his production instead of concealing the exploitative relations within it. Extending the subcontracting process into other mediums, he takes the additional, logical step of hiring performers to complete his performance art. These performers complete variations of endurance-based activities that are quite familiar to the art community as a genre of performance art that has been practiced by Chris Burden and Marina Abramović, among other artists. However, where other artists hire manufacturers or craftsmen with specific skills or young artists out of art school, Sierra selects his assistants and workers from a social class that usually has no place in the process of art production and performance. It is also a population that is rarely present at international art exhibitions or in galleries. In strong contrast to the work of the Border Film Project, Sierra's works stage the social and economic interrelation between prosperous individuals, the prime audience of contemporary art production, and the workers who make that prosperity possible.

One recalls the legendary accounts of Andy Warhol's boorish—if not robber-baron-like—behavior as the "manager" of the Factory, his hyper-productive Manhattan studio of the mid 1960s. It is said that Warhol often did not pay his employees for their work, or that he required that they meet with him and ask for their pay before he would give it.[13] However, rarely is such exploitation of "hired help" on the part of renowned artists held up for analysis; art history and criticism see it as somehow irrelevant to art.

Ironically, art-historical discourse continues to maintain that the workings and dealings, or business practices, that have come to define the artist's studio after minimalism—when increasingly the production of actual objects and images is contracted out by the artist, to be done by others—is still of less importance than the actual objects that are produced. The accusation that Sierra pays his laborers to do "useless" work rings hollow in the sphere of art production where these performances take place, since artistic labor has always been "useless" and distinct from the means-ends utilitarianism of other kinds of production. It is notoriously difficult to identify the specific use value of art. One can say that on many levels Sierra's labor is similarly useless, as it produces art. As has been suggested, his work is more accurately described as contemporary "ethnographic realism," which, in antagonistic fashion, reveals as delusional the art community's self-image as progressive and "democratic."[14]

The network Multiplicity (also known as multiplicity.lab), an "agency for territorial investigations" dedicated to research, is based in the Department of Architecture at the Politecnico di Milano. The architect Stefano Boeri, one of the founders of the group, describes its research projects as "eclectic atlases," or collections of data, that are used to generate models of the flux that constitutes particular spaces. Projects have produced models of urban Milan, and, in the case of *USE—Uncertain States of Europe*, part of Dutch architect Rem Koolhaas' project *Mutations* (2000), of the entire territory of Europe. As the various projects of this essentially analytic enterprise unfold, histories and layers of meaning are accessed and excavated as by-products.[15]

In the process of charting data for the Mediterranean territory, the Multiplicity project *ID: A Journey through a Solid Sea* (2002) uncovered what is known as the "Malta boat tragedy" of 1996, when a boat carrying over 500 sank near Portopalo, Sicily, killing 283 Pakistani, Indian, and Sri Lankan migrants who were aboard. Multiplicity refers to this disaster as *Solid Sea Case 01: The Ghost Ship*, using underwater film footage by the Italian newspaper *La Repubblica*, and interviews with survivors. This project is presented on the Multiplicity website as well as through multi-channel video installations the group has realized in museums and galleries in Europe and Africa. Multiplicity maps this area as the "solid" convergence of huge numbers of trajectories and paths of mobility, a space that is also constituted by the markers of human trafficking across it, a "human geography." They therefore do not chart space in terms of traditional demarcations such as national and State borders, but as flows of identities across and through it. While *ID* is in part a memorial to a particular injustice suffered by migrants in the late twentieth century—a *Raft of the Medusa* for the era of globalism—it makes use of that tragedy to assert a new topography of territories. Multiplicity's global geography includes and represents these territories, the flows of people across areas that have previously remained uncharted.

Media/Informatics Activism; New-Media Art

The vast network of global media, including print media, television, and the internet, is another key component of contemporary globalism. This network cements large US, European, and Japanese corporations' control of the release and dissemination of information, one outcome of the deregulation of network radio and television in these countries. This deregulation began in the US in the 1970s and was mostly enacted during the Reagan administration in the 1980s, when the Federal Communications Commission's regulatory power was considerably curtailed. This action loosened governmental control of radio and television transmissions, and allowed for wide-scale privatization of these concerns as commercial, for-profit enterprises. An earlier criterion, that media stations be devoted to the public interest—having to do with public-service and educational programming—was no longer required. Other countries have similarly deregulated aspects of their national media networks since the 1980s. As is often noted, the concentration of media control into the hands of a small group of corporate interests in advanced industrial countries has arguably homogenized the look and content of the media worldwide. It has also led to the criticism that media coverage is increasingly filtered through the long- and short-term interests, and profit-driven goals, of these corporations and their business partners.

Since the 1990s artists have positioned themselves within this globalized media landscape to critique the nature of its representations—which because of its tie to photography and film the public widely understands as "truth"—or even to sabotage the stability of this corporate structure in the name of "correcting" it. Alfredo Jaar's installations address the power of photojournalistic images as presumed documents and markers of real events in the global media. He is drawn to cataclysmic events in developing countries. His art critiques how contemporary photojournalism's images of disaster, conflict, and violence, primarily under the control of corporate collections like Corbis or Getty Images, are merged into a general spectacle culture that contains them as local and of little significance for its dominant markets/audiences. Jaar instead advocates a humanism for the photographic images of such terrible events that retains their tie to the empathetic witnessing of the suffering and trauma of others.[16]

Jaar's *Rwanda Project* (1994–2000), a series of photo and text installations, in part focuses on the representation of one of many awful massacres of people gathered at the Ntarama Church, south of Kigali, Rwanda, during the spring of 1994.[17] The photographs that Jaar includes in 1996's *The Eyes of Gutete Emerita* (**Figure 7.7**)

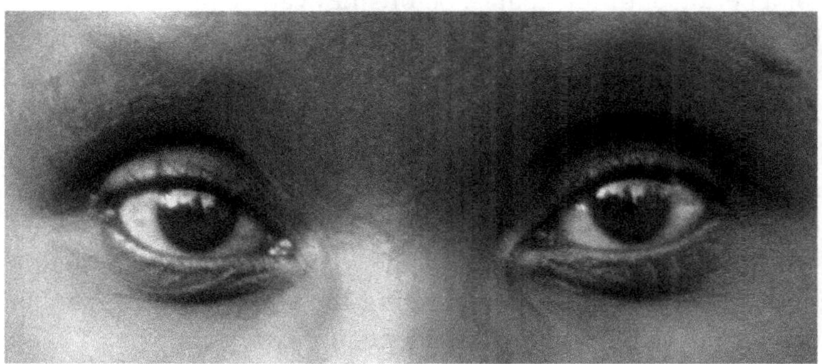

7.7   Alfredo Jaar, *The Eyes of Gutete Emerita* (1996) (from the series *The Rwanda Project*, 1994–8)

only depict this subject's eyes; the massacre of her husband and sons is not represented aside from her accounts, reproduced as texts throughout the installation. Thus we only know of the event as it was witnessed by a survivor, the young woman Gutete Emerita, and not as another photograph of dead bodies to which we have no relation. Another room of the installation features an enormous light table piled high with thousands of slides of the same image of Gutete Emerita's eyes. Jaar reminds us of the sheer number of photographs that pass before our eyes each day, and suggests that we might maintain our humanity in the midst of this visual torrent in considering the injustice suffered by one person at a time.

The media and network art team the Yes Men (Igor Vamos and Jacques Servin, aka, respectively, Mike Bonanno and Andy Bichlbaum), based in New York City but active globally, describe their work as "identity correction," "disinformation," or "culture jamming." They have produced numerous websites and performances, as well as two films, *The Yes Men* (2003) and *The Yes Men Fix the World* (2009). Impersonating media spokesmen for various multinational corporations or government agencies both online and in person, the two artists plant elaborate hoaxes concerning these same corporations in the mainstream media. Some are widely distributed. This dissemination of their statements lends legitimacy to Yes Men disinformation statements for a period of time—that is, before they can be refuted by actual corporate public-relations personnel. In order to gain maximum publicity and media exposure, and thereby embarrass corporate and political entities, the Yes Men make use of fake websites and press releases as mainstays of the media, along with in-person appearances or performances at the traditional corporate venue of the convention or conference.[18]

The Yes Men's most effective disinformation campaign **(Figure 7.8)** took place surrounding the 20-year anniversary of one of the worst industrial accidents in history, the 1984 Union Carbide Corporation (UCC) chemical spill in Bhopal, India, that killed 3,787 people at the time, and is estimated to have caused between 15,000 and 20,000 deaths altogether. Since the accident

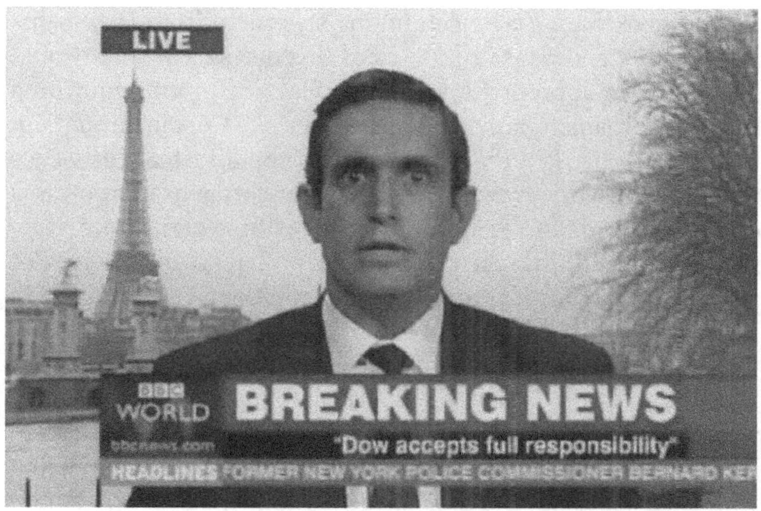

7.8   The Yes Men/"Jude Finisterra," still from televised interview on
the BBC on December 3, 2004

there had been competing legal actions concerning the responsibility for the disaster and for restitution for victims and survivors.
UCC was purchased by Dow Chemical in 2001. Since that time
the Dow corporation maintains that UCC acted responsibly in the
aftermath of the leak, provided adequate clean-up at the former
facility, and delivered adequate medical facilities and supplies to
the affected population. A number of lawsuits in both Indian and
US courts continue to dispute these claims to the present day. In
2004 the Yes Men created a faux Dow corporate website concerning the anniversary of the Bhopal Disaster. Through this website
the artists, presumed to be Dow employees, were contacted by
the BBC for a television interview regarding Bhopal. In this interview, on December 3, 2004, "Jude Finisterra," in reality Yes Man
Bichlbaum/Servin, stated that Dow had decided to compensate
the Bhopal community fully for the disaster through liquidation
of the UCC, worth approximately 12 billion US dollars. In the
few hours' before Dow was able to issue a statement refuting this
misrepresentation as a hoax, its share price fell 4.2 percent on a

European exchange. The debunking statement from Dow—that it would not compensate victims of this disaster in what would have been an appropriate way—was featured prominently on a number of mainstream online news sites like Google throughout the day that marked the anniversary of the disaster. Thus Dow was forced to foreground its own lack of compensation on this critical day, and the Yes Men were successful in generating negative publicity against the corporation, perhaps with the idea of shaming this entity into an adequate settlement with survivors in Bhopal. A predictable wave of corporate-generated condemnation for their hoax followed, including the accusation that the Yes Men falsely and "cruelly" raised the hopes of Bhopal survivors that they would receive better settlements. In response to this criticism the artists traveled to Bhopal where they filmed their meeting with local activists, who first staged a public mock strangulation of the two artists for the cameras. The artists were then thanked for their efforts in publicizing the city's continuing struggle for compensation and justice in the wake of the disaster.

In this case the corporation in question, Dow Chemical, found itself having to respond on the record with statements that debunked the unauthorized ones the Yes Men had made on its behalf. In the process true corporate spokesmen are forced to underscore their company's unethical positions in neglecting the public interest, and in evading the rule of law. In their manipulation of mainstream media the Yes Men make use of several conditions that characterize it, particularly in its online manifestations. Their impersonations of corporate and government personnel rely on the anonymity that the internet affords, along with its ability to disseminate unverified information very rapidly. Their projects evidence that at present it is still possible for almost anyone to gain access to this technology and disseminate information through it.

The Yes Men therefore expand the tradition of guerrilla media art or culture jamming that began with the American artist Mel Chin in 1996. Chin, along with a team of artists, the GALA Committee, designed objects used on the set for several episodes of the prime-time television series *Melrose Place*. They introduced odd objects on camera that planted their own meaningful narratives regarding wider social and political issues within this soap opera—for example, a Chinese food takeout container featuring slogans from the Tiananmen Square protests, or bed linens used in an after-sex scene decorated with a pattern of unrolled condoms. Media artworks by Chin and the Yes Men apply the culture-jamming technique of *détournement*, first introduced by Guy Debord and the Situationist International in the 1960s, to the psychogeography of the media landscape. They "détourne" given cultural entities (for example, websites or complete television programs) by reproducing or appropriating them to render them familiar, but then amend them with slight alterations that critique its parent. The Yes Men might also be connected to the media-art practice of plagiarism, a Neoist media strategy. Culture-jamming media artists pierce the veil of the otherwise smooth workings of the mass media under corporate control, thereby interrupting and exposing its usual and ethically questionable functions and practices.

Though corporate interests and monopolies have established themselves in the manufacture of the hardware and software designs for the browsers and servers that constitute the internet, the control and oversight of newer media technology of the internet is less settled and more contested. This has become clear not only through the success of media artists like the Yes Men, but also in the rise of internet activists like Julian Assange, who edits WikiLeaks, a site that publishes, with its print-media partners, classified data about instances of global corporate or institutional malfeasance or, famously, US governmental or military communications regarding the conduct of foreign wars in Iraq and Afghanistan. The current contestation of the control of the internet is further evidenced in the successful activities of "hacktivist" groups like Anonymous and LulzSec, who have in the name of migrants' rights hacked into the websites of US and Italian police agencies in order to vandalize and open classified information to public scrutiny. Such hacking activities, even as activism, certainly raise a number of moral and ethical concerns.

Within this general contestation of technology, new-media artists are focused on asserting the public's right to retain control of the internet as a public domain or on raising awareness of the scope of internet use that surrounds them, including activity that carries out operations of surveillance on private citizens. The Radical Software Group (RSG) is a collective of artists and programmers that includes the media scholar and programmer Alexander Galloway. The group engages with digital culture and "network environments" in part by designing interfaces.[19] The most extensively developed of these is *Carnivore*, both a search engine and a tool or platform to be used by other new-media artists. RSG calls its software *CarnivorePE* (the last two letters standing for "personal edition"), since it was appropriated from the US Federal Bureau of Investigation's edition (also called "Carnivore"), a software program for electronic wiretapping or digital surveillance (the agency later retitled the software to the less-threatening "DCS-1000"). Unlike the FBI version, the RSG edition of the software harvests data drawn only from volunteers and is installed on specific networks; Galloway has therefore called it a "site-specific installation."[20] The data harvested can then be used to characterize the types of exchanges on the network it is installed on.

The second level of *CarnivorePE* has to do with the processing of this data, which it leaves open-ended so that additional "clients" or artistic programmers can do the processing of the data according to their particular aesthetic or artistic vision, perhaps with an eye to sketching the contours or personality of the activity of a particular network at a given time. One of many examples of a client or artistic interface provided on the *Carnivore* website is by Scott Sona Snibbe, entitled *Stars Fueled by Network Traffic* (2002, **Figure 7.9**). Snibbe describes the work as a "field of stars that are fueled by network traffic," the "constellation of fixed and transient hosts" that characterize local networks.[21] The star-images are generated by an IP address on the network one is using, or that is being accessed by that network. *CarnivorePE* is free and available for download on the same website. In a sense, it extends the data-harvesting power of digital surveillance to anyone who wants to use it. Given the second level of the *CarnivorePE* program, it also assures that this collected data cannot be used for devious or criminal purposes, but rather only to produce visual and sound

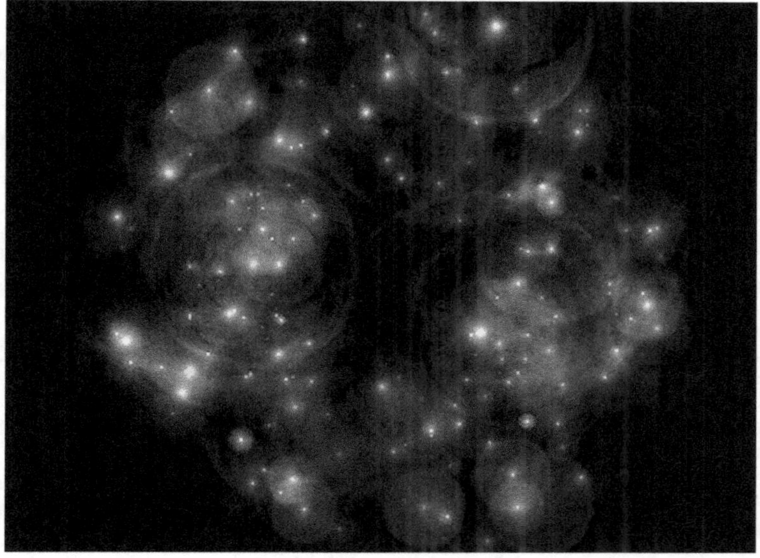

7.9   Scott Sona Snibbe, *Stars Fueled by Network Traffic* (Radical Software
Group Carnivore client, 2002)

artworks. Since the inception of the *Carnivore* program, other artists,
like the Norwegian sound-art group Thorns Ltd., have made use
of similar network-stream data to generate material, as they did at
the Site Santa Fe Biennial in the sonic work, *0.0 Santa Fe* (2006).

It has been questioned whether the RSG program is critical of
other electronic surveillance programs that are engaged for the purposes of law enforcement or even national security, since it basically
replicates the same kind of (intrusive) data collection on specific
individuals' use of the internet on a given network. Galloway has,
however, asserted that the group was generally supportive of such
digital surveillance since it can provide the data source that is a
critical and necessary component for digital or new-media art.[22] He
also believes that in granting free access to surveillance software
to everyone, network users/viewers would become more aware of
the prevalence of these programs in their everyday lives.

The Raqs Media Collective, based in Delhi, was formed in 1992
by Monica Narula, Jeebesh Bagchi, and Shuddhabrata Sengupta.

They note that "Raqs" could be seen as a version of the internet "FAQ," but referring instead to "rarely asked questions"; it also points to the Urdu, Persian, and Arabic word meaning "dance." This collective takes a stance parallel to that of the RSG in its insistence that the internet be used to facilitate access to, and the open exchange and dissemination of, diverse artistic visions. Raqs advocates this openness primarily through its adherence to the notion of "copyleft," a redefinition of copyright licensing that allows for the free availability of a given work. Copyleft has also been forwarded by other entities such as the non-profit organization Creative Commons. Raqs' first projects were designed to include the input and work of the local population of Delhi. Working both in actual physical space as well as on the spaces of the internet, its project *28.28 N/77.15 E:: 2001/02 (An Installation on the Coordinates of Everyday Life in Delhi)* of 2002 (**Figure 7.10**) was realized as a physical installation, and also as an online exhibition at their

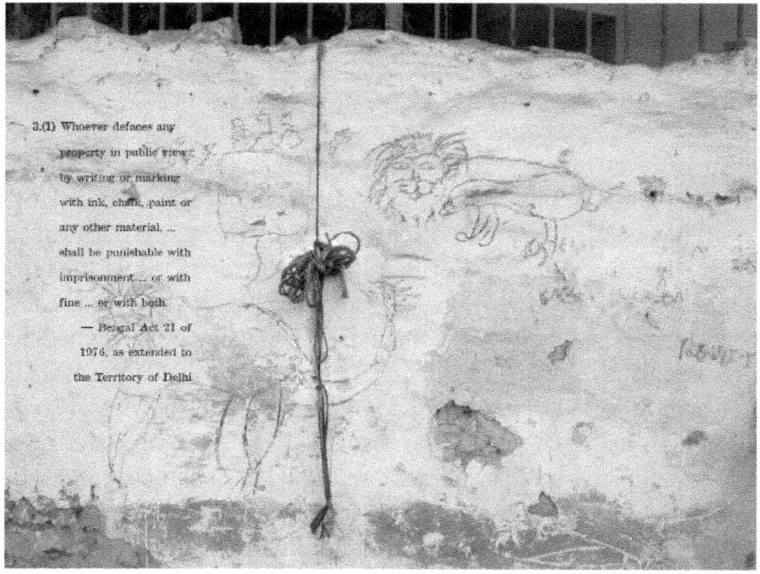

7.10   Raqs Media Collective, *28.28 N/77.15 E:: 2001/02 (An Installation on the Coordinates of Everyday Life in Delhi)* (2002)

Creative Commons "laboratory," "Open Platform for Unlimited Signification" (OPUS).[23] Both realizations of the work featured sounds, images, and texts that Raqs had collected about the urban spaces of Delhi seen from various points of view. The OPUS site encouraged further use, distribution, and amending of these representations that could in turn also be altered and disseminated, digitally or otherwise, after they had been uploaded. OPUS invites participants to submit their "recension," which they define as a version of reality "contraindicative of the notion of hierarchy." The recension is not to be understood within the usual priority given to an original as opposed to a copy. Thus a Raqs recension is somewhat similar to the "clients" that can be generated with the use of *Carnivore*, only as a platform OPUS does not require specialized programming skills, merely the ability to upload or download items to the site.

28.28 N/77.15 E:: 2001/02 is then a work that is open-ended. Raqs produces works and installations that are mutable objects—to borrow the language of programming—but that remain tied to aspects of localized urban space. Through the use of OPUS as a channel, local spaces like those in Delhi are rendered highly cosmopolitan by means of their very multiplicity, their ability to mutate, and their wide availability as digital art. Raqs also serves as a kind of bridge for open creativity, even of non-artists, in terms of representing the urban spaces in which many live as spaces of a world citizenry. Additionally, Raqs serves as a conduit for the flow of these multiple viewpoints and visions into the institutional spaces of the art community. This collective uses digital technology to agitate for a new inclusiveness within the realm of contemporary art, and urges that it be used as a tool in decentralizing art institutions.

protestAR:

#OCCUPYWALLSTREET
and #arOCCUPYWALLSTREET

In 2011, the Canadian activist organization Adbusters issued a call for coordinated protests in the US against the widening gap in income between middle-class Americans and the most affluent citizens, and the accompanying rise in political influence by the latter group. Their recruiting poster featured the image of an icon of the prosperity of the American finance system, the sculpture *Charging Bull* by Arturo Di Modica, located near Wall Street. In Adbusters' digitized photomontage, the bull sculpture is crowned by a dancer in a graceful pose. The call established Wall Street—the finance center of the US and hub of the economic crash that occurred in 2008—as the target of protest. Perhaps the need for direct action had been precipitated by public frustration over economic stagnation: the media focused on an obstreperous US Congress over the summer of 2011, as it delayed for weeks its standard authorization for the funding of bills it had already passed. Three years after the US financial crisis and the onset of the global recession, economic growth remained weak and high levels of unemployment persisted in many major US cities. Additionally, data released by independent organizations and the US Congressional Budget Office indicated that by 2007 the concentration of income and national wealth in the US at the top one percent had effectively doubled since 1980.[1]

Hundreds of demonstrators answered the call for protest on September 17, 2011; since they were not allowed to picket or occupy Wall Street itself because they lacked permits, the protesters moved to Zuccotti Park, a nearby landlord-controlled, quasi-public park. Due to this unusual arrangement, the police were not empowered to remove protesters from the park as the landlord of the property declined to request police assistance in clearing it. Several hundred demonstrators began to camp and live in the park, a situation made possible by donations of food and other necessities from sympathizers nationwide, along with a high level of organization and coordination on the part of the demonstrators. On October 15, sympathy marches and protests—dubbed "Occupy London" or similar—took place nationally and globally, and in world financial centers including Zurich, London, Rome, Frankfurt, Paris, and Tokyo.

Michael Kimmelman, an art critic for the *New York Times*, heralded the Occupy Wall Street "movement" in Zuccotti Park as a re-emergence of the Aristotelian polis, in that it succeeded in reinstating the importance of a "proper city" and "face-to-face conversation" to the civic order that, in antiquity, extended only as far as the human voice could carry.[2] On the one hand it appears that Kimmelman was correct; he invoked Kent State in 1970 and Tahrir Square in 2011 as similar realizations of the ideal polis situated in public space. Yet the laptops and smartphones that the Zuccotti Park protesters frequently recharged at generators or "media centers" in the park complicated any notion of the primacy of the place of this park in New York to the discussions that marked the protest. The site of this demonstration was a place where community can and did happen—largely due to the coordination possible through social media like Twitter and Facebook. It was also a hub on the global network that linked this group of individuals to other demonstrators in "public" spaces. Another part of this global protest involved the currently fading notion of true public space, open to and controlled by a public sphere of democratic exchange and discourse. Instead it is the power of the no-place of the internet and a loosening of the power of physical space that has made Occupy Wall Street an occurrence that took place in many other sites globally.

Making use of the technical possibilities that smartphones offer in public space, Manifest.AR, a group of internet-based artists, is using its work to resist the social and legal conventions that control and police actual physical space in urban centers.[3] The group instead prefers to "augment" or meld physical space with virtual ones, and with virtual images, in an act of (digital) trespass and refusal. The group links its AR ("augmented reality") work to the situationist notion of psychogeography; as Guy Debord described this endeavor in 1955, it was to encompass study of the "laws" and "effects" of the geographical or physical environment on individual behavior or on the psyche. Debord realized these studies by means of the "aimless" urban wandering he termed the *dérive*, along with other strategies. Manifest.AR alters our perception of physical space through new applications available on handheld devices that make use of augmented-reality technology. "Augmented reality" produces live, real-time images of the "real world" that are modified with computer imagery. AR does not offer the immersion of virtual reality, which instead offers a depiction of another, simulated world. AR is most widely used in media coverage of sports; in US football broadcasts, for example, the computer-generated image of a line marking where the ball must be carried in order to achieve a first down is an AR-generated effect; it enhances an actual camera image with a computer-generated one.

Manifest.AR now regularly mounts counter-exhibitions of virtual artworks "within" the confines of museums and galleries that otherwise would have excluded them from displaying physical artworks in their spaces. In October 2010 the group realized *We AR in MoMA* in using an AR browser available on smartphones.[4] After loading this application, the visitor to MoMA could visit each floor to view, through their phone, virtual works by Manifest. AR artists such as Mark Skwarek and Tamiko Thiel that were "installed" (in a simulated way) on each floor. The group issued an international call to other AR artists to place their virtual works in the museum as well. In this piece, the artists worked digitally in order to occupy a restricted space, which had to do with making their works viewable within an exclusive art institution.

Manifest.AR similarly puts out a global call for ARart participation—an "augmented-reality occupation"—in conjunction with Occupy Wall Street. For the demonstration, these entities refer to themselves using the hashtags that are used as search markers for Twitter and that appear in the body of Twitter messages: #arOC-CUPYWALLSTREET and #OCCUPYWALLSTREET. AR artists are able to create their own browser content and link it to others coordinated by Manifest.AR. Its blog states that the entire financial district of New York City was blanketed with these artwork augmentations; the group has also introduced augmentations to other cities like Washington DC. Artwork augmentations are created by means of the group's augmented-reality app, which they have called "protestAR." One protestAR work by Mark Skwarek features still images of protesters waving American flags, banners and placards that feature slogans like "Jail bankers not protesters!" It is therefore possible that a pedestrian in the financial district who has downloaded the application can then point his or her phone to a street area that in physical reality around him or her is divided and restricted with multiple barriers, and see the protestAR of that same space filled with Occupy Wall Street demonstrators **(Figure E.1)**. In accessing *Money Grab* by Todd Margolis (2011), one can see dollar bills fluttering down from

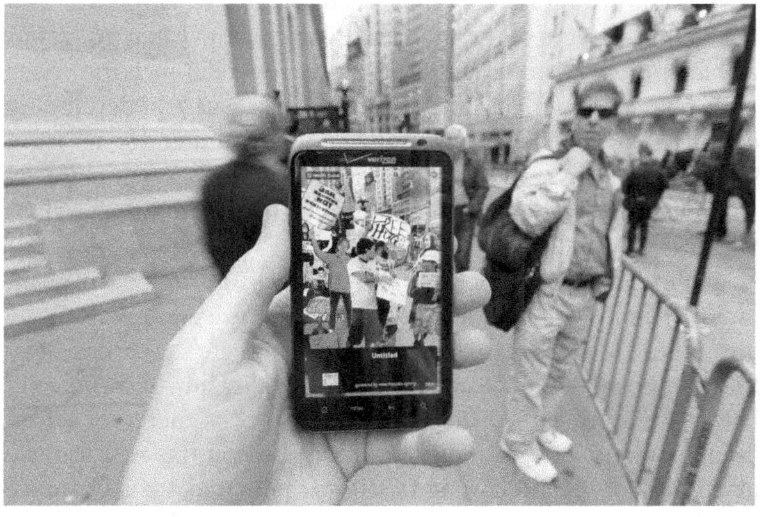

E.1   Mark Skwarek, ProtestAR, Wall Street (2011)

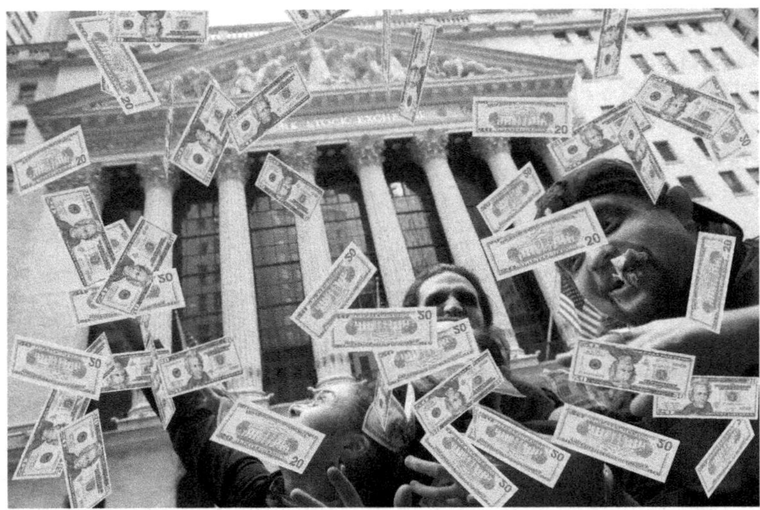

E.2   Todd Margolis, *Money Grab* (2011)

the sky like rain onto the cleared Wall Street area (**Figure E.2**). In the Wall Street-centered realization of his ARwork *Water wARs* (2011), John Craig Freeman inserts other aspects of protest into the charged spaces of the financial district: in it virtual images of a shanty town surrounded by water barrels reference the crises and refugees generated by the lack of clean water in developing countries, or "emerging markets," another unintended result of global corporate activity or "development" that is criticized by the alter-globalization movement, which Freeman traces back or "brings" to Wall Street.

Other works in #arOCCUPYWALLSTREET are global in span, and can be downloaded well beyond the immediate Wall Street area. These ARworks can pinpoint other corporate targets of protest that can be related to Occupy Wall Street's agenda of countering corporate greed and malfeasance. Such works therefore create ready-made images of protest, and can be manipulated to raise awareness of certain corporate sites as potential areas of future physical-space occupation and protest. Tamiko Thiel's *Reign of Gold* (2011) asks participants around the world to email their screenshots of the work—showing $50 gold coins cascading from the sky—at their favorite site of protest. Her own realization of the work features several buildings on Wall Street including an entrance to the New York Stock Exchange (**Figure E.3**), which is then seen in a blizzard of coins. Another user viewed *Reign of Gold* at the Tokyo headquarters of the Tokyo Electric Power Company, which has handled grievances associated with the nuclear disaster at the Fukushima Daiichi Nuclear Power Plant in Japan, which took place in March of 2011.

Ultimately these AR works are well suited to generate iconic imagery of occupation as a means of resistance to and refusal of the customary relations and exclusivity of the status quo. As the technology of AR improves and allows for a greater accuracy of photographic reproduction, AR images will take on increasing visual power. The quality of the AR image will soon match that of other digital photographic images, making the AR component of a

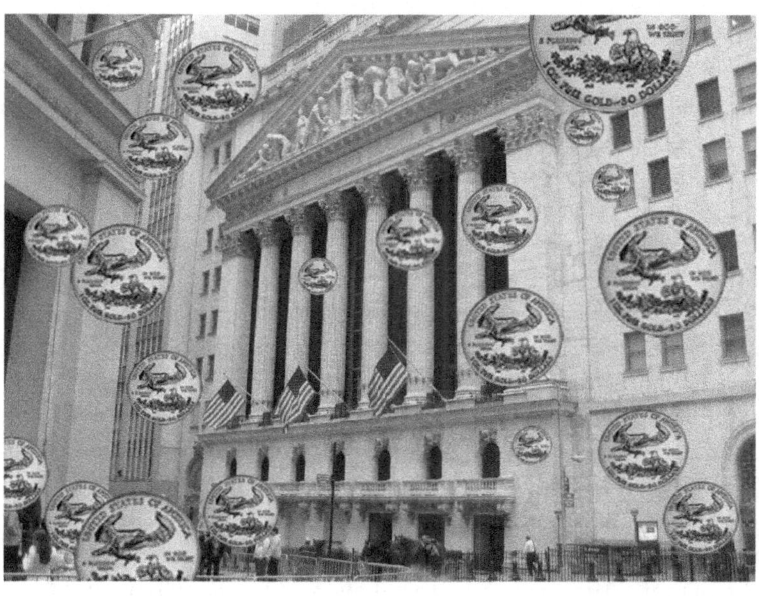

E.3   Tamiko Thiel, *Reign of Gold* (New York Stock Exchange, Broad Street façade, 2011)

photograph almost imperceptible. AR artworks will become indistinguishable from "regular" photographs, and will be circulated as such within the stream of mass-media and internet images. They will take on photography's indexical quality, or, the assumption of the "straight" photograph's tie to a moment that was actually encountered in the physical world, as a "document" of a particular moment that has the character of physical evidence. The provocative occupations and interventions of AR will take on an aspect of the "real," allowing for culture-jamming art and a radical expansion of the art community and its audience. This will realize an explosion of digital art that will parallel the moment of video art's appearance on broadcast television in the late 1960s and 1970s.

It is of course the case that ARart is restricted to a certain viewer who has access to smartphones, or new mobile handheld hardware and software. This technology is currently exclusive to urban centers of developed countries, and can otherwise only be accessed by means of the profit-oriented networks that are established in these countries. A demand for the modernizing of telecommunications globally, and for the right of citizens of developing countries (which the anthropologist and activist David Graeber has called the "global south") to gain entrance to global telecommunications networks and its technologies, must become an additional concern of the alter-globalization movement. It is quite likely that artists sympathetic to these goals will continue to play a major role in bridging the divide between the realms of art and "everyday life." As they have in the recent past, artists will remain active in generating new meanings. The realm of art stimulates new ways of thinking; it rejects stale ideologies that confer status upon geographical centers and onto privileged sub-populations while marginalizing others. It is within the realm of art that we can begin to consider the possibility of realizing the ideal polis in a "glocal" way. Art can envision a polis that may be simultaneously local and global because of the communication that global networks make possible; the polis can extend across the planet. Artists continue to believe and to know that what they do is political. In this way, art continues to be a full participant in realizing social, political, and economic change.

notes

Introduction

1   See especially Michel Foucault, *The Archeology of Knowledge*, trans. A.M. Sheridan Smith (New York, NY: Harper & Row, 1972).

2   On the issue of nation-building and art, see the work of Albert Boime, particularly *Art in an Age of Revolution, 1750–1800* (Chicago, IL: University of Chicago Press, 1987) and *Art in an Age of Counterrevolution, 1815–1848* (Chicago, IL: University of Chicago Press, 2004).

3   Heinrich Heine's art criticism and its ties to socialism are examined in Margaret Rose, "The politicization of art criticism: Heine's 1831 portrayal of Delacroix's *Liberté* and its aftermath," *Monatshefte* lxxiii/4 (Winter 1981), pp. 405–14, and Susanne Zantop, ed., *Paintings on the Move: Heinrich Heine and the Visual Arts* (London and Lincoln, NE: University of Nebraska Press, 1989).

4   See Henri, Comte de Saint-Simon [or possibly Olinde Rodrigues], "The artist, the savant, and the industrialist," in *Art in Theory 1815–1900: An Anthology of Changing Ideas*, eds Charles Harrison and Paul J. Wood (London: Blackwell Publishers Ltd., 1998), pp. 38–41.

5   See Timothy J. Clark, *Farewell to an Idea: Episodes from a History of Modernism* (New Haven, CT: Yale University Press, 1999).

6   On Picasso's difficult and changing reception in the GDR see, for example, Brigitta Milde, "Picasso in der DDR," in *Picasso et les femmes* [exh. cat.], eds

Ingrid Mössinger and Beate Ritter (New York, NY: Kunstsammlungen Chemnitz, 2002), pp. 372–85.

7   See Moira Roth, "The aesthetic of indifference," *Artforum* xvi/3 (November 1977), pp. 46–53.

8   See Susan Buck-Morss, *Dreamworld and Catastrophe: The Passing of Mass Utopia in East and West* (Cambridge, MA: MIT Press, 2000) and Boris Groys et al., *Dream Factory Communism: The Visual Culture of the Stalin Period* [exh. cat.] (Ostfildern-Ruit: Hatje Cantz, 2003).

9   See, for example, Blake Stimson and Gregory Sholette, eds, *Collectivism after Modernism: The Art of Social Imagination After 1945* (Minneapolis, MN: University of Minnesota Press, 2007).

10 See Terry Smith et al, eds, *Antinomies of Art and Culture: Modernity, Postmodernity, Contemporaneity* (Durham, NC: Duke University Press, 2008).

11 Jack Burnham, "Systems esthetics," *Artforum* vii/1 (September 1968), pp. 30, 31. Available at http://monoskop.org/images/e/e6/Burnham_Jack_1968_Systems_Esthetics.pdf (accessed February 6, 2013).

12 See, for example, Nina Felshin, ed., *But Is It Art?: The Spirit of Art as Activism* (Seattle, WA: Bay Press, 1994).

Chapter 1 · State-Sponsored Art During the Cold War

1   See Andrei Aleksandrovich Zhdanov, *Essays on Literature, Philosophy, and Music* (New York, NY: International Publishers, 1950).

2   See Ulrich Krempel, ed., *Alexander Deineka, Malerei, Graphik, Plakat* [exh. cat.] (Düsseldorf: Städtische Kunsthalle, 1982) and Toby Clark, *Art and Propaganda in the Twentieth Century* (London: Calmann and King Ltd., 1997), pp. 91–3.

3   On this shift see Francis Frascina, "Introduction," in *Pollock and After: The Critical Debate*, ed. Francis Frascina (London and New York, NY: Routledge, 2000), pp. 113–29, and Nancy Jachec, *The Philosophy and Politics of Abstract Expressionism, 1940–1960* (Cambridge: Cambridge University Press, 2000).

4   See Serge Guilbaut, "Postwar painting games: the rough and the slick," in *Reconstructing Modernism: Art in New York, Paris, and Montreal 1945–1964*, ed. Serge Guilbaut (Cambridge, MA: MIT Press, 1990), pp. 30–84.

5   On Picasso's complicated relationship with the PCF see Sarah Wilson, "'La beauté révolutionnaire'? Réalisme socialiste and French painting 1935–1954," *Oxford Art Journal* iii/2 (October 1980), pp. 61–9, and Gertje Utley, *Picasso: The Communist Years* (New Haven, CT: Yale University Press, 2000).

6   See also Francis Frascina, "The politics of representation," in *Modernism in Dispute: Art since the Forties*, ed. Paul Wood (New Haven, CT: Yale University Press, 1993), pp. 77–169.

7   Ibid., p. 137.

8   See Renato Guttuso, *Guttuso* [exh. cat.] (London: Whitechapel Art Gallery, 1996) and James Hyman, *The Third Way: Renato Guttuso and Realism in Europe* (London: James Hyman Gallery, 2003). Available at http://www.jameshymangallery.com/pages/publication/509.html (accessed February 6, 2013).

9   Alberto Moravia, *Man as an End: A Defense of Humanism*, trans. Bernard Wall (New York, NY: Farrar, Straus & Giroux, 1965), p. 243.

10   See Gertje Utley, *Picasso: The Communist Years* (New Haven, CT: Yale University Press, 2000), pp. 101–16.

11   As reported in ibid., pp. 208ff.

12   See Frascina, "Introduction." As of a few years ago, the FBI files on Picasso were available free of charge via the agency's "Electronic Reading Room" at http://foia.fbi.gov/room.htm. At the time of writing the scanned documents have been removed from the website and the reader must purchase copies. A for-profit website will also sell you a CD with the Picasso FBI file documents for about £6 or $10.

13   Ibid.

14   See Alfred H. Barr, Jr., "Is modern art communistic?," *New York Times* (December 14, 1952) and Joseph A. Barry, "The two Picassos: politician and painter," *New York Times Magazine* (May 6, 1951).

15   Frascina, "Politics of representation," p. 141.

16   Gabriele Mucchi, "Leninfriedenspreis für Picasso: Ein Gruss Gabriele Mucchis an Pablo Picasso," *Bildende Kunst* 8 (1962), p. 409.

17   Clement Greenberg, "Picasso at seventy-five," rpt. in *Clement Greenberg: The Collected Essays and Criticism, Volume 4: Modernism with a Vengeance 1957–1969*, ed. John O'Brian (Chicago, IL: University of Chicago Press, 1986), p. 30.

18   See Hans F. Secker, *Diego Rivera* (Dresden: Verlag der Kunst, 1957).

19 See Elisabeth Malkin, "Rivera, Fridamania's other half, gets his due," *New York Times* (December 25, 2007).

20 An excellent and extensive catalog was produced to accompany the exhibition: Okwui Enwezor, ed., *The Short Century: Independence and Liberation Movements in Africa 1945–1994* [exh. cat.] (New York, NY: Prestel, 2001).

21 On Cold War Angolan art, see Delinda J. Collier, *Art in a State of Emergency: Figuring Angolan Nationalism, 1953–2007* [Ph.D. dissertation, Emory University, 2010].

22 See Irving Sandler, *The Triumph of American Painting: A History of Abstract Expressionism* (New York, NY: Harper and Row, 1976).

23 See Jachec, *Philosophy and Politics*, pp. 1–16.

24 Ibid., pp. 184ff.

25 B. Alan Bowness, "The American invasion and the British response," *Studio International* clxxiii/890 (June 1967), pp. 285–93.

26 On the reception of American abstract expressionism in West Germany, see Kurt Winkler, "II. Documenta '59, Kunst nach 1945," in *Stationen der Moderne* [exh. cat.], ed. Berlinische Galerie (Berlin: Berlinische Galerie, 1988), pp. 429–30, and Michael Nungesser, "Flammenwerfer der Kunst und tanzender Derwisch. David Alfaro Siqueiros und Jackson Pollock, ihre unterschiedliche Rezeption in Deutschland, Ost und West," in Jürgen Harten et al., *Siqueiros/Pollock Pollock/Siqueiros* [exh. cat.] (Düsseldorf: Städtische Kunsthalle and DuMont, 1995), pp. 83–100.

27 This phrase is taken from Serge Guilbaut, *How New York Stole the Idea of Modern Art: Abstract Expressionism, Freedom, and the Cold War* (Chicago, IL: University of Chicago Press, 1985), an account of the postwar shift of the international art market and its ideological implications for visual modernism.

28 Jachec has explored this shift in her chapter "A new radicalism and the counter-enlightenment." See Jachec, *Philosophy and Politics*, pp. 105–56.

29 See the chapter "The discrediting of collectivist ideology," in ibid., pp. 17–61.

30 See ibid., pp. 219ff.

31 On the Cold War aspects of Immendorff and Schönebeck see Claudia Mesch, "*Bonjour Monsieur Courbet*: realist painting and the defector dialectic," in *Modern Art at the Berlin Wall: Demarcating Culture in the Cold War Germanys* (London: I.B.Tauris, 2009), pp. 104–61.

32 See a number of books by Groys including *The Total Art of Stalinism: Avant-Garde, Aesthetic Dictatorship, and Beyond* (Princeton, NJ: Princeton University Press, 1992).

Chapter 2 · Post-Colonial Identity and the Civil-Rights Movement

1 Chika Okeke, "Modern African art," in *The Short Century: Independence and Liberation Movements in Africa, 1945–1994* [exh. cat.], ed. Okwui Enwezor (New York, NY: Prestel, 2001), p. 29.

2 Ibid., p. 30.

3 On this idea see Olu Oguibe, "'We were there too': the true location of Ernest Mancoba's modernism," in *Documenta Magazine No. 1 2007: Modernity?* [exh. cat.] (Cologne: Taschen, 2008), pp. 138–9.

4 Okwui Enwezor, "The short century: independence and liberation movements in Africa 1945–1994, an introduction," in *The Short Century: Independence and Liberation Movements in Africa 1945–1994* [exh. cat.], ed. Okwui Enwezor (New York, NY: Prestel, 2001), p. 12.

5 Ibid., pp. 12–13.

6 See also Henry Glassie, *Prince Twins Seven-Seven: His Art, His Life in Nigeria, His Exile in America* (Bloomington and Indianapolis, IN: Indiana University Press, 2010).

7 See Okeke, "Modern African art," p. 33

8 "Art and freedom," *The Grove Encyclopedia of Islamic Art and Architecture*, Vol. 2 (Oxford: Oxford University Press, 2009), p. 226.

9 See Okeke, "Modern African art," p. 34.

10 See Mary Schmidt Campbell, "Tradition and conflict: images of a turbulent decade 1963–1973," in *Tradition and Conflict: Images of a Turbulent Decade 1963–1973* [exh. cat.] (New York, NY: Studio Museum, 1985), pp. 45–68.

11 See Paul Von Blum, "Charles White: an artist for humanity's sake," *The Journal of Pan African Studies* iii/4 (December 2009), pp. 27–36.

12 Campbell, "Tradition and conflict," p. 79.

13 See also Steve Cannon et al., *David Hammons: Rousing the Rubble* [exh. cat.] (Cambridge, MA: MIT Press and New York, NY: ICA, 1991).

14 See "Frédéric Bruly Bouabré," *Documenta 11_Platform 5: Exhibition* [exh. cat.], ed. Okwui Enwezor et al. (Ostfildern-Ruit: Hatje Cantz, 2002), pp 208–11.

15 On Adéagbo see Kasper König, Homi Bhabha, and Viktoria Schmidt-Linsenhoff, *DC: Georges Adéagbo* [exh. cat.] (Cologne: König, 2004).

Chapter 3 · The Anti-War and Peace Movements

1 Lucy R. Lippard, *Get the Message? A Decade of Art for Social Change* (New York, NY: E.P. Dutton, 1984), p. 2.

2 On the *Peace Tower* see also Francis Frascina, "'There' and 'here'; 'then' and 'now': the Los Angeles artists' Tower of Protest (1966) and its legacy," in *Art, Politics and Dissent: Aspects of the Art Left in Sixties America* (Manchester: Manchester University Press, 1999), pp. 57–107.

3 See Irving Petlin, Mark di Suvero, and Rirkrit Tiravanija, "1000 Words: Peace Tower," *Artforum* xliv/7 (March 2006), pp. 252–7.

4 On David Davis' art see Claudia Mesch, "A discipline for modern urban space: David E. Davis's public sculptures since 1975," in *David E. Davis: Artist and Humanist, Sculpture 1967–2002* (Cleveland, OH: Sculpture Center Press, 2003), pp. 22–7.

5 See Marc Wiznia, "Protests marked Vietnam war era at Yale," *Yale Daily News* (March 28, 2001).

6 See Mark Rosenthal, "'Unbridled' monuments; or, how Claes Oldenburg set out to change the world," in Marla Prather et al., *Claes Oldenburg: An Anthology* [exh. cat.] (New York, NY: Guggenheim Museum, 1995), pp. 255–62.

7 See Germano Celant, "The sculptor versus the architect," in Marla Prather et al., *Claes Oldenburg: An Anthology* [exh. cat.] (New York, NY: Guggenheim Museum, 1995), p. 380.

8 The hotel opened the room to the public to commemorate the 40th anniversary of the performance in 2009. See "Amsterdam remembers John and Yoko's bed-in," *NRC Handelsblad* (March 19, 2009).

9 On the *Bed-In* see Midori Yoshimoto, *Into Performance: Japanese Women Artists in New York* (New Brunswick, NJ: Rutgers University Press, 2005), pp. 110ff.

10 See "John Lennon on The David Frost Show 1969 part 1" and "John Lennon on The David Frost Show 1969 part 2." Available at http://www.youtube.com/watch?v=g2jKFZVIQv0 and http://www.youtube.com/watch?v=e6neIqDt8rU (accessed February 6, 2013).

11 On the peace sign see Ken Kolsbun, and Michael S. Sweeney, *Peace: The Biography of a Symbol* (Washington DC: National Geographic, 2008).

12 The performance is described in Lucy R. Lippard, *A Different War: Vietnam in Art* (Seattle, WA: Whatcom Museum of History and Art and Real Comet Press, 1990), pp. 24–6. See also Jon Hendricks and Jean Toche, *GAAG: The Guerrilla Art Action Group, 1969–1976: A Selection* (1978; New York, NY: Printed Matter Inc., 2011). My thanks to Jon Hendricks for clarifying aspects of this important performance.

13 See Katy Kline and Helaine Posner, eds, *Leon Golub and Nancy Spero: War and Memory* [exh. cat.] (Cambridge, MA: MIT List Visual Arts Center, 1994).

14 Friedrich Wilhelm Nietzsche, *The Gay Science*, trans. Josefine Nauckhoff and Adrian Del Caro (Cambridge: Cambridge University Press, 2001), p. 177.

15 Susan Sontag, "Looking at war: photography's view of devastation and death," *New Yorker* (December 9, 2002), pp. 82–98; revised and published as *Regarding the Pain of Others* (New York, NY: Farrar, Straus & Giroux, 2003).

16 See Vicki Goldberg, "News photographs as catalysts: the television era," in *The Power of Photography: How Photographs Changed Our Lives* (New York: Abbeville Press, 1991), pp. 216–51. See especially pp. 226–46.

17 See Hal Foster, "Who's afraid of the neo-avant-garde?," in *The Return of the Real: The Avant-Garde at the End of the Century* (Cambridge, MA: MIT Press, 1996), pp. 1–34.

18 The poster and demonstration are discussed in Lippard, *Get the Message?*, pp. 8ff., and in Francis Frascina, "The politics of representation," in *Modernism in Dispute: Art since the Forties*, ed. Paul Wood (New Haven, CT: Yale University Press, 1993), pp. 106–9.

19 Lippard, *A Different War*, pp. 27–8.

20 This description is available at http://hadjithomasjoreige.com (accessed February 6, 2013). On their art see also Peter Weibel and Bruno Latour, eds, *Iconoclash* [exh. cat.] (Karlsruhe: ZKM Zentrum für Kunst und Medientechnologie, and Cambridge, MA: MIT Press, 2002).

21 See the Atlas Group Archive website. Available at http://www.theatlasgroup.org/ (accessed February 6, 2013).

22 See Carolyn Christov-Bakargiev et al., *Documenta (13): The Guidebook* [exh. cat.] (Ostfildern-Ruit: Hatje Cantz, 2012), p. 400.

23 See Laura Hoptman et al., *54th Carnegie International 2004–2005* [exh. cat.] (Pittsburgh, PA: Museum of Art, Carnegie Institute, 2004), pp. 142–4.

24 Hal Foster, "Vision quest: the cinema of Harun Farocki," *Artforum* xliii/3 (November 2004), pp. 156–61.

Chapter 4 · Feminisms

1 See, for example, Maura Reilly and Linda Nochlin, eds, *Global Feminisms: New Directions in Contemporary Art* [exh. cat.] (London and New York, NY: Merrell, 2007).

2 Linda Nochlin, "Why have there been no great women artists?," *ARTnews* (January 1971), pp. 22–39. Available at http://www.fehe.org/index.php?id=686 (accessed February 6, 2013).

3 Ibid., p. 39.

4 Judy Chicago and Miriam Schapiro, "A feminist art program," *Art Journal* xxxi/1 (Autumn 1971), pp. 48–9.

5 See Arlene Raven, "Womanhouse," in *The Power of Feminist Art: The American Movement of the 1970s, History and Impact*, eds Norma Broude and Mary D. Garrard (New York, NY: Abrams, 1994), pp. 48–64.

6 As has been widely discussed in, for example, Amelia Jones, ed., *Sexual Politics: Judy Chicago's* Dinner Party *in Feminist Art History* [exh. cat.] (Berkeley, CA: University of California Press, 1998) and Helen Molesworth, "Cleaning up in the 1970s: the work of Judy Chicago, Mary Kelly and Mierle Laderman Ukeles," in *Rewriting Conceptual Art*, eds Michael Newman and Jon Bird (London: Reaktion Books, 1999), pp. 107–22.

7 See Gloria Feman Orenstein, "Recovering her story: feminist artists reclaim the great goddess," in *The Power of Feminist Art: The American Movement of the 1970s, History and Impact*, eds Norma Broude and Mary D. Garrard (New York, NY: Abrams, 1994), p. 184.

8 Notably Lucy R. Lippard, "The pains and pleasures of rebirth: European and American women's body art," in *From the Center: Feminist Essays on Women's Art* (New York, NY: E.P. Dutton, 1976), pp. 121–38.

9 Cited in Amelia Jones, "The rhetoric of the pose: Hannah Wilke and the radical narcissism of feminist body art," in *Body Art/Performing the Subject* (Minneapolis, MN: University of Minnesota Press, 1998), p. 183.

10 See ibid.

11 Joan Jonas, "Panel remarks," *The New Television: A Public/Private Art*, eds Douglas Davis and Allison Simmons (Cambridge, MA: MIT Press, 1977), p. 71.

12 These performances and others are described in Elsa Longhauser et al., *Valie Export: Ob/De+Con(Struction)* [exh. cat.] (Philadelphia, PA: Goldie Paley Gallery, 1999).

13 On this performance and her others see Dan Cameron et al., *Carolee Schneemann: Up to and Including Her Limits* [exh. cat.] (New York, NY: New Museum, 1997).

14 On this work see Mary Kelly, *Post-Partum Document* (Boston, MA: Routledge & Kegan Paul, 1983).

15 See Trinh T. Minh-ha, "Difference: 'a special Third World women issue,'" in *Woman Native Other* (Bloomington, IN: Indiana University Press, 1989), pp. 79–116.

16 Ibid., pp. 102–4.

17 On Neshat's work see Eleanor Heartney, "Shirin Neshat: living between cultures," in Eleanor Heartney et al., *After the Revolution: Women Who Transformed Contemporary Art* (Munich and New York, NY: Prestel, 2007), pp. 230–51.

18 See Thierry N'Landu, "Le Groupe Amos," in *Documenta 11_Platform 5: Exhibition* [exh. cat.], ed. Okwui Enwezor et al. (Ostfildern-Ruit: Hatje Cantz, 2002), p. 102.

19 See Okwui Enwezor, "The production of social space as artwork: protocols of community in the work of Le Groupe Amos and Huit Facettes," in *Collectivism After Modernism: The Art of Social Imagination after 1945*, eds Blake Stimson and Gregory Sholette (Minneapolis, MN: University of Minnesota Press, 2007), pp. 223–52.

20 The flyer is reproduced in ibid., p. 237.

21 See bell hooks, *Feminism is for Everybody: Passionate Politics* (Cambridge, MA: South End Press, 2000).

Chapter 5 · Gay Identity/Queer Art

1 Herbert Marcuse, *Eros and Civilization: A Philosophical Inquiry into Freud* (1955; Boston, MA: Beacon Press, 1966), p. 50.

2   Kenneth E. Silver, "Modes of disclosure: the construction of gay identity and the rise of pop art," in *Hand-Painted Pop: American Art in Transition 1955–62*, ed. Russell Ferguson (New York, NY: Rizzoli and Museum of Contemporary Art, Los Angeles, 1992), pp. 179–204.

3   See Mimi Swartz, "Living the good lie," *New York Times Magazine* (June 19, 2011).

4   See Thomas Crow, "Saturday disasters: trace and reference in early Warhol," *Art in America* (May 1987), pp. 128–36.

5   See Richard Meyer, "Most wanted men: homoeroticism and the secret of censorship in early Warhol," in *Outlaw Representation: Censorship and Homosexuality in Twentieth-Century American Art* (Boston, MA: Beacon Press, 2002), pp. 95–158.

6   Ibid., pp. 128–35.

7   Ibid., pp. 150–3.

8   On Fassbinder see Laurence Kardish, ed., *Rainer Werner Fassbinder* [exh. cat.] (New York, NY: Museum of Modern Art, 1997) and Al LaValley, "The gay liberation of Rainer Werner Fassbinder: male subjectivity, male bodies, male lovers," *New German Critique* 63 (Autumn 1994), pp. 108–37.

9   See Kaja Silverman, "Masochistic ecstasy and the ruination of masculinity in Fassbinder's cinema," in *Male Subjectivity at the Margins* (London and New York, NY: Routledge, 1992), pp. 214–96.

10 Thomas Elsaesser, "The new German cinema's Germany," in *New German Cinema: A History* (New Brunswick, NJ: Rutgers University Press, 1989), p. 228.

11 On this group see Kynaston McShine, ed. *BerlinArt* [exh. cat.] (New York, NY: Museum of Modern Art and Prestel, 1987).

12 This claim was made by Benjamin Buchloh in "Figures of authority, ciphers of regression: notes on the return of representation in European painting," *October* 16 (Spring 1981), pp. 39–68.

13 Most of Cihlarz's oeuvre can be found on the database of his extensive website: http://www.salomeberlin.de (accessed February 6, 2013).

14 On these paintings see Donald Kuspit, "The stranger in the city: Rainer Fetting's sense of self," in *Rainer Fetting Selbst/Self Portraits 1973–1998* [exh. cat.] (Berlin: Neuer Berliner Kunstverein and Nicolaische Verlagsbuchhandlung, 1999), pp. 24–8.

15 An excellent timeline of the development of the disease can be found at the website for the 2006 PBS documentary *Frontline: The Age of Aids*.

Available at http://www.pbs.org/wgbh/pages/frontline/aids (accessed February 6, 2013).

16 Douglas Crimp, "AIDS: cultural analysis/cultural activism," *October* 43 (Winter 1987), p. 3.

17 Jesse Green, "When political art mattered," *New York Times Magazine* (December 7, 2003).

18 See the ACT UP Oral History Project website. Available at http://www.actuporalhistory.org (accessed February 6, 2013).

19 Douglas Crimp, "Melancholia and moralism: an introduction," in *Melancholia and Moralism: Essays on AIDS and Queer Politics* (Cambridge, MA: MIT Press, 2002), p. 26.

20 On Wojnarowicz see the excellent overview in Peter F. Spooner, "David Wojnarowicz: a portrait of the artist as X-ray technician," in *Suspended License: Censorship and the Visual Arts*, ed. Elizabeth C. Childs (Seattle, WA: University of Washington Press, 1997), pp. 333–65.

21 Ibid., pp. 344–6.

Chapter 6 · Environmental Art

1 Paul Schmelzer, "Paul Schmelzer interviews Rirkrit Tiravanija," in *Land, Art: A Cultural Ecology Handbook*, ed. Max Andrews (London: RSA, 2006), p. 60.

2 See Amy Franceschini, "Artist-as-citizen/scientist-as-citizen: Future-farmers interviews Jonathan Meuser," in *Land, Art: A Cultural Ecology Handbook*, ed. Max Andrews (London: RSA, 2006), pp. 134–7.

3 See Jack Burnham, "Systems esthetics," *Artforum* vii/1 (September 1968), pp. 30–5. Available at http://monoskop.org/images/e/e6/Burnham_Jack_1968_Systems_Esthetics.pdf (accessed February 6, 2013).

4 Aldo Leopold, *A Sand County Almanac, and Sketches Here and There* (New York, NY: Oxford University Press, 1949), p. 204.

5 See Rachel Carson, *Silent Spring* (Boston, MA: Houghton Mifflin, 1962).

6 Hans Haacke (January 1965 manifesto), as cited in Jack Burnham, "Hans Haacke—wind and water sculpture," rpt. in *Land and Environmental Art*, eds Jeffrey Kastner and Brian Wallis (London and New York, NY: Phaidon Press, 1998), p. 252.

7 See Robert Smithson, "A tour of the monuments of Passaic, New Jersey,"

in *Robert Smithson: The Collected Writings*, ed. Jack Flam (Berkeley and Los Angeles, CA: University of California, 1996), pp. 68–74.

8   See Jeffrey Kastner, "There, now: from Robert Smithson to Guantanamo," in *Land, Art: A Cultural Ecology Handbook*, ed. Max Andrews (London: RSA, 2006), pp. 22–32.

9   Robert Smithson, "Proposal (1972)," in *Robert Smithson: The Collected Writings*, ed. Jack Flam (Berkeley and Los Angeles, CA: University of California, 1996), p. 354, as cited in Kastner, "There, now," p. 22.

10 Alan Sonfist, "Natural phenomena as public monuments" [statement delivered at the Metropolitan Museum of Art, New York, 1968], rpt. in *Land and Environmental Art*, eds Jeffrey Kastner and Brian Wallis (London and New York, NY: Phaidon Press, 1998), p. 258.

11 The first part of a lecture by Clare Patey, entitled "Feeding the world: the ultimate design challenge," can be viewed online. Available at http:// www.youtube.com/watch?v=DJ-KNh5l_BE (accessed February 6, 2013).

12 See the Harrison Studio, the artists' extensive website. Available at http:// theharrisonstudio.net/ (accessed February 6, 2013).

13 On Beuys' project see Lynne Cooke, "7000 Oaks" (New York, NY: Dia Art Foundation, 1995–2004). Available at http://www.diaart.org/sites/ main/7000oaks/essay.html (accessed February 6, 2013).

14 See the account in Thomas Niemeyer, "Die Arbeit des Koordinationsbüros 7000 Eichen," in *Joseph Beuys Documenta-Arbeit*, eds Veit Loers and Pia Witzmann (Ostfildern-Ruit: Edition Cantz, 1993), pp. 228–38.

15 Richard Demarco, "Conversations with artists," *Studio International* cxcv/996 (September 1982), p. 46.

16 See Niemeyer, "Die Arbeit," p. 236.

17 See Carola Platzek, "Ines Doujak: the continuity of colonialist practices," trans. Jeanne Haunschild, in *Documenta Magazine No. 2 2007: Life!* (Cologne: Taschen, 2007), pp. 136–41.

18 On the memorial see the Remember Saro-Wiwa website. Available at http://remembersarowiwa.com (accessed February 6, 2013).

19 See Svetlana Alpers, "The studio, the laboratory, and the vexations of art," in *Picturing Science, Producing Art*, eds Peter Galison and Caroline Jones (New York, NY: Routledge, 1998), pp. 401–17.

20 See Beatriz da Costa, "PigeonBlog" (2006). Available at http:// beatrizdacosta.net/Pigeonblog/statement.php (accessed February 6, 2013).

21 See Emily Gertz, "Pigeons write a smog blog," *Plenty* (July 2006). Available at http://www.mnn.com/earth-matters/climate-change/stories/pigeons-write-a-smog-blog (accessed February 6, 2013).

22 Superfund is the popular title of a US program that deals with sites containing abandoned hazardous waste. It was initiated by the Comprehensive Environmental Response, Compensation, and Liability Act of 1980, and gives the EPA the authority to enforce and oversee the cleanup of these sites by those responsible, or to collect fines that make such a cleanup possible.

Chapter 7 · Anti-Globalization

1 See Terry Smith, "Introduction: the contemporaneity question," in *Antinomies of Art and Culture: Modernity, Postmodernity, Contemporaneity* (Durham, NC: Duke University Press, 2008), pp. 1–22.

2 Thomas Hirschhorn, "Text for Flugplatz Welt/World Airport," in Thomas Hirschhorn et al., *Thomas Hirschhorn* (London: Phaidon Press, 2004), pp. 133–4.

3 See Achille Bonito Oliva, *Alighiero Boetti: Bringing the World into Art 1993/1962* [exh. cat.] (Milan: Electa, 2009).

4 Mierle Laderman Ukeles, "Maintenance art manifesto" (1969), rpt. in *Theories and Documents of Contemporary Art*, eds Kristine Stiles and Peter Selz (Berkeley, CA: University of California Press, 1996), p. 622.

5 Mierle Laderman Ukeles, "Sanitation manifesto!" (1984), rpt. in *Theories and Documents of Contemporary Art*, eds Kristine Stiles and Peter Selz (Berkeley, CA: University of California Press, 1996), p. 624.

6 Ibid., pp. 624–5.

7 United Nations, "45/158: International convention on the protection of the rights of all migrant workers and members of their families." Available at http://www.un.org/documents/ga/res/45/a45r158.htm (accessed February 6, 2013).

8 On the film see also Klaus Ottmann, "From the other side (*Le l'autre côté*)," in *Chantal Akerman: Moving through Time and Space* [exh. cat.], ed. Terrie Sultan (Houston, TX: Blaffer Gallery and D.A.P./Distributed Art Publishers, 2008), pp. 28–39.

9 The project is detailed in Rudy Adler, Victoria Criado, and Brett Huneycutt,

Border Film Project: Photos by Migrants & Minutemen on the US–Mexico Border (New York, NY: Abrams, 2007).

10 See Chris Kraus, "Border film project show," *Artforum* xlv/6 (February 2007), pp. 256–7.

11 See, for example, Claire Bishop, "Antagonism and relational aesthetics," *October* 110 (Fall 2004), pp. 51–79.

12 On Sierra's art see Teresa Margolles, "Santiago Sierra" [interview], *Bomb* 86 (Winter 2004), pp. 62–9.

13 As recounted by various Factory alumni in the film *Superstar: The Life and Times of Andy Warhol* (1990), directed by Chuck Workman. See also Caroline A. Jones, "Andy Warhol's Factory, 'commonism,' and the business art business," in *Machine in the Studio: Constructing the Postwar American Artist* (Chicago, IL: University of Chicago Press, 1996), pp. 189–267.

14 On this point see Bishop, "Antagonism and relational aesthetics," p. 70.

15 See the Multiplicity website. Available at http://www.multiplicity.it (accessed February 6, 2013).

16 On Jaar's strategies see Abigail Solomon-Godeau, "Lament of the images: Alfredo Jaar and the ethics of representation," *Aperture* 181 (Winter 2005), pp. 36–47.

17 On Jaar's views regarding war see Alfredo Jaar, *Alfredo Jaar: Geography = War* [exh. cat.] (Richmond, VA: Virginia Museum of the Arts, 1991).

18 See the Yes Men website. Available at http://theyesmen.org (accessed February 6, 2013).

19 See the Radical Software Group, *Carnivore* [software application, 2001–]. Available at http://r-s-g.org/carnivore (accessed February 6, 2013).

20 On this project see also Matthew Mirapaul, "Cybersnooping for sounds and images, not suspects," *New York Times* (October 1, 2001). Available at http://www.nytimes.com/2001/10/01/arts/arts-online-cybersnooping-for-sounds-and-images-not-suspects.html?pagewanted=all (accessed February 6, 2013).

21 The work is available at http://www.snibbe.com/projects/interactive/fuel (accessed February 6, 2013).

22 As cited in Mirapaul, Matthew, "Cybersnooping."

23 See the OPUS (Open Platform for Unlimited Signification) website. Previously available at http://www.opuscommons.net/templates/doc/index.html (accessed June 12, 2012; link no longer working).

Epilogue · protestAR: #OCCUPYWALLSTREET and #arOCCUPYWALLSTREET

1 On these statistics see US Center on Budget and Policy Priorities, "Tax data show richest 1 percent took a hit in 2008, but income remained highly concentrated at the top: recent gains of bottom 90 percent wiped out." Available at http://www.cbpp.org/cms/index.cfm?fa=view&id=3309 (accessed February 6, 2013). See also US Congressional Budget Office, *Trends in the Distribution of Household Income Between 1979 and 2007* (Washington DC: Congress of the United States and the Congressional Budget Office, 2011).

2 Michael Kimmelman, "In protest, the power of place," *New York Times* (October 16, 2011).

3 On the group see the AR Occupy Wall Street website. Available at http://protestars.wordpress.com (accessed February 6, 2013).

4 Bruce Sterling, "Augmented reality: AR uninvited at MOMA NYC," *Wired* (October 6, 2010). Available at http://www.wired.com/beyond_the_beyond/2010/10/augmented-reality-ar-uninvited-at-moma-nyc (accessed February 6, 2013).

further reading

General

Boime, Albert, *Art in an Age of Revolution, 1750–1800* (Chicago, IL: University of Chicago Press, 1987).

——*Art in an Age of Counterrevolution, 1815–1848* (Chicago, IL: University of Chicago Press, 2004).

Bradley, Will, and Charles Esche, *Art and Social Change: A Critical Reader* (London: Tate Publishing, 2007).

Clark, Timothy J., *Farewell to an Idea: Episodes from a History of Modernism* (New Haven, CT: Yale University Press, 1999).

Clark, Toby, *Art and Propaganda in the Twentieth Century* (London: Calmann and King Ltd., 1997).

Felshin, Nina, ed., *But Is It Art?: The Spirit of Art as Activism* (Seattle, WA: Bay Press, 1994).

Foster, Hal, *The Return of the Real: The Avant-Garde at the End of the Century* (Cambridge, MA: MIT Press, 1996).

Mouffe, Chantal, *On the Political* (New York, NY: Routledge, 2005).

Rose, Margaret, "The politicization of art criticism: Heine's 1831 portrayal of Delacroix's *Liberté* and its aftermath," *Monatshefte* lxxiii/4 (Winter 1981), pp. 405–14.

Roth, Moira, "The aesthetic of indifference," *Artforum* xvi/3 (November 1977), pp. 46–53.

Smith, Terry, "Introduction: the contemporaneity question," in *Antinomies of Art and Culture: Modernity, Postmodernity, Contemporaneity* (Durham, NC: Duke University Press, 2008), pp. 1–22.

Stimson, Blake, and Gregory Sholette, eds, *Collectivism after Modernism: The Art of Social Imagination After 1945* (Minneapolis, MN: University of Minnesota Press, 2007).

Texte zur Kunst 80: Political Art? (December 2010).

Zantop, Susanne, ed., *Paintings on the Move: Heinrich Heine and the Visual Arts* (London and Lincoln, NE: University of Nebraska Press, 1989).

Chapter 1 · State-Sponsored Art During the Cold War

Barr, Jr., Alfred H., "Is modern art communistic?," *New York Times* (December 14, 1952).

Bowness, B. Alan, "The American invasion and the British response," *Studio International* clxxiii/890 (June 1967), pp. 285–93.

Caute, David, *The Dancer Defects: The Struggle for Cultural Supremacy During the Cold War* (Oxford: Oxford University Press, 2003).

Collier, Delinda J., *Art in a State of Emergency: Figuring Angolan Nationalism, 1953–2007* [Ph.D. dissertation, Emory University, 2010].

Enwezor, Okwui, ed., *The Short Century: Independence and Liberation Movements in Africa 1945–1994* [exh. cat.] (New York, NY: Prestel, 2001).

Frascina, Francis, "The politics of representation," in *Modernism in Dispute: Art since the Forties*, ed. Paul Wood (New Haven, CT: Yale University Press, 1993), pp. 77–169.

——*Art, Politics and Dissent: Aspects of the Art Left in Sixties America* (Manchester: Manchester University Press, 1999).

——"Introduction," in *Pollock and After: The Critical Debate*, ed. Francis Frascina (London and New York, NY: Routledge, 2000), pp. 113–29.

Gale, Matthew, "London and Ferrara, Renato Guttuso," *Burlington Magazine* cxxxviii/1121 (August 1996), pp. 554–6.

Guilbaut, Serge, "Postwar painting games: the rough and the slick," in *Reconstructing Modernism: Art in New York, Paris, and Montreal 1945–1964*, ed. Serge Guilbaut (Cambridge, MA: MIT Press, 1990), pp. 30–84.

Guttuso, Renato, *Guttuso* [exh. cat.] (London: Whitechapel Art Gallery, 1996).

Hyman, James, *The Third Way: Renato Guttuso and Realism in Europe* (London: James Hyman Gallery, 2003). Available at http://www.

jameshymangallery.com/pages/publication/509.html (accessed February 6, 2013).

Jachec, Nancy, *The Philosophy and Politics of Abstract Expressionism, 1940–1960* (Cambridge: Cambridge University Press, 2000).

Mesch, Claudia, *Modern Art at the Berlin Wall: Demarcating Culture in the Cold War Germanys* (London: I.B.Tauris, 2009).

Milde, Brigitta, "Picasso in der DDR," in *Picasso et les femmes* [exh. cat.], eds Ingrid Mössinger and Beate Ritter (New York, NY: Kunstsammlungen Chemnitz, 2002), pp. 372–85.

Moravia, Alberto, *Man as an End: A Defense of Humanism*, trans. Bernard Wall (New York, NY: Farrar, Straus & Giroux, 1965).

The New American Painting [exh. cat.] (New York, NY: Museum of Modern Art, 1959).

Nungesser, Michael, "Flammenwerfer der Kunst und tanzender Derwisch. David Alfaro Siqueiros und Jackson Pollock, ihre unterschiedliche Rezeption in Deutschland, Ost und West," in Jürgen Harten et al., *Siqueiros/Pollock Pollock/Siqueiros* [exh. cat.] (Düsseldorf: Städtische Kunsthalle and DuMont, 1995), pp. 83–100.

Utley, Gertje, *Picasso: The Communist Years* (New Haven, CT: Yale University Press, 2000).

Wilson, Sarah, "'La beauté révolutionnaire'? Réalisme socialiste and French painting 1935–1954," *Oxford Art Journal* iii/2 (October 1980), pp. 61–9.

Winkler, Kurt, "II. Documenta '59, Kunst nach 1945," in *Stationen der Moderne* [exh. cat.], ed. Berlinische Galerie (Berlin: Berlinische Galerie, 1988), pp. 429–30.

Zhdanov, Andrei Aleksandrovich, *Essays on Literature, Philosophy, and Music* (New York, NY: International Publishers, 1950).

Chapter 2 · Post-Colonial Identity and the Civil-Rights Movement

Archive Adéagbo [website]. Available at http://www.jointadventures.org/adeagbo/archive.htm (accessed February 6, 2013).

CAACART, Contemporary African Art Collection [website]. Available at http://www.caacart.com/artist_page.html (accessed February 6, 2013).

Campbell, Mary Schmidt, "Tradition and conflict: images of a turbulent decade

1963–1973," in *Tradition and Conflict: Images of a Turbulent Decade 1963–1973* [exh. cat.] (New York, NY: Studio Museum, 1985), pp. 45–68.

Cannon, Steve, et al., *David Hammons: Rousing the Rubble* [exh. cat.] (Cambridge, MA: MIT Press and New York, NY: ICA, 1991).

Martin Riches, William T., *The Civil Rights Movement: Struggle and Resistance*, 2nd ed. (New York, NY: Palgrave Macmillan, 2003).

Oguibe, Olu, "'We were there too': the true location of Ernest Mancoba's modernism," in *Documenta Magazine No. 1 2007: Modernity?* [exh. cat.] (Cologne: Taschen, 2008), pp. 138–9.

Okeke, Chika, "Modern African art," in *The Short Century: Independence and Liberation Movements in Africa, 1945–1994* [exh. cat.], ed. Okwui Enwezor (New York, NY: Prestel, 2001), pp. 29–36.

Powell, Richard J., *Black Art and Culture in the 20th Century* (London: Thames & Hudson, 1997).

Pruitt, Sharon, "The spiral group: defining African American art during the civil rights movement," in *Engines of the Black Power Movement: Essays on the Influence of Civil Rights Actions, Arts, and Islam*, ed. James L. Conyers, Jr. (Jefferson, NC: McFarland & Company, 2007), pp. 5–20.

Sontag, Deborah, "Headless bodies from a bottomless imagination," *New York Times* (June 17, 2009).

Thompson, Bridget, "Open letter regarding 'The African Spiritual Expression of Ernest Mancoba,'" *Third Text* xix/4 (July 2005), pp. 420–2.

Von Blum, Paul, "Charles White: an artist for humanity's sake," *The Journal of Pan African Studies* iii/4 (December 2009), pp. 27–36.

Chapter 3 · The Anti-War and Peace Movements

"Amsterdam remembers John and Yoko's bed-in," *NRC Handelsblad* (March 19, 2009).

The Atlas Group Archive [website]. Available at http://www.theatlasgroup. org (accessed February 6, 2013).

Bird, Jon, *Leon Golub* [exh. cat.] (London: Reaktion Books, 2000).

Cotter, Suzanne, ed., *Out of Beirut* [exh. cat.] (Oxford: JRP/Ringier/Modern Art, 2007).

Ebony, David, *Botero: Abu Ghraib* (New York, NY: Prestel, 2006).

Foster, Hal, "Vision quest: the cinema of Harun Farocki," *Artforum* xliii/3 (November 2004), pp. 156–61.

Goldberg, Vicki, *The Power of Photography: How Photographs Changed Our Lives* (New York, NY: Abbeville Press, 1991).

Hendricks, Jon, and Jean Toche, *GAAG: The Guerrilla Art Action Group, 1969–1976: A Selection* (1978; New York, NY: Printed Matter Inc., 2011).

Kline, Katy, and Helaine Posner, eds, *Leon Golub and Nancy Spero: War and Memory* [exh. cat.] (Cambridge, MA: MIT List Visual Arts Center, 1994).

Kolsbun, Ken, and Michael S. Sweeney, *Peace: The Biography of a Symbol* (Washington DC: National Geographic, 2008).

Kuspit, Donald, *The Existential/Activist Painter: The Example of Leon Golub* (New Brunswick, NJ: Rutgers University Press, 1986).

Lippard, Lucy R., *Get the Message? A Decade of Art for Social Change* (New York, NY: E.P. Dutton, 1984).

——*A Different War: Vietnam in Art* (Seattle, WA: Whatcom Museum of History and Art and Real Comet Press, 1990).

Petlin, Irving, Mark di Suvero, and Rirkrit Tiravanija, "1000 Words: Peace Tower," *Artforum* xliv/7 (March 2006), pp. 252–7.

Prather, Marla, et al., *Claes Oldenburg: An Anthology* [exh. cat.] (New York, NY: Guggenheim Museum, 1995).

Sontag, Susan, "Looking at war: photography's view of devastation and death," *New Yorker* (December 9, 2002), pp. 82–98.

——*Regarding the Pain of Others* (New York, NY: Farrar, Straus & Giroux, 2003).

Weibel, Peter, and Bruno Latour, eds, *Iconoclash* [exh. cat.] (Karlsruhe: ZKM Zentrum für Kunst und Medientechnologie, and Cambridge, MA: MIT Press, 2002).

Wiznia, Marc, "Protests marked Vietnam war era at Yale," *Yale Daily News* (March 28, 2001).

Chapter 4 · Feminisms

Broude, Norma, and Mary D. Garrard, eds, *The Power of Feminist Art: The American Movement of the 1970s, History and Impact* (New York, NY: Abrams, 1994).

Chicago, Judy, and Miriam Schapiro, "A feminist art program," *Art Journal* xxxi/1 (Autumn 1971), pp. 48–9.

Enwezor, Okwui, "The production of social space as artwork: protocols of community in the work of Le Groupe Amos and Huit Facettes," in *Collectivism After Modernism: The Art of Social Imagination After 1945,* eds Blake Stimson and Gregory Sholette (Minneapolis, MN: University of Minnesota Press, 2007), pp. 223–52.

hooks, bell, *Feminism is for Everybody: Passionate Politics* (Cambridge, MA: South End Press, 2000).

Jonas, Joan, "Panel remarks," *The New Television: A Public/Private Art*, eds Douglas Davis and Allison Simmons (Cambridge, MA: MIT Press, 1977), p. 71.

Jones, Amelia, "Power and feminist art (history)," *Art History* xviii/3 (September 1995), pp. 435–43.

——"The rhetoric of the pose: Hannah Wilke and the radical narcissism of feminist body art," in *Body Art/Performing the Subject* (Minneapolis, MN: University of Minnesota Press, 1998), pp. 151–96.

Jones, Amelia, ed., *Sexual Politics: Judy Chicago's Dinner Party in Feminist Art History* [exh. cat.] (Berkeley, CA: University of California Press, 1998).

Kelly, Mary, *Post-Partum Document* (Boston, MA: Routledge & Kegan Paul, 1983).

Longhauser, Elsa, et al., *Valie Export: Ob/De+Con(Struction)* [exh. cat.] (Philadelphia, PA: Goldie Paley Gallery, 1999).

Mark, Lisa Gabrielle, ed., *Wack! Art and the Feminist Revolution* [exh. cat.] (Cambridge, MA: MIT Press, 2007).

Molesworth, Helen, "Cleaning up in the 1970s: the work of Judy Chicago, Mary Kelly and Mierle Laderman Ukeles," in *Rewriting Conceptual Art*, eds Michael Newman and Jon Bird (London: Reaktion Books, 1999), pp. 107–22.

N'Landu, Thierry, "Le Groupe Amos," in *Documenta 11_Platform 5: Exhibition* [exh. cat.], ed. Okwui Enwezor et al. (Ostfilcern-Ruit: Hatje Cantz, 2002), p. 102.

Nochlin, Linda, "Why have there been no great women artists?," *ARTnews* (January 1971), pp. 22–39. Available at http://www.fehe.org/index.php?id=686 (accessed February 6, 2013).

Pollock, Griselda, "Screening the Seventies: sexuality and representation in feminist practice—a Brechtian perspective," in *Vision and Difference: Femininity, Feminism and the Histories of Art* (London and New York, NY: Routledge, 1988), pp. 155–99.

Reilly, Maura, and Linda Nochlin, eds, *Global Feminisms: New Directions in Contemporary Art* [exh. cat.] (London and New York, NY: Merrell, 2007).

Trinh T. Minh-ha, *Woman Native Other* (Bloomington, IN: Indiana University Press, 1989).

Chapter 5 · Gay Identity/Queer Art

Blessing, Jennifer, *Rrose is a Rrose is a Rrose: Gender Performance in Photography* [exh. cat.] (New York, NY: Abrams and Guggenheim Museum, 1997).

Crimp, Douglas, and Adam Rolston, *AIDS Demo/Graphics* (Seattle, WA: Bay Press, 1990).

———*Melancholia and Moralism: Essays on AIDS and Queer Politics* (Cambridge, MA: MIT Press, 2002).

Crow, Thomas, "Saturday disasters: trace and reference in early Warhol," *Art in America* (May 1987), pp. 128–36.

Escoffier, Jeffrey, "Herbert Marcuse," *glbtq: An Encyclopedia of Gay, Lesbian, Bisexual, Transgender, and Queer Culture*. Available at www.glbtq.com/social-sciences/marcuse_h.html (accessed February 6, 2013).

Frontline: The Age of Aids (documentary, 2006). Available at http://www.pbs.org/wgbh/pages/frontline/aids (accessed February 6, 2013).

Green, Jesse, "When political art mattered," *New York Times Magazine* (December 7, 2003).

Kardish, Laurence, ed., *Rainer Werner Fassbinder* [exh. cat.] (New York, NY: Museum of Modern Art, 1997).

Kuspit, Donald, "The stranger in the city: Rainer Fetting's sense of self," in *Rainer Fetting Selbst/Self Portraits 1973–1998* [exh. cat.] (Berlin: Neuer Berliner Kunstverein and Nicolaische Verlagsbuchhandlung, 1999), pp. 24–8.

LaValley, Al, "The gay liberation of Rainer Werner Fassbinder: male subjectivity, male bodies, male lovers," *New German Critique* 63 (Autumn 1994), pp. 108–37.

Marcuse, Herbert, *Eros and Civilization: A Philosophical Inquiry into Freud* (1955; Boston, MA: Beacon Press, 1966).

Meyer, Richard, *Outlaw Representation: Censorship and Homosexuality in Twentieth-Century American Art* (Boston, MA: Beacon Press, 2002).

Sedgwick, Eve, *Epistemology of the Closet* (Berkeley, CA: University of California Press, 1990).

Silver, Kenneth E., "Modes of disclosure: the construction of gay identity and the rise of pop art," in *Hand-Painted Pop: American Art in Transition 1955–62*, ed. Russell Ferguson (New York, NY: Rizzoli and Museum of Contemporary Art, Los Angeles, 1992), pp. 179–204.

Spooner, Peter F., "David Wojnarowicz: a portrait of the artist as X-ray technician," in *Suspended License: Censorship and the Visual Arts*, ed. Elizabeth C. Childs (Seattle, WA: University of Washington Press, 1997), pp. 333–65.

Swartz, Mimi, "Living the good lie," *New York Times Magazine* (June 19, 2011).

Thomsen, Christian Braad, *Fassbinder: The Life and Work of a Provocative Genius*, trans. Martin Chalmers (Minneapolis, MN: University of Minnesota Press, 2004).

Chapter 6 · Environmental Art

Andrews, Max, ed., *Land, Art: A Cultural Ecology Handbook* (London: RSA, 2006).

Boettger, Suzaan, *Earthworks: Art and the Landscape of the Sixties* (Berkeley, CA: University of California Press, 2004).

Burnham, Jack, "Systems esthetics," *Artforum* vii/1 (September 1968), pp. 30–5. Available at http://monoskop.org/images/e/e6/Burnham_Jack_1968_Systems_Esthetics.pdf (accessed February 6, 2013).

Carson, Rachel, *Silent Spring* (Boston, MA: Houghton Mifflin, 1962).

Cooke, Lynne, "7000 Oaks" (New York, NY: Dia Art Foundation, 1995–2004). Available at http://www.diaart.org/sites/main/7000oaks/essay.html (accessed February 6, 2013).

Gertz, Emily, "Pigeons write a smog blog," *Plenty* (July 2006). Available at http://www.mnn.com/earth-matters/climate-change/stories/pigeons-write-a-smog-blog (accessed February 6, 2013).

Groener, Fernando and Rose-Marie Kandler, eds, *7000 Eichen, Joseph Beuys* (Cologne: König, 1987).

The Harrison Studio [website]. Available at http://theharrisonstudio.net (accessed February 6, 2013).

Henri, Comte de Saint-Simon [or possibly Olinde Rodrigues], "The artist, the savant, and the industrialist," in *Art in Theory 1815–1900: An Anthology of Changing Ideas*, eds Charles Harrison and Paul J. Wood (London: Blackwell Publishers Ltd., 1998), pp. 38–41.

J. Craig Venter Institute [website]. Available at http://www.jcvi.org/cms/home (accessed February 6, 2013).

Kastner, Jeffrey, "There, now: from Robert Smithson to Guantanamo," in

Land, Art: A Cultural Ecology Handbook, ed. Max Andrews (London: RSA, 2006), pp. 22–32.

Kastner, Jeffrey, and Brian Wallis, eds, *Land and Environmental Art* (London and New York, NY: Phaidon Press, 1998).

Leopold, Aldo, *A Sand County Almanac, and Sketches Here and There* (New York, NY: Oxford University Press, 1949).

Loers, Veit, and Pia Witzmann, eds, *Joseph Beuys Documenta-Arbeit* (Ostfildern-Ruit: Edition Cantz, 1993).

PigeonBlog [website]. Available at http://www.pigeonblog.mapyourcity.net (accessed February 6, 2013).

Platzek, Carola, "Ines Doujak: the continuity of colonial practices," trans. Jeanne Haunschild, in *Documenta Magazine No. 2 2007: Life!* (Cologne: Taschen, 2007), pp. 136–41.

Preemptive Media [website]. Available at http://www.preemptivemedia.net (accessed February 6, 2013).

Remember Saro-Wiwa [website]. Available at http://remembersarowiwa.com (accessed February 6, 2013).

Smithson, Robert, "A tour of the monuments of Passaic, New Jersey" and "Proposal (1972)," in *Robert Smithson: The Collected Writings*, ed. Jack Flam (Berkeley and Los Angeles, CA: University of California, 1996), pp. 68–74, 354.

Stiftung 7000 Eichen (7,000 Oaks Foundation) [website]. Available at http://www.7000eichen.de (accessed February 6, 2013).

Tisdall, Caroline, *Joseph Beuys* [exh. cat.] (New York, NY: Guggenheim Museum, 1979).

Chapter 7 · Anti-Globalization

Adler, Rudy, Victoria Criado, and Brett Huneycutt, *Border Film Project: Photos by Migrants & Minutemen on the US–Mexico Border* (New York, NY: Abrams, 2007).

Bishop, Claire, "Antagonism and relational aesthetics," *October* 110 (Fall 2004), pp. 51–79.

Dery, Mark, *Culture Jamming: Hacking, Slashing and Sniping in the Empire of Signs* (Westfield, NJ: Open Magazine Pamphlet Series, 1993). 2010 revised reprint available at: http://markdery.com/?page_id=154 (accessed February 6, 2013).

Gallo, Rubén, *New Tendencies in Mexican Art: The 1990s* (New York, NY: Palgrave Macmillan, 2004).

Galloway, Alexander, *Protocol: How Control Exists after Decentralization* (Cambridge, MA: MIT Press, 2004).

Graeber, David, *Debt: The First 5,000 Years* (New York, NY: Melville House, 2011).

Hirschhorn, Thomas, "Text for Flugplatz Welt/World Airport," in Thomas Hirschhorn et al., *Thomas Hirschhorn* (London: Phaidon Press, 2004), pp. 133–4.

Jaar, Alfredo, *Alfredo Jaar: Geography = War* [exh. cat.] (Richmond, VA: Virginia Museum of the Arts, 1991).

Jones, Caroline A., "Andy Warhol's Factory, 'commonism,' and the business art business," in *Machine in the Studio: Constructing the Postwar American Artist* (Chicago, IL: University of Chicago Press, 1996), pp. 189–267.

Klein, Naomi, *No Logo: No Space, No Choice. No Jobs* (New York, NY: Picador, 1999).

———*The Shock Doctrine: The Rise of Disaster Capitalism* (New York, NY: Metropolitan Books, 2008).

LulzSec [website]. Previously available at http://lulzsecurity.com (accessed June 12, 2012; link no longer working).

Margolles, Teresa, "Santiago Sierra" [interview], *Bomb* 86 (Winter 2004), pp. 62–9.

Mirapaul, Matthew, "Cybersnooping for sounds and images, not suspects," *New York Times* (October 1, 2001). Available at http://www.nytimes.com/2001/10/01/arts/arts-online-cybersnooping-for-sounds-and-images-not-suspects.html?pagewanted=all (accessed February 6, 2013).

Multiplicity [website]. Available at http://www.multiplicity.it (accessed February 6, 2013).

Oliva, Achille Bonito, *Alighiero Boetti: Bringing the World into Art 1993/1962* [exh. cat.] (Milan: Electa, 2009).

OPUS (Open Platform for Unlimited Signification) [website]. Previously available at http://www.opuscommons.net/templates/doc/index.html (accessed June 12, 2012; link no longer working).

Ottmann, Klaus, "From the Other Side (*De l'autre côté*)," in *Chantal Akerman: Moving through Time and Space* [exh. cat.], ed. Terrie Sultan (Houston, TX: Blaffer Gallery and D.A.P./Distributed Art Publishers, 2008), pp. 28–39.

Radical Software Group, *Carnivore* (software application, 2001–). Available at http://r-s-g.org/carnivore (accessed February 6, 2013).

Raqs Media Collective [website]. Available at http://www.raqsmediacollective. net (accessed February 6, 2013).

Smith, Terry et al, eds, *Antinomies of Art and Culture: Modernity, Postmodernity, Contemporaneity* (Durham, NC: Duke University Press, 2008).

Ukeles, Mierle Laderman, "Maintenance art manifesto" (1969), rpt. in *Theories and Documents of Contemporary Art*, eds Kristine Stiles and Peter Selz (Berkeley, CA: University of California Press, 1996), pp. 622–4.

———"Sanitation manifesto!" (1984), rpt. in *Theories and Documents of Contemporary Art*, eds Kristine Stiles and Peter Selz (Berkeley, CA: University of California Press, 1996), p. 624.

United Nations, "45/158: International convention on the protection of the rights of all migrant workers and members of their families." Available at http://www.un.org/documents/ga/res/45/a45r158.htm (accessed February 6, 2013).

Yergin, Daniel, and Joseph Stanislaw, *The Commanding Heights: The Battle for the World Economy* (New York, NY: Touchstone, 1998).

The Yes Men [website]. Available at http://theyesmen.org (accessed February 6, 2013).

The Yes Men, "Dow chemical just says 'yes' to Bhopal," in *Network Art: Practices and Positions*, ed. Tom Corby (New York, NY: Routledge, 2006), pp. 173–84. Unedited version available at http://theyesmen. org/dowtext (accessed February 6, 2013).

Epilogue · protestAR: #OCCUPYWALLSTREET and #arOCCUPYWALLSTREET

AR Occupy Wall Street [website]. Available at http://protestars.wordpress. com (accessed February 6, 2013).

Debord, Guy, "Introduction to a critique of urban geography," *Les Lèvres nues* 6 (1955). Available at http://library.nothingness.org/articles/SI/en/ display/2 (accessed February 6, 2013).

Graeber, David, "Occupy Wall Street rediscovers the radical imagination," *Guardian* (September 25, 2011). Available at http://www.guardian.co.uk/ commentisfree/cifamerica/2011/sep/25/occupy-wall-street-protest (accessed February 6, 2013).

Kimmelman, Michael, "In protest, the power of place," *New York Times* (October 16, 2011).

Sholette, Gregory, "Occupology, swarmology, whateverology: the city of (dis)order versus the people's archive," *Art Journal* online (Winter 2011). Available at http://artjournal.collegeart.org/?p=2395 (accessed February 6, 2013).

Sterling, Bruce, "Augmented reality: AR uninvited at MOMA NYC," *Wired* (October 6, 2010). Available at http://www.wired.com/beyond_the_beyond/2010/10/augmented-reality-ar-uninvited-at-moma-nyc (accessed February 6, 2013).

US Center on Budget and Policy Priorities, "Tax data show richest 1 percent took a hit in 2008, but income remained highly concentrated at the top: recent gains of bottom 90 percent wiped out." Available at http://www.cbpp.org/cms/index.cfm?fa=view&id=3309 (accessed February 6, 2013).

US Congressional Budget Office, *Trends in the Distribution of Household Income between 1979 and 2007* (Washington DC: Congress of the United States and the Congressional Budget Office, 2011).

index